THE ROCKS
BEGIN TO SPEAK

by LaVan Martineau

KC PUBLICATIONS
LAS VEGAS, NEVADA

Book design by K. C. DenDooven.

Drawings and photographs by author.

First Edition. First printing, January, 1973
          Second printing, November, 1976
          Third Printing, February, 1987
          Fourth Printing, December, 1990
          Fifth Printing, July, 1994

Library of Congress 72-85137 . ISBN 0-916122-30-1

KC Publications, Inc.
3245 E. Patrick Lane, Suite A
Las Vegas, Nevada 89120

Printed in the United States of America.

Dedicated to Edrick Bushhead,
James and Mabel Yellowjacket,
and Wendel John

Contents

Foreword

Rock writings—are these perplexing markings a systematic, widespread method of communication? Are they actually written records of man—historical accounts of events, battles, and other important happenings throughout the ages?

The general consensus of archeologists and anthropologists has been that a particular rock writing had significance only to the writer, his family, or, at most, his tribe. But, like many others who have been drawn again and again to these mysterious markings, I felt the answer must involve much more than this.

These ancient and not-so-ancient people were busy eking out a means of life, day after day, often in a harsh land. Why would they take the time and spend the energy to carve these drawings, often very intricate, if indeed they meant so little? The symbols don't make sense as letters, often present a cluttered and untidy appearance, and are not in a linear flow of lines! And why are they often bunched together, in odd locations, in hard-to-reach places? Like others, I wondered, shook my head, and went on to things I could better understand.

It was left for someone with a new approach and a new attitude to find the key to this riddle—someone with a unique combination of knowledge of Indian ways and languages, and skill in modern methods of decoding. And this man has come forward—the right man with the right tools at the right point in time: LaVan Martineau.

I first met LaVan at a Ute Sun Dance in northern Utah, during the time I was publishing a quarterly magazine. LaVan's ideas fascinated me. Even more, his persistence in testing those ideas impressed me. He showed me several notebooks filled with sketches, photos, references, and notes. I could only listen—interested, not then fully convinced. But I did notice the dog-eared, thumb-worn pages of his notebooks—indications of a dedicated man.

He said he could read petroglyphs as recorded information, and his ideas made such sense to me that I published a series of his articles in my magazine. And now we have his book—the culmination of many, many years of hard work and single-minded perseverance.

LaVan was reared during his teens by Indian families. He understands their ways. More importantly, he understands and *lives* by their ideals, philosophies, and attitudes. He speaks several Indian languages fluently. Other Indians discuss matters with him freely and frankly.

The most significant of the Indian languages to LaVan is the sign language, which he understands and "speaks." For it is upon the sign language that many of the symbols of rock writing are based. This is only logical. A visual sign language would have been a natural first common language for various tribes from whom widely different spoken languages had evolved.

Sign language was sufficient for face-to-face meetings. But some means had to be found by which events and important information could be more permanently recorded. Apparently man was no different centuries ago than he is today in one respect. The need to leave a record of his existence and to communicate with future generations was just as compelling to the ancient historian as it is to his modern counterpart.

LaVan's findings corroborate those of early scholars. They, too, had concluded that the pictography they found among American Indian tribes was based on the sign language, and was a definite system of communication.

As we look to the future, we must also look to the past. The art of communication can be traced back for centuries. Yet it is hard to believe that a system as complex as ancient Chinese or Egyptian hieroglyphics was *basic*. Something simpler had to come before—a common denominator which was the forerunner of written language. LaVan believes it was the pictography of the Indian and his predecessors. He deserves to be heard—*must* be heard.

Read this book with an open mind. It presents a totally new approach to an age-old mystery. Just as other "unsolvable" puzzles have been resolved, so must the mystery of rock writing. This could well be one of the most significant discoveries of our time. We think so!

K. C. DenDooven
PUBLISHER

Preface

It has been many years since the hills last rang to the sound of an Indian chiseling his message upon the rocks and the now-forgotten trails felt the tread of his moccasined feet.

Since that time many Indian tribes have become extinct, and their languages and cultures lost. Those that remain only linger in the rags of a forgotten glory; even the memory of practices once so basic to their ways of life has faded or slipped away entirely. Tribes who, according to early scholars, were quite fluent in the sign language in the nineteenth century (Paiute, Pima, Papago, Maricopa, Zuni, and Arizona Apache, for example) no longer retain even a memory of having once used it.

Likewise, the art of pictography of the ancients has vanished. An Indian may gaze upon rock writings with the same curiosity that a white man might exhibit. And if you ask an Indian who it was who wrote them and what they signify, it is quite likely he will merely shrug his shoulders. Some tribes, fortunately, have been a little more reluctant to adandon their cultures. Strongholds of Indian tradition, religion, and cultural traits still exist in scattered pockets throughout the nation.

It was, in fact, an ancient custom in which the Paiute still takes pride that decided the course of my life, and led to my study and work with Indian rock writings. Southern Paiutes have no word for *orphanage*, and will not permit a child to be left alone. After the funeral of my father (my mother had died a few years before, when I was ten), a one-armed Paiute named Edrick Bushhead came to me, saying, "Come stay with me and be my son, since you have no place to go." Underaged, ignored by relatives and by county welfare, I gratefully accepted.

Long before his death, my father had rented a house in the little Paiute village just within the city limits of Cedar City, Utah, and as a youth many of my playmates had been Indian boys. Now, as Edrick's son, this village became my permanent home. Other Paiutes assisted Edrick with my upbringing. Maimie

Merrycats (anglicized Paiute for *American*) took pride in calling me her son. James and Mabel Yellowjacket, and Wendel John from the Shivwits band of Paiutes were others of my many foster parents who took pains to teach me their language, songs, and customs — all of which so greatly influenced my life.

It is no wonder that my outlook was the same as the people who so unselfishly gave me their love and care. Even now, I live and work as the Indian, cherishing many of his edifying customs and traditions. Their nomadic ways are still an integral part of my life, with which I am content.

My interest in competitive and ceremonial Indian war dancing took me as a youth, and later as a man, to many Indian reservations dotted with a few remaining tipis. There I learned the universal sign language from tribes still practicing it—Ute, Northern Arapaho, Comanche, Otoe, Pawnee, and others.

I felt just as at home among these tribes as I did with the Paiutes, and in fact spent several years on other reservations — particularly with the San Carlos Apaches, whose language, customs, and sandpainting symbology I studied with great interest.

Among these many friends were Indians who could speak several languages fluently. Many more had memorized hundreds of unwritten Indian songs. Needless to say, I was never hampered with any misgivings concerning the intelligence of the American Indian!

And there was never any question in my mind who it was who had written upon the rocks in the hills surrounding our little Paiute villages and near the reservations where I lived in the southern parts of Utah and Nevada, and on the Arizona Strip.

I often overheard it said that the panels had been written by the Hopi — *Mookweetch* as they are still called in Paiute — and by invading war parties from Plains Indian tribes. Paiutes themselves laid claim to many of the writings. Traditional Hopi whom I met in later life did not falter in saying that it was indeed their ancestors who had written upon the rocks, and that they tell of migrations, histories, disputes, and land claims. Some Hopi even attempted to read the panels to me, for fortunately a few of the symbols are still understood throughout the various Hopi clans.

Thus circumstance, rather than design, led to my involvement with rock writings, and took me to those places where Indian tradition illuminated subjects long kept in the dimness of neglect and disuse.

My interest in deciphering Indian rock writings had its roots in 1956, in a conversation with an anthropologist friend for whom I had recently made some models of various old-time Indian arrows. Our discussion involved some petroglyphs near an archeological site which he had excavated. He said it was his opinion that the panels were *not* the work of the inhabitants of the ruins—because of the fact that the petroglyph symbols did not *also* appear on the pottery found at the site. This argument aroused my interest, since it seemed so unfounded. Is the English alphabet commonly used as a decoration upon the dishes of white men?

It also seemed peculiar that the anthropologists I met, who it would seem should be knowledgeable in the field, showed little interest in rock writings, and would only quote theories which I knew to completely disregard the numerous Paiute stories about *tumpe poop* (tŭm-pe pō-ŏp — rock writing).

Adding to this frustration was the fact that the best-known books on the subject at that time (and indeed since) consisted basically of either site information only, or of some unproven and undocumented assumptions regarding meanings and origins. As I became more and more aware of this lack of any real evidence or interest, it seemed possible that harm to the heritage of the American Indian might be a consequence. For this reason I took upon myself the responsibility for continuing the study of rock writings in the light of what *Indians* had to say concerning them — a study begun by scholars early in America's history. The information supplied to these scholars by Indian informants was being ignored by those to whom I thought the responsibility belonged.

No small part of my motive for attempting to defend the American Indian amidst this unfortunate neglect was the great debt of gratitude I owed him.

Destiny in the unlikely form of the United States Air Force provided a situation which was to prove to be of incalculable help in this pursuit. While serving in Korea, the Air Route Traffic Control Center in which I worked shared a quonset hut and adjacent rooms with the cryptography department. Adding to my good luck, seven of my eight tentmates worked in this crypto department. I, by proximity, became keenly interested in the subject and eventually, having already had the required security clearance, learned from my more experienced tentmates many of the principles used in deciphering codes and ciphers. Obtaining knowledge of cryptanalysis in this manner was especially fortuitous, since authoritative books on the subject would have been very difficult to obtain because of the military value of this science.

In the course of my research, any preconceived ideas I may have entertained were weighed and abandoned in the balancing scales of cryptanalysis—a science which allows no mixing of fact and fancy. Success in this field depends upon its leading the follower to the truth. It does not bend to accommodate preconceptions.

Other than the few glimmerings of light shed by Indian informants, the scope of rock writings was unknown to me at the outset. The findings presented here are, in many instances, far from what I anticipated they would be. Cryptanalysis, like a horse given reign who instinctively finds his way home, led me through darkness to the ultimate truth that rock writing was indeed a full-fledged pictography.

An abundance of material is an absolute prerequisite in any cryptanalytic study. It soon became apparent that an extensive compilation would be necessary — one which would require full-time effort. As a nomad, I traveled wherever my needs took me — collecting sketches, photographs, and site maps of panels located throughout the United States, Mexico, and Canada. (In Utah alone, I recorded and mapped 253 sites for purposes of this study.) In the interest of thoroughness, I searched out and consulted every publication — old and new — which contained sketches, photos, and theories. Each of these was studied for possible merit.

My Indian friends again came to aid me. Many friends among the Southern Paiute, Northern Ute, and San Carlos Apache generously gave me room and board at the critical times in this research. This hospitality — which demands nothing in return and is so much a part of the ancient tradition of nomadic Indian tribes —allowed me to devote nearly all of my time to study, and most of my meager resources to paying the costs of color photography and the expenses of hundreds of field trips required to do the job thoroughly and well. Thus, in seeking to repay a debt of gratitude, it has only increased.

I had not anticipated publishing the findings of my cryptanalytic research until the time came when it was possible to read the entire system fluently. My underlying purpose was to wait until all doubt regarding the exact meaning of each symbol was removed by extensive cryptanalytic application.

It became apparent, however, that such undue caution would keep these findings from the public for many long years. It was therefore decided to publish what is now known, at the same time reserving the right to change or refine in future publications any symbol translation, as the evidence may dictate. Likewise, if others should offer corrections substantiated by reliable cryptanalytic methods, the appropriate changes will be made.

It will take lifetimes and the dedication of more than just one man to exhume the body of evidence and recall the spirit of a great vanished people as manifested in their writings. This work is offered on the strength of its scientific merits and documentation only, in the hope that it might be of some aid in the monumental task of resurrecting the lost heritage of a trampled Indian culture.

LaVan Martineau

The Rocks Begin to Speak

Part I

1.

Art and the Mysterious Sheep

A STUDY OF A COMPLETELY UNKNOWN WRITING SYSTEM is very much like tracking an elusive animal whose trail has grown cold. But no matter how dim the trail, there are always a few signs that leap to the trained eye of the tracker.

In the final stages of its journey through history, Indian pictography has left a broad and still-warm trail filled with many signs that even the most unskilled tracker could hardly overlook. In the groping early years of this study, most of these clues were stumbled upon, quite by accident—clues which proved beyond a doubt, even before the aid and support of actual symbol translations, the purpose and structure of America's rock writings.

In most works concerned with these mysterious markings, the term *rock writing* is seldom applied to them, in spite of the fact that this is the very term the Indians themselves have always used, and would thus seem to be the most appropriate one. (*Tŭm-'pe pō-'ōp*, for instance, means rock writing in Paiute. Other tribes have equally specific words.)

This omission is due largely to the fact that most scholars have never accepted the premise that these markings were indeed *writing*. The existence in the languages of many Indian tribes of a *word* for writing (in the sense of recording information for others to read) proves, at least, that picture writing was long accepted as writing by the Indian. And who but the American Indian himself is more qualified to say whether it is or is not?

The existence of such a writing system among the Indians offers a solution to the mystery, so long ignored, of why tribes had their own words for *reading* and *writing*. Such words were not borrowed from English or Spanish, nor are they descriptive (as are many of their words denoting modern gadgets). They are retained from a recent time when the Indians practiced their own form of picture writing.

Although the idea that rock writing is indeed writing is in opposition to

Rock writing is used in this work when discussing any messages left upon rocks, whether painted or pecked. *Pictography* (picture writing) is used to refer to writing upon any and all substances, including rocks. *Petroglyphs* are those panels which have been inscribed in the rock in some manner. *Pictographs* refer to painted panels or to one of the symbols of pictography.

Fig. 1. This panel from the Santa Clara River in Utah appears to consist merely of artistic designs devoid of meaning. However, all the basic symbols in its makeup are very common to Indian pictography.

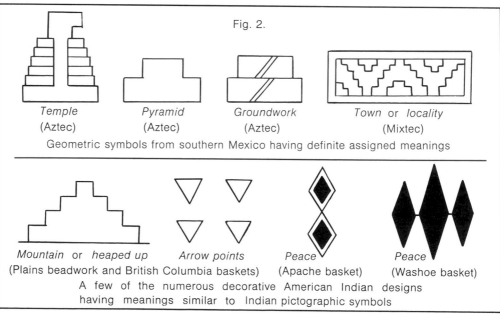

Fig. 2.

| *Temple* (Aztec) | *Pyramid* (Aztec) | *Groundwork* (Aztec) | *Town* or *locality* (Mixtec) |

Geometric symbols from southern Mexico having definite assigned meanings

| *Mountain* or *heaped up* (Plains beadwork and British Columbia baskets) | *Arrow points* | *Peace* (Apache basket) | *Peace* (Washoe basket) |

A few of the numerous decorative American Indian designs having meanings similar to Indian pictographic symbols

Puerco River, Ariz.

some theories set forth in modern publications on the subject, it does not disagree too drastically with others. The general feeling of most "experts" is that rock writing was meant to be understood, but only by the writer or local band.

Interesting, but unsupported, theories have been postulated that rock writings were of no more significance than as "art," "doodles," "hunting records," and "hunting magic." A few theorists have even ventured to state that the Indians were not responsible for *any* of the rock writings in America, or that they acquired such practices, along with the sign language, from the white man himself!

It is not difficult to see from the frequently occurring symbols resembling mountain sheep, and from the many artistic designs, why theories developed that they had to do with hunting magic, or were merely drawings. It was decided that, in order to determine the accuracy of these theories and to establish the purpose of these confusing symbol types and their relationships to other symbols, the first step should be a concentrated analysis of these particular symbols themselves. After all, the best way to split a big chunk of knotty wood is to strike it right in the heart of its largest knot!

It can be said of almost any writing system that it contains a certain degree of inherent artistic beauty or value. This would be especially true of a picture-writing system, even though this is not its basic purpose. The problem was to find out whether panels with artistic design—such as those from the Southwest shown in figures 1 and 46—were basically intended as art, or were in fact written communication.

At first such panels looked as if they could contain no meaning whatever. Adding to this impression was the fact that similar designs occurred on older pottery types from the same southwestern vicinity. But careful comparison revealed that these panels did not contain the artistic balance and symmetry that many pottery designs exhibited.

Also, each of these apparent designs can be broken down into basic symbols common to numerous panels having no semblance of artistic design. In other words, these designs are composed of basic symbols common to most rock writings, and thus manifest a definite linguistic trait.

Extensive compilation also revealed that symbols of geometric, pottery-like design had a noticeable geographic concentration in the ancient and modern Pueblo civilizations of the Southwest. It was observed that symbols of this type were also very common throughout the ancient cultures and advanced civilizations of Mexico. They appear upon the seals of officials (Franch 1958), and are common in the translated Aztec manuscripts. That some of these symbols represent towns, stepped buildings, and pyramids (figure 2) is common knowledge among scholars. This knowledge led to the interpretation of similar symbols found so abundantly near the ruins of the less advanced peoples of the Southwest—cultures which utilized similar building techniques.

In the beadwork designs of the Plains Indians, who did not build stone houses, pyramid-type symbols retain a related meaning—that of a rocky mountain or hill. Other bead (or quillwork) and basketry design elements found throughout the country and not just within the Southwest—diamonds, triangles, and

Fig. 3. This panel from Pintura, Utah, uses rock incorporation in such a unique and suggestive manner (the rock knob itself represents a hill) that the meaning of this clockwise spiral becomes self-evident. (The incomplete circle in which this spiral is enclosed should not be confused with the spiral itself.)

Fig. 4. Rock incorporation as used by the Pueblo Indians of New Mexico

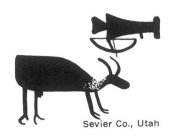

Sevier Co., Utah

zigzag lines—have a symbolic value as well as artistic appeal. These meanings have been retained, having been handed down to a few Indian craftsmen who have related them to modern students (figure 2). Many of these artistic symbols are identical in meaning to similar symbols in Indian pictography recently deciphered, revealing that it had a noticeable influence in the decorating of pottery, basketry, and quillwork. This is in direct opposition to the theory that pottery and other designs influenced the content of Indian pictography.

The "art" theory is diminished further when it is discovered that the floral symbol is almost completely non-existent in the great number of rock writings occurring throughout the country. Only a few panels containing symbols resembling flowers have been found, and none of these resemble the floral designs of the woodland areas of the East. The rarity with which they occur shows an almost complete disregard for the art-inspiring flower—incredible if we are to believe rock writings are only "pretty pictures."

The art theory is also weakened by the animal and human figures in pictography, the majority of which are highly abstract and far from realistic. Nor are the lone abstract lines and circles found on isolated rocks acceptable as appropriate art renderings.

A fact which carried much weight in deciphering rock writings and establishing their purpose was the discovery that the rocks and rock surfaces used for inscribing symbols were often very unusual. Smooth, seemingly ideal writing surfaces were often completely ignored in favor of uneven surfaces. If artistic expression had been the intent, smooth and accessible surfaces would surely have been used.

Some symbols followed cracks in the rocks, ended, or were purposely placed at the rock's edge. Natural holes or other rock features were often embodied in the makeup of a symbol. Examples of this may be found in figure 3, and in the man in figure 4, in which natural holes are utilized as eyes and mouth. These examples actually employ rock features to add to the meaning of a panel. Such use has been termed *rock incorporation*. Similar examples are plentiful throughout America and in many parts of the world. This practice is completely foreign to the principles of art, but in a pictography it serves the useful functions of clarifying or conveniently abbreviating symbols. Inscribing on stone was no easy task!

Almost everyone who has seen the mystifying symbol of an animal resembling a mountain sheep has been curious to know its purpose. Such scenes as those in which sheep are being shot at by men with bows and arrows naturally prompt theories that they illustrate hunting episodes, or that they are ritual figures once used in hunting magic.

But such theories do not hold up under close examination. Hunting was so

7

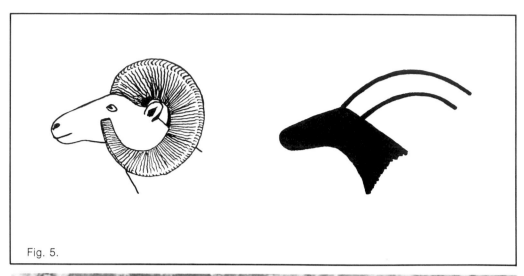

Fig. 5.

Fig. 6. Note the true-to-life thickness at the base of this ram's horn and the tapering curl at its end. Also note the short tail. These realistic features indicate this example was intended to be an actual depiction of a mountain sheep.

Flathead Co.,
Mont. *(pictograph)*

common among Indians that it would hardly have merited such one-sided and profuse depictions. Indian legends commemorate only the *unusual* hunt or the *unusual* animal. Futhermore, mountain-sheep symbols are found in some areas where there is no proof that this animal ever existed!

Such theories obviously are based upon the assumption that symbols resembling mountain sheep serve no other purpose than their actual depiction. The weakness here is that symbols in which the horns go straight back over the head resemble a *goat* more than they do a mountain sheep, whose horns have an outward and downward spiral which often ends pointing toward the front. (Compare the sketch of a realistic sheep in figure 5 with the assumed sheep representation in the same figure.) Also, the assumed mountain-sheep symbol is *never* depicted with a realistic tapering horn, even on the numerous large or life-sized examples.

On the other hand, realistic depictions of *actual* mountain sheep seldom *overlook* this feature, unless the symbol is unusually small. (Note the realistic example of a true mountain-sheep depiction in figure 6. This panel from Three Rivers, New Mexico was, according to archeologists, inscribed between 900 and 1400 A.D. by the Jornado branch of the Mogollon culture.)

Also significant is the fact that the mountain-sheep symbol in question occurred with hundreds of variations—two heads, five legs, square bodies, and numerous other abstract appendages (figure 7). If these actually were true-to-life pictures of mountain sheep, then there must have been a wild array of the species roaming the country at the time! "Poor art," used as an explanation by some, does not adequately explain the existence of two heads and three legs!

In the pictography of the Dakota Indians, we find many similar examples of highly abstract symbols resembling animals and humans. These unusual symbols are arranged in abstract combinations to portray personal names (figure 8), and are a basic part of Indian pictography.

Another curious fact, one which fails to support "hunting" theories, is that the sheep was very rarely portrayed in a *dead* position—that is, with the head pointing straight down, or on its back with feet pointing straight up. If these symbols were actual hunting scenes, or served as hunting magic, then this type of occurrence would be much more frequent.

Numerous animal pictures throughout the East and among the Zuni, Blackfoot, Hopi, Navajo and other tribes show realistic depictions with a "heart line"— a line drawn from the mouth to a visible heart (figure 9). Among the Ojibwa, who *did practice hunting magic in connection with pictography,* this heart line, often pierced with an arrow, was always included in the depiction of the particular animal whose death was to be hastened with the aid of magic. Such depictions

Fig. 7. These are but a few examples from a collection of many rock writings using sheep-like symbols. The completely unrealistic features prove they were *not* intended to actually depict mountain sheep.

Eagle-Bear   Horned-Horse   Grasp   Four-Crows   Female-Elk-Boy   Flat-Iron

Fig. 8. Personal names from the Dakota census records demonstrate that abstract symbols were part of the basic makeup of Indian pictography (Mallery).

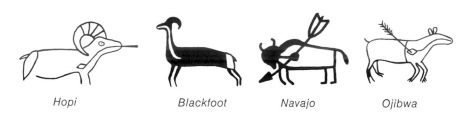

Hopi   Blackfoot   Navajo   Ojibwa

Fig. 9. Examples of true hunting-magic symbols used in realistic animal depictions are found in widely separated locations amid dissimilar cultures. The line from the mouth to the heart represents the voice of the hunter reaching to the heart of the animal, thus controlling or bringing it near so that it may be killed more easily. The animal's mouth is used to imply that of the hunter's, eliminating the need to draw an additional figure. (Note, in two examples, the arrows indicating successful kills.)

Duchesne Co., Utah

were sketched on birch bark or in the sand, and were believed helpful in the hunt (Tanner 1830). This heart-line symbol is therefore the only known symbol which is a *true* hunting-magic symbol. Since this heart line is completely absent on so-called mountain-sheep symbols, the sheep must serve a completely *different* purpose.

Another important feature entirely lacking on symbols assumed to be mountain sheep is the distinguishing white rump and white nose, as shown on the realistic Hopi and Blackfoot examples in figure 9.

Further study also revealed that sheep symbols have a high frequency rate along the Columbia River, one of the best fishing locations in the world. Surprisingly, *fish* symbols are rare along this river. Likewise, sheep symbols have a high frequency rate in areas where buffalo and deer were plentiful, but in many of these areas buffalo and deer symbols are rarely found! It would seem that the opposite should hold true. Sheep symbols may also be found in Israel, Afghanistan, Turkey, Central Asia, Siberia, Italy, and other areas. The common occurrence of this symbol throughout the world, even in areas where meat was plentiful, suggests a reason for its existence not related to hunting.

What, then, was the *real* purpose of this mysterious sheep symbol?

One of the first definite clues leading to its discovery came with the realization that they occurred at a high frequency rate together with figures of men behind shields—panels which were unmistakably battle accounts. Hunting magic and the hunting of mountain sheep have no relationship or affinity with warfare. Also, symbols of sheep with men riding them have been found mixed among symbols of wagons and men on horseback, and even in conjunction with trains and buildings. Again, there is no affinity or logic in such cases. It must be concluded that most of these sheep symbols do not represent mountain sheep at all, but have another altogether different purpose.

There is probably no better way to express animated action and direction of travel than with neutral animal or human forms. Such symbols are natural methods of depicting such ideas as *running, walking, climbing, lying down,* and *direction*—simply by the attitude of the figure itself. Any pictography would be incomplete and much more cumbersome if this convenient method of substitution were overlooked. Employed in this capacity, **the sheep symbol provided a simple method with which to express action or direction**—a fact which explains its presence in topics unrelated to each other in panels located throughout the world.

The term *sheep* is therefore dropped and the term *goat* or *horned quadruped* applied, *for convenience only,* in referring to this symbol, so that it will not be confused with those symbols actually *intended* as mountain sheep. The term

Chart 1.

A	B	C

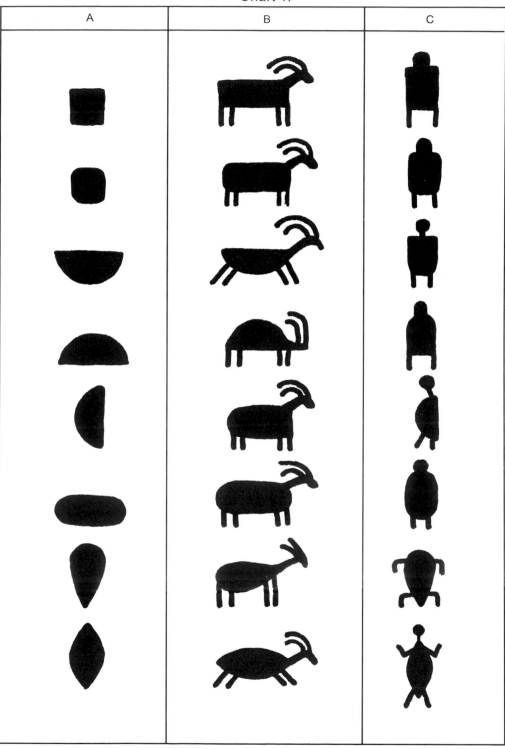

Washington Co., Utah

goat, then, will be used as a *symbol term only,* and will not refer to a domestic or wild goat, or any living animal.

Once this basic principle was understood, it was easy to prove with the aid of a simple scientific test. A list of many different, yet common, goat symbols was established (chart 1). It was found that each of these symbols could be broken down into very common basic symbols. Column *A* gives examples of such symbols, and represents a breakdown of the goat forms in column *B.* The basic symbols in column *A* were selected from panels which did not contain goats, and thus showed definite composition for purposes of communication when compared with the symbols in column *B.*

A similar breakdown of human and abstract deer symbols reveals that they, too, serve the purpose of expressing various actions and meanings. They also serve as phrases and ideograms, and as such do not always represent deer or any particular individual. (Note the same basic symbol breakdown of human figures in column *C* of chart 1). This important discovery throws light on the structure of Indian pictography. At the same time, it is shown to be, not surprisingly, identical to the structure of spoken Indian languages. This principle is exemplified in the well known anglicized Aztec word *montezuma.* This name ("the chief shoots to heaven when he is angry") is actually the incorporation of several words into one. This trait is so common in Indian languages that many early writers appropriately termed them *incorporating, agglutinative,* and *polysynthetic* languages. These terms can also be applied to Indian rock writing, which has the same predominant structure.

Chart 2 demonstrates that the Indian was adept at expressing abstract ideas by using this same principle. Column *A* presents two or more symbols combined to form short phrases or sentences. This type of combination, wherein symbols are only *attached* to other symbols, is called *symbol combination.* Column *B* presents a breakdown into the independent forms used in composing the combinations in column *A.*

Column *C* is a similar, but more abbreviated, method of combining symbols to create phrases, in a manner not unlike spoken practices. This principle is called *symbol incorporation,* and is accomplished by blending two symbols so that each shares part of its form with the other. This is also a very common practice in spoken Indian languages, where two or more words drop or abandon part of their makeup to blend into one word. Column *D* shows the basic symbols used in this blending.

The consistency with which these principles occur, their abundant use in Indian rock writing, and their affinity to spoken-language practices present an almost conclusive case for classing Indian pictography as a highly developed writing system—even before any translations have been attempted.

Chart 2.

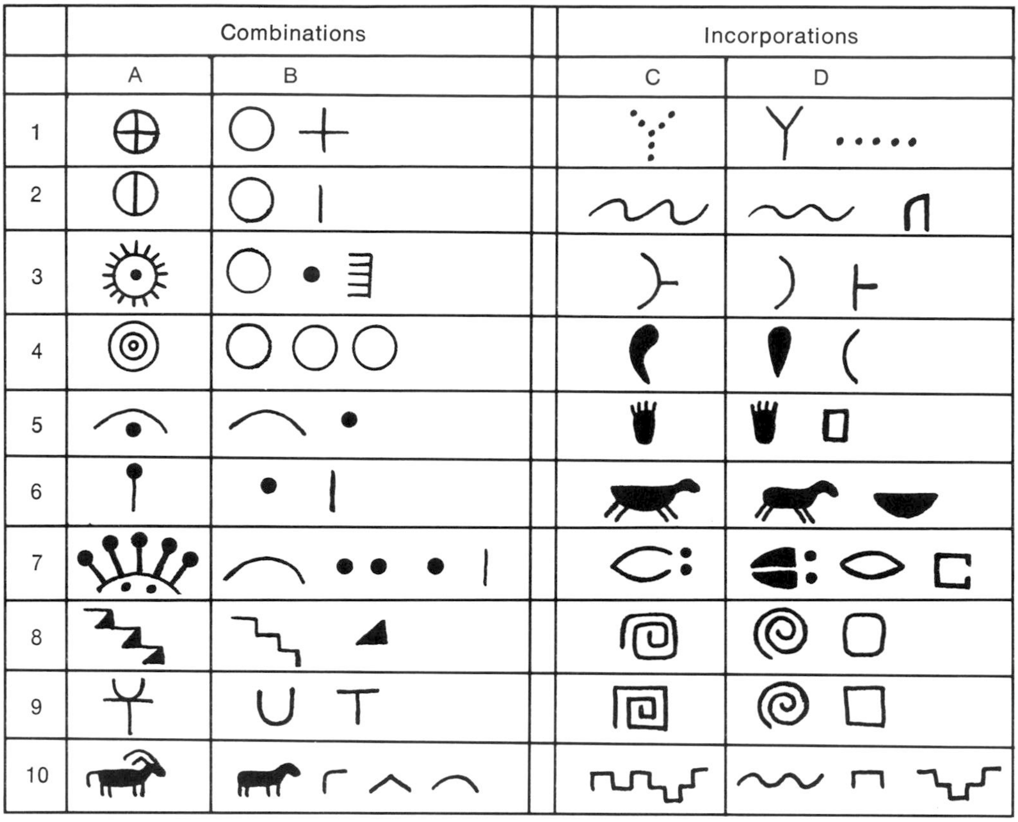

		Combinations			Incorporations	
		A	B		C	D
1	⊕	○ +			⋮Y⋮	Y .....
2	⊕	○ |			∿	∿ ⌐
3	☀	○ • ☰			}⁻	) ⊢
4	◎	○ ○ ○			(	❜ (
5	⌢•	⌢ •			♅	♅ □
6	⸠	• |			🐑	🐑 ⌣
7	⚊⚊⚊	⌢ •• • |			⊂⋮	◀⋮ ◇ ⊏
8	⚡	⌐ ◢			▣	◉ ▢
9	⅄	U T			▣	◉ ▢
10	🐏	🐑 ⌐ ∧ ⌒			�ↄᓚᔦᓫ	∿ ⊓ ⅄⌐

The hundreds of variations of combinations and incorporations of goats, animals, human and abstract symbols existing in rock writings point to a broad range of meaning. It was a very extensive pictography in which almost every human expression was attempted. If this were not so, or if Indian pictography had been fairly crude, these linguistic traits would instead be quite limited and not nearly so numerous. That linguistic traits *do* exist definitely invalidates those theories that Indian rock writings served basically as either hunting magic, hunting accounts, or art!

The broad range of expression covering many topics has produced an interesting result in twentieth-century studies of rock writing. A complete pictography naturally contains hundreds of symbols. Each topic would not, nor could not, use them all. This results in many panels having a completely different appearance. (Compare the panels presented in this work.) This outward dissimilarity has prompted scholars to classify topics and symbols into "styles." For example, nonrepresentational symbols have been labeled "abstract styles," while goats were classed as "representational style."

We now know that styles do not exist as such, but are in reality different stories using a broad dictionary of symbols, thus demonstrating the wide scope of expression possible in Indian pictography.

14

2.

The Rocks Break Their Silence

ONE OF THE GREATEST REWARDS in the study of rock writing comes when symbols themselves can be deciphered. The acquisition of a few known symbol meanings which could be used to relate to symbols of unknown meanings and thus decipher the bulk of this system was the most difficult task of the project. One by one these wedges were obtained; and, as the number of known symbols increased, so did the rapidity with which Indian pictography could be understood. Eventually stories began to unfold, and sleeping histories from a remote age stirred amidst surroundings quite unlike the day they were inscribed.

The story of this long process of deciphering, still underway, would actually fill volumes if the histories of the deciphering of all the symbols were presented here. Each was a project in itself, involving many mistakes, elimination processes, and tests until its true meaning was ultimately established; and there were as many projects as there were unknown symbols.

No accurate count can be made yet, but perhaps no writing system except Chinese exceeds Indian pictography in the number of symbols used. Space permits presentation of only a small cross-section of the history behind a few of the first symbols cracked.

The science used to decipher Indian rock writings is *cryptanalysis*. This word includes the Greek *kryptos* (hidden, covered, or secret); hence, "an analysis of that which is secret or hidden." This science is employed by the military intelligence in the deciphering of unknown codes and ciphers. Since its purpose is to solve the mysteries presented by unknown systems of communication, cryptanalysis is right at home in deciphering the forgotten writing systems of ancient languages. It has already been used very productively for this purpose. (A more comprehensive study of the science of cryptanalysis in regard to deciphering rock writings is presented in the chapter, "Cryptanalysis, the Forgotten Tool.")

One of the prerequisites of deciphering any writing system with cryptanalytic methods is a complete symbol list. Access to numerous examples of the more common symbols in as many varied positions of affinity (relationship in meaning one symbol bears to associated symbols) as possible is of further help. The process of acquiring such a list necessitates a great amount of field work in recording (sketching and photography.) Books with many photographs and *accurate* sketches are rare; for this reason extensive field work becomes all the more necessary.

The initial field work was confined to specific cultural areas, in case the examples obtained had only local significance. The first area covered was Iron County, Utah. Next came Sevier County and parts of Wayne County, Utah.

In this period from 1956 to 1960, few symbols were actually deciphered, although many had been assigned tentative meanings. All but a few of these first guesses were eventually scrapped when they failed to pass the tests of consistency (having the same meaning each time used), the basic requirement of any writing system which is meant to be understood. (It is this principle of consistency which makes cryptanalysis effective.)

The deciphering of the first symbols was far from being a sudden, dramatic discovery. Large complicated panels with the most interesting stories could not be read until the principles of symbol incorporation and symbol combination, which comprise much of the system's structure, were thoroughly understood, and until many of the individual symbols were successfully analyzed. In early attempts many combinations and incorporations were each considered just one symbol. Since this was an erroneous assumption, all attempts to decipher them naturally failed. The symbol structure of Indian pictography is quite simple once understood, but this understanding took many years to achieve.

Efforts were concentrated upon smaller panels, in order that symbols utilizing complicated combinations and incorporations could be temporarily avoided. These panels often consisted of only one or two symbols, but they came to be invaluable. If they were indeed communication, their meanings had to be complete in themselves. They also had to be appropriate to their locations and to the fact that they were occasionally found in positions isolated from other panels. In most cases these symbols were puzzlingly abstract, but time soon revealed that abstract symbols were actually the easiest ones to crack.

Panels in Washington County, Utah, (recorded after Sevier and Wayne counties) proved valuable in providing these lone symbols which all but deciphered themselves. From the 120 sites in this county personally visited, many panels were found scattered far up the sides of boulder-strewn hills. The reason for this was that the rocks more suitable for writing were not always at the base of the hill; often they were in scattered, inconspicuous places higher up. After recording information upon such an out-of-the-way rock, the author would place

Clark Co., Nev.

on a conspicuous rock, symbols directing passers-by to the hidden panel. Panels giving such directions are therefore termed *locators.*

Locators are not found in many sites where the writings are plainly visible. It was for this reason that Iron, Sevier and Wayne counties—with their long cliff faces and canyons where most writings could readily be seen—did not provide many early deciphering clues when study was first begun there.

The first locator deciphered was symbol *a* of figure 10. An Indian friend had just discovered an unusual panel, missed in earlier trips because it was hidden. At the same time, I stumbled upon two little dots which lined up and pointed straight at the hidden panel. Looking further, two more dots were found which also lined up and located this same panel. I then realized that these two different sets of dots were acting as locators for that very panel. Educated guesses as to the meanings of these highly suggestive dots were that they were either two "eyes" directing, or two dots representing footsteps going a short distance in the direction pointed. There was no way of proving either meaning until many more examples had been deciphered. This process of elimination would take time and considerable field work, but the geographical evidence sufficed for the moment.

The discovery of these first two locators did not assume the impression of importance that they perhaps should have, and it was not until several others were found in like manner that their value was fully realized.

The next locator (*b*) was a straight line, also pointing directly at a hidden panel. The tentative meaning *go,* or *go in this direction,* was assigned to it. Later research revealed that this line, rather than meaning *go,* was more likely a pointing finger to indicate direction, much as a modern arrow does. In some cases where this line was vertical, it varied from this meaning and appeared to represent the abbreviated figure of a man minus all appendages, or the numeral *one.*

When countless examples of this finger symbol were found, not only in Utah, but in the area of the Hohokam in southern Arizona (a completely different cultural area), the importance of locators was established beyond doubt. They were afterward searched out with the eagerness of a prospector.

In reverse situations it was found that hidden panels could be used to "locate the locators." In other words, hidden panels could be used to establish which of the many panels strewn along the foot of a hill were the actual locators.

Many locators consisting of different symbols were soon found, and the list of tentatively read symbols increased. The geographic evidence provided by the locators gave much-needed encouragement. They also became the all-important cryptanalytic wedges which for years had been so elusive.

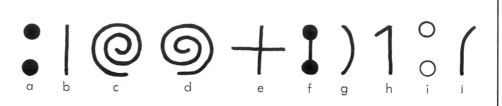

Fig. 10. The first simple locators deciphered

The more common simple locators first found and deciphered appear as symbols *c* through *j* in figure 10. (The number of times each of these symbols were discovered used as locators is given below.) The tentative meanings assigned to these locators, though often crude, are as follows:

Fig. 11. This petroglyph (long, chalked line) on the rock in the foreground can be readily seen from the foot of this hill. It serves as an excellent locator for the water-retaining rock in the center.

Springdale, Utah

(*c*) *Going up*: This symbol in seven examples located panels directly above it. The concept behind this meaning is probably patterned after the upward spiral of an eagle as it gains altitude. In the sign language, an identical spiral is used to denote this same idea; an opposite movement indicates *going down*.

(*d*) *Coming down* or *descending*: Five examples of this symbol located panels below it.

(*e*) *Cross over*: Ten examples of this symbol were found in which something had to be crossed in order to reach a hidden panel.

(*f*) *Writings* or *talk* (two heads with a line indicating speech): Six examples of this symbol pointed at hidden panels.

(*g*) *Go around*: Ten examples were located in which one had to veer around something in the path to the hidden panels.

(*h*) *Near* or *close*: Six examples were located near writings. Such is the case in figure 11, showing an example in which this symbol locates a nearby water pocket not visible from the foot of the hill.

(*i*) *Looking*: Eleven examples in which these two eyes lined up and pointed at a hidden panel were found. In one example, each eye appeared on the opposite side of the rock. In this case, it located a panel around the corner of the hill. In another example, both eyes appeared side by side and barely touched the top of a rock. With this incorporated-rock meaning, it meant, "Look near the top of the hill." Other panels were inscribed there.

(*j*) *Missed* (a bent stick): Eight examples of this line pointed at panels as if to say, "You missed something in this direction."

Many of these symbols, besides the pointing fingers already mentioned, were found used as locators with identical meanings in two different cultural areas: the Virgin River branch of the Anasazi of southern Utah and southern Nevada, and the Hohokam of southern Arizona. This was the first indication that this system might have widespread usage. Since then, many of these symbols have been found used with identical meaning in panels in many dissimilar and far-flung cultural areas throughout the West.

These symbols, with their convincing and nearly conclusive geographic evidence, were the first symbols deciphered in which other than cryptanalytical evidence could be provided to prove meaning. They were then used as the necessary known symbols, or affinity checks, required in relating and deciphering unknown symbols.

From the examples in figure 10, we can see that all lone symbols are not locators, and all locators do not locate panels—some locate waterholes, caches, and other things of importance to the Indians.

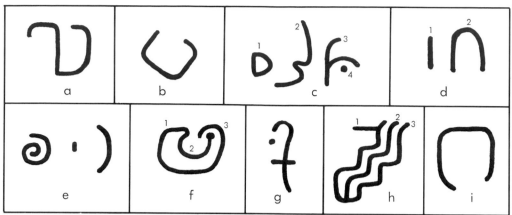

Fig. 12. Larger locators

Meanwhile, locators of a more complicated nature were found. These were easily read because of the peculiar position of the hidden object, thus increasing the list of known symbols. The first few of these larger locators, all found in Washington County, appear in figure 12. Symbol *a* is located on the east face of a large boulder; on the opposite side is a large panel not readily visible. The right half of this symbol—a *D* with the top missing—is a very common symbol. It represents the right half, or side, of a circle—hence its meaning *side*. The two right angles direct the seeker two turns to the left, placing him around and behind the rock in question. The author was saying, "From this side, go around the end and behind," or, more loosely, "Go around behind this rock."

Symbol *b* represents three *turns,* and is found on a rock on which writings appearing on the opposite end can be reached by going around either side of the

Fig. 13. The arrow indicates the position of symbol *f* in figure 12, which depicts and locates the hidden water-retaining rock in the foreground.

20

Valencia Co., N. Mex.

rock. The open area of this symbol indicates the location of the writings, or the point which is reached by going around either side. Locators *a* and *b* substantiate each other. Both use an identical round-cornered right angle to indicate a turn.

Panel *c* shows the right half of a circle, or *side (1)*, already explained; the outline of a cluster of boulders containing a little cove or indentation (2); the symbol *missed (3)*; and a dot (object) covered by a curved line (4). The last symbol is identical to the sign language *hidden*, in which the closed right hand is placed under the palm of the left. The substance of this panel is, "On the side by the little cove there is something hidden which might be missed." These symbols locate a large panel which one would normally fail to see while traveling in this direction.

In panel *d, 1* represents an abbreviated man, or perhaps a finger pointing *up; 2* represents the profile of the large rock on which it appears. On the left side of the same large rock is a larger panel which could easily be overlooked were it not for this locator. This symbol therefore represents a pointing finger or man standing on the left side of the rock where the hidden panel appears.

Panel *e* contains three simple symbols; their meanings have already been discussed. The accuracy of these previous translations was verified by the fact that they could be read with ease, and because the information they contained proved correct. This panel occurs high upon the side of a mountain at the base of a short vertical cliff. There is but one passageway to the top; it is a little way to the right of this panel. This *around* symbol describes the course of travel necessary to reach the top by means of the passage. The panel loosely reads, "Ascend to the top, ahead, by going around to the right." *Top* is indicated by the coil's outer line ending on top of itself. *Ahead* is shown by the finger which points straight up and to the ultimate destination. This pointing finger is short, thus utilizing an ingeniously simple method of implying *near*.

Panel *f* represents a rock (*1*), with a waterhole in it (2). The symbol *hidden* (3) is incorporated into the rock's shape, indicating that the waterhole is not visible from the point at which the reader stands. Stated more simply, it depicts a hidden waterhole lying straight ahead (figure 13). The arrow indicates the position of the panel locating this particular waterhole—one which plays an important part in Southern Paiute mythology. Note the smooth area on this rock, worn from centuries of use.

In panel *g,* the dot represents *here,* the cane-like symbol means *turn around,* and the incorporated cross indicates *across.* This panel simply says, "Cross over, turn around, and you will come to something." These instructions give the exact position of a hidden panel. To reach it one must cross over the top of the rock containing the locator, then down the opposite side. This panel can be reached

Fig. 14.

from the top in this manner only, due to its peculiar and almost inaccessible position in a crevice parallel to the side of a cliff.

Panel *h* locates an entrance into a nearby underground cavern situated in a confusion of huge lava boulders. In this symbol combination, *1* represents the ground surface; the middle line (*2*) indicates movement—*going under*, or "passing down through a stepped entrance and into a cavern" (*3*). The middle line (*2*) reaches all the way to the bottom of this cavern, indicating that it is a dead end.

Panel *i* is another cavern locator. It shows an entrance or opening in the bottom of a symbol representing a deep container, or *an entrance into something deep.*

In this same vicinity is a larger panel (figure 14) locating yet another cavern. Symbol *a* represents an enclosed, stepped cavern, this time incorporating the top of the rock into it to represent the ground surface. Symbol *b* represents a cavern branching from the main one and dead ending, or *turning around,* as indicated by the line curving upward. Symbol *c* shows steps and a very irregular or crooked

Virgin River, Utah

line, indicating a *crooked* cavern. Symbol *d* is a head pointing downward, indicating a person *going down* in this direction. Symbol *e* denotes the necessity of movement *around*.

All of these cavern locators locate nearby caverns of the type they describe and in the immediate area, thus providing the geographic evidence necessary to support these loose translations.

In the numerous locators in all the foregoing examples, a fair degree of consistency in symbol meaning is maintained. Consistency is the ultimate proof that a translation is accurate, even though it may need some refinement in meaning—only to come in time, with further comparisons.

Besides the confirming evidence of consistency, geographic conditions substantiating meanings were met in every case, giving further proof and making the use of these guidelines feasible in these early translations. (Many other locators have since been found, but space does not permit their inclusion here.)

Resemblances to the sign language were noticed in the symbols *hidden, cross over, going up, coming down, going around, close, going under,* and the pointing finger. These were considered only curious coincidences and were not pursued at the time.

It has been shown repeatedly that the symbols deciphered had a geographic significance in their use as locators. Many of these were also found on numerous undeciphered panels, all of which could not have been locators. This prompted an early assumption that all panels with an abundance of these symbols were maps. Many, but by no means all, did indeed eventually prove to be maps. (Indians did not use maps in the sense that we do today. They were sometimes left as information for the benefit of war parties who might return home after an absence of perhaps many months to find that their band had moved on. War parties may have left maps in enemy territory, giving locations of good springs or good raiding areas for the benefit of war parties of the same tribe to follow. Migrating Indians may very appropriately have left maps of their migrations—travels which may have covered thousands of miles.) Topic-affinity tests also revealed that some of these geographic symbol meanings were pertinent to battles containing descriptions of locations and movements, and some applied to several other topics as well.

However, it was from the translations of these early locator symbols that many of the larger and more interesting panels were read. It is worth repeating that this was accomplished by using these known symbols in conjunction with pertinent cryptanalytic principles. The following examples show how larger panels were eventually read by using these known symbols as penetrating wedges to isolate a topic.

Fig. 15. The first flood account deciphered (from Washington County, Utah)

FLOODS DESCEND

The first example deciphered of a descending coil used as other than a locator appears in figure 15. This panel was in a small wash adjacent to a hillside puebloan village found in Washington County, Utah. The panel suggested its own meaning, once the significance of the coil was known. Logic, elimination by affinity, and geographic evidence accomplished the rest.

The coil represents "something" coming down from off the top of a hill. The most logical explanation, in conjunction with other symbols, was that it was a flash flood. The small dot at the top of this symbol represents the point of origin of the flood and its smallness at this point. The line extending from this dot to the coil represents the slope of the hill, the path of the flood. The two dots through which this "flood" travels indicate *passing through,* just as in the sign language, and the large dot on this line shows that the flood increased in size as it de-

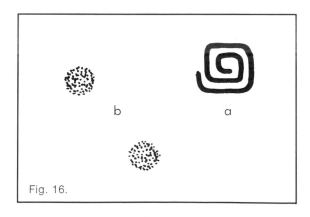
b   a

Fig. 16.

24

Hurricane, Utah

scended. Rock incorporation purposely places this panel near the top of the rock to clarify the flood's point of origin. Examination of the area reveals the actual path of this flood and some of the damage it inflicted on this once-inhabited hillside.

Also appearing in this wash is the symbol of an upside-down man. This symbol—according to examples in the pictography of eastern states—means *dead.* Someone had been killed in this flood. These two panels tell the story and at the same time give warning to future inhabitants of the site.

In the South Mountains of Phoenix, Arizona, another coil was found in the bottom of a wash, or bedrock, in a position slightly protected from flood water. This lone incorporation is almost identical to symbol *a* in figure 16. It was first thought to be a locator, but since it was at an elevation lower than the panels it obviously was not acting in that capacity. A breakdown of this incorporation appears in chart 2, line *8.* As this coil was in the "descending" form, the incorporated round-cornered square must be eliminated as a descriptive locality symbol. The only translation which made the meaning of this panel complete in itself was "coming down upon (someone's) property," the squared effect resembling property lines. (Contrary to popular belief, many Indian tribes did recognize ownership.) It was therefore tentatively considered to be nothing more than a flood warning in a very appropriate place—the mouth of a dangerous and large wash.

Back in Utah, within a hundred yards of the first discovered flood story, this same flood symbol appeared (symbol *a,* figure 16). If the translation of the southern Arizona symbol was correct, then it was evident that the Utah panel concerned yet another flood story. Thus some of the guesswork was eliminated in what proved to be a complicated story which took considerable time and extensive affinity checks to unravel.

This rock contains symbols on two sides and on its top. The incorporated coil (*a*) and the two large dots (*b*) in figure 16 are on one side. These large dots, or "eyes," line up and point at the area destroyed by the flood, the evidence of which can still be seen. These two dots are larger than ones found acting as panel locators, therefore their size must indicate further meanings—the most logical, appropriate, and suggestive was *big eyes,* or *astonishment* at seeing the flood coming down. These eyes incorporate the additional meaning of *wet,* hence *flood,* by employing a scattered pecking technique which duplicates the appearance of droplets of water. This technique may be observed incorporated into several of the symbols on this rock.

In examples on other panels, this scattered pecking technique varies in meaning, but in all examples its concept is related to "small and scattered" parti-

25

Fig. 17. Another interesting account of a flash flood

Fig. 18.

26

Washington Co., Utah

cles, implied by the essence of this technique. It therefore does not mean *wet* in all instances. In this case, however, the *cupped hand* (*water*) symbol (*a* in figure 17)—a part of the same panel as figure 16—which had been deciphered earlier in conjunction with waterholes, indicates the topic and thus acts as a determinative in distinguishing *wet* from other possible meanings.

This *water* symbol is placed on the side of the highest knob or peak of this rock to indicate *water from near the top of the hill.* This is an excellent example of the value of rock incorporation in reducing the amount of pecking necessitated, by eliminating the symbol for *hill* and *near the top. Coming down* also did not need to be written again, since its meaning was inferred by pointing the water symbol downward.

The spiraling flood symbol may again be seen on the top side of this rock (*b*). This symbol appropriately reveals that a flood came down over a village from beneath the top of the mesa. The horizontal line represents the ground surface, and *beneath* is implied by the placing of the coil under this line. In other words, it indicates a flash flood originating below the crest (where such floods normally originate).

Symbol *c* represents the idea of "not leaving any tracks." It is a leg with doubled foot lines, meaning *nothing there,* evidently coming from the idea that people are greatly subject to surprise when they have not first seen the tracks of their enemy. The flood likewise took the inhabitants of the area by surprise.

The rubbed or mutilated area (*d*) in this panel is a method of saying *destruction.* The faint symbols under this rubbed area were destroyed or ruined by abrasion. It is an appropriate method of indicating that some dwellings or people had been destroyed or ruined.

Figure 18, of an adjacent rock, tells the entire story. Symbol *a* is a picture of a *wet* man overrun by a flood. The outstretched arms mean *barring,* or *standing in the path.* The bowl-shaped symbol (*b*), of a shape similar to the cavern locator, indicates *deep.* Opposite to this is the symbol for *high* (*c*), which is probably derived from the shape of a mound. In this case it is made *wet* to show that it is a "mound" of *water.* The vertical lines indicate *in front of,* accomplished by placing the lines in front of these two symbols. The flood, then, was *high* and *deep,* and *someone was in front of it.*

SURPRISING IMPLICATIONS

Aside from the geographic evidence afforded in the narration of these two flood accounts and the consistency shown, these panels also provide evidence relating pictography to the universal sign language. According to Mallery (1881), the sign language was once used as a means of communication by nearly all

Chart 3.

A	B
Beneath or Under	Bad Spring Under Earth (Ojibwa)
Mound, Heap, or Hill	Mound or Heap (Dakota)
Talk	Intense Talk (Ojibwa)
A Dead Person	Dead (Iroquois)
Going Up or Ascending	Medicine Animal Ascending Out of His Hole (Winnebago)
Wet	Liquid (Mixtec)
Hidden	Hidden (Ojibwa)
Rock	Rock (Blackfoot)
Eyes	Eyes (Many Tribes)
Eyes	Eyes (Many Tribes)

The symbols in column *A* are all from Washington County, Utah, and compare remarkably in both shape and concept to the documented symbols in column *B* which come from other tribes located throughout the continent.

Fig. 19. The war symbol in the fore-ground (two arrowheads pointing at each other) can be easily seen from the top of this cliff. One arrowhead utilizes rock incorporation in that it is extended down over the side of the rock (arrow) to say, "war down over the side of the cliff." This symbol very appropriately locates the large panel in the background. This descriptive war story (note the shield figure) is not vis-ible from the cliff top except in the out-of-the-way position from which this photograph was taken.

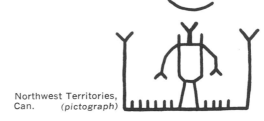

Northwest Territories,
Can.   *(pictograph)*

tribes from Alaska to Mexico. Its use overcame the difficulties posed by extreme differences in languages. The symbols for *passing through, water, in front,* and *coming down* bear close resemblances to movements for such concepts in the sign language, thus substantiating this claim.

The relationship of many symbols already discussed to those appearing in eastern pictography was also established by similarities in meanings (chart 3). With this new knowledge, deeper studies were inaugurated into the sign language and into eastern pictography. These studies proved very beneficial in later work, but prior to these discoveries, no relationship had been even remotely considered.

The works of several well known scholars in the last century present this same conclusion: Indian pictography was a widespread system based upon the sign language. Many of these arguments and the works in which they appear are discussed in a later chapter, "The Red Man's Trampled Pencil."

It is worth noting that the majority of the foregoing panels are from one cultural locality—Washington County, Utah. The feasibility of initially concentrating work in one cultural area was based on the assumption that consistency would be more pronounced within such a confined area than it would among many dissimilar cultural areas. Later, however, these symbols were found to exist with the same consistency in meaning in different cultural areas, thus implying a widespread use of this writing system. (An excellent example of a locator of a panel having a completely different topic comes from the dissimilar cultural area of the Galisteo Basin, New Mexico, and appears with its interpretation in figure 19.)

Chart 4 presents a consistency table in which the numerals represent the number of times each symbol in this chapter has been read with the same meaning. It does not cover any panels not discussed, although many do exist which could appropriately be added to this table. In order to avoid redundancy, consistency tables are not presented with each panel translated. A master table (chart 8) covering many symbols used in this work does, however, appear in the chapter, "Conclusions." This chart, showing frequencies with which symbols are used with the same meanings, proves their consistency beyond any doubt.

It was, however, the locators presented in this chapter which paved the way for the deciphering of many more complicated panels. The known symbols obtained from these locators became useful cryptanalytic wedges. Together with the new, unsolicited (and indeed unexpected) help of the sign language, and the aid of a few known symbols from eastern pictography, they greatly facilitated the process of decipherment.

There was no particular order in which panels were deciphered—many of them were studied at the same time. Each panel was considered read when its

Chart 4.

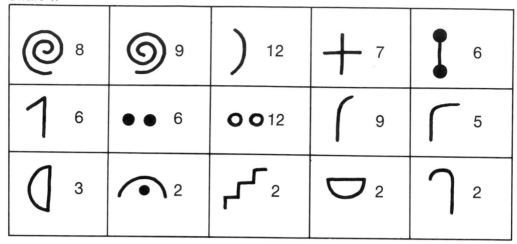

basic message was obtained. This generally occurred after a sufficient number of known symbols on each panel could be read.

After recognizing clues pointing to the general use of this system throughout the country, panels from many areas were studied, and some read. The confines of the area in which pictography was used is still undetermined. However, this study eventually led to field work encompassing areas from the Northwest Territories in Canada to the State of Oaxaca in Mexico. At the time of this writing, 1800 sketches and thousands of photographs from hundreds of sites had been accumulated.

Study is no longer confined to one cultural locality. Nevertheless, it was in one fruitful place—Washington County, Utah—that the turning point was reached in this demanding study which had then spanned twelve slow-to-yield years. Now the uphill climb levels off. New translations are being acquired, gathering momentum with almost the same intensity as that of the floods depicted centuries before.

3.

Through the Eyes of the Indian

THE IMPORTANT THING TO REMEMBER in reading rock writings is that, although this pictographic system can be translated into English (or any language), it was written *by* and *for* people of various cultures quite unlike our own. Cultural traits and linguistic idioms are so inextricably woven into its fabric that some panels may be difficult, if not impossible, for persons unacquainted with these ancient usages to read. But for the Indian living in that time—himself a part of this heritage —reading the writings left for him upon the rocks was a simple matter.

Obviously, then, the student who is serious about the study of rock writings must acquaint himself with as much information regarding pertinent Indian cultures as may be available. Scientific publications — such as the annual reports of the Bureau of Ethnology and anthropological papers of various colleges—contain useful information; however, the great bulk of Indian cultural information is, unfortunately, not yet recorded. Some of the more popular books, because of the lack of authoritative research and the tendencies of their authors to put personal interpretations (usually wrong) on pertinent data, are of doubtful value.

Documented and authoritative cultural information dating to before the arrival of the European to this land is extremely scarce, and consists almost solely of accounts handed down from generation to generation. (The areas in which subordinate evidence in translating is weak or lacking has been intentionally avoided in this work; the panels studied here, with few exceptions, are concerned with those topics on which reliable and sufficient historical, cultural, or geographic information is available.) A great number of prehistoric panels, however, can be read almost in their entirety; the subjects of these panels reveal a high percentage of battle accounts, disputes, and migrations. Their full value, however, cannot be realized until tribal identities are established and until the ancient idioms of these panels can be thoroughly understood in the light of the cultural backgrounds in which they were used.

There is no doubt that panels of this type will eventually be brought out of cultural darkness into the light of understanding with the aid of a thorough compilation and analysis of all existing panels in each area. Cryptanalytical methods are available which will help in extracting the full value of most of these panels, adding greatly to our knowledge of Indian history. But in the meantime the would-be reader of Indian rock writing must be constantly aware of these cultural difficulties and make allowances for them.

A thorough understanding of Indian pictography cannot be attained without some knowledge and feel for the sign language. There is no one book containing all the signs of the sign language, but one of the best and most nearly complete books on the subject is W. P. Clark's *The Indian Sign Language,* published in Philadelphia in 1885. This is a rare book, but recent reprints may be found in some larger libraries. This work contains no pictures but does give descriptions of signs which are not only adequate but are presented with insight into many aspects of Indian culture. *Universal Indian Sign Language,* written and published by William Tomkins (3044 Lawrence Street, San Diego), contains illustrations of almost all the signs in Clark's book. These two publications complement each other. In the *First Annual Report of the Bureau of Ethnology (1879-80),* Colonel Garrick Mallery gives much useful information not contained in either of these books. Other books on the sign language are also available.

Efficiency in reading increases as understanding of the sign language, known pictography, and Indian cultures increases. None of these essentials can be overlooked if findings are to be accurate to any degree. The sign language varies slightly from area to area; this must also be considered in deciphering symbols derived from it. Variations may also have occurred in rock writings and sign language from era to era, but this has not yet been proven.

Not all symbols of pictography are patterned after the sign language. Some concepts can be depicted better in a written symbol than in a hand sign. For example, why try to depict the sign-language *moccasin* — bringing both hands up over the feet as if putting on a pair of moccasins? It is much simpler to draw the moccasins themselves. Indian pictographic symbols are based on the sign language *only* where convenience and simplicity dictate.

A feature of pictography applied on rocks is that it is often more abbreviated than that drawn on softer materials, and therefore may appear simpler and more abstract. This abbreviation constitutes a great saving in the time and energy required to write upon hard stone. Writing upon bark or buckskin required much less time and energy, allowing the writer the option of adding more artistic detail. Recognizing those symbols which have been abbreviated is important, although it is sometimes quite difficult to do until experience in reading is acquired.

A certain type of abbreviation or omisson is necessary in *all* pictography, a result of the fact that each of the appendages and body parts of human and animal figures has an assigned meaning of its own. For example, legs equal the various actions of legs; arms equal the actions of arms; and eyes mean *looking,* or have other related meanings. Therefore, if the author's intent was to say only one thing,

Apache Co., Ariz.

all other body parts had to be omitted. The inclusion of other body parts would also have included their unwanted meanings. This accounts for the fact that many faces do not have eyes, and many bodies lack arms or legs, resulting in a sometimes startling appearance which may not be especially appealing aesthetically. The inclusion of all body appendages may be a part of art, but it is not a part of pictography.

It must be apparent by now that there is much to consider in the study of rock writings if they are to be translated accurately. A knowledge of Indian linguistic and cultural traits is much more important than learning long complicated scientific terms applied to pictography. The Indian reader of that day had only the advantages of his background and the symbols he was taught; he had no need for terms of structural classification.

The key to the simplicity of pictography, as in the sign language, lies in the fact that most of its symbols are self-interpreting, granted the reader has the proper cultural background with which to work. If the concept behind all the basic symbols (whether derived from the sign language or not) is thoroughly understood, then all the combinations, incorporations, and other uses can be figured out. It is obviously, then, more important to memorize the few hundred basic symbols and their concepts than it is to memorize the thousands of sentences and phrases formed by combinations and incorporations.

THE OLD MAN OF THE DALLES

Figure 20 exemplifies the difficulties which may be encountered in attempting to read a panel without having some knowledge of the Indian culture of the area in which the panel occurs—in this case, The Dalles, Oregon. The panel represents an old man traveling past one of the famous fishing spots of this area. His body is in profile, and his head is turned front view, indicating that he is looking over at a fisherman as he walks past. His age is signified by the bent body and cane, identical to symbols for *old man* in eastern and plains pictography and in the sign language. This old man is also *naked* or *very poor,* indicated by the absence of a belt or crotch line. (This method of saying *naked* is the same in eastern pictography.) The upper hand with the discernible palm is the sign-language *good,* accomplished by extending the right hand, palm down, away from the body on a level with the heart. This indicates a *level,* hence *good,* trail out from the heart.

The crux of this message and the key cultural idiom in the panel which identifies it as a fishing topic is the triangular symbol, an arrowhead, on this old man's buttocks. Without it, this panel would not convey anything of importance.

Research into the ways of the Indians of this area reveals that it was a custom among fisherman at this place to leave fish on the rocks near their fishing spots. Those passing by who wanted a fish could take one. However, if the fisherman could not spare them, he would indicate this to a passing Indian by slapping his

33

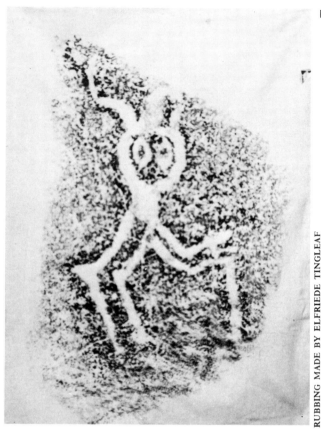

Fig. 20. The "Old Man" of The Dalles

RUBBING MADE BY ELFRIEDE TINGLEAF

own buttocks. This visual method of communication was necessary — shouting could not be heard above the roar of the falls (Seaman 1967).

The arrowhead on the old man's buttocks therefore indicates they were not slapped or *hurt,* since the arrowhead is pointing away from his body and is doing no harm. This panel might then be translated, "It is good that a fisherman should not slap his buttocks and keep a weak, poor old man passing by from taking the fish he needs." This admonition to generosity was probably for the benefit of all the needy and weak—not just the aged.

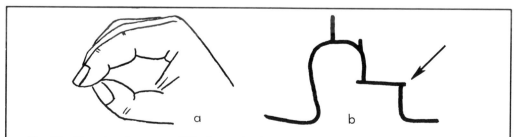

Fig. 21. The sign-language *little* is made by protruding the tip of the index finger "a little way" beyond the tip of the thumb (a). Symbol b incorporates a similar protrusion (arrow) into steps leading upward.

Utah Co., Utah

This translation aptly demonstrates just how necessary an understanding of the sign language, known pictography, and local cultural information is to the reading of panels such as this one. Lack of cultural understanding and the difficulties in obtaining it are two of the reasons why Indian pictography has not been fully deciphered.

This particular panel illustrates another common principle employed in Indian pictography. The author of this panel combines the actions of the fisherman and the old man into one symbol by drawing the arrowhead on the old man's buttocks. If he had not done this he would have had to inscribe a second figure — that of the fisherman, either in the act of slapping his own buttocks or with the arrowhead placed upon them. This probably would have meant another hour's hard work, so the motive for the incorporation of the action of two parties into one is not hard to understand. Modern-day readers, because of the ambiguity this combining presents, may not appreciate this labor-saving device; however, to Indian readers of that day and that area, no such ambiguity existed. Many a panel will be encountered in which the Indian author took for granted a certain amount of cultural and picture-writing knowledge on the part of the reader. He could not, of course, foresee that his work would be labeled as meaningless by illiterate people from another land!

Indian pictography, in its absence of sounds and because of its principles of symbol combination and incorporation, presents other inherent problems which must be considered in reading it. One of these problems is the necessity of combining or incorporating one symbol into all other symbols in constructing a phrase, where such combination of meanings is necessary. This cannot always be done. The shape of many symbols will not allow others to be combined with or incorporated into them without sacrificing clarity and distorting meaning. Indian pictography bridges this gap by providing several methods of saying the same thing—each of which can be clearly understood and conveniently used with other appropriate symbols.

For example, the concept *little* is expressed in the sign language as shown in figure 21 (*a*). This same sign is incorporated into the steps proceeding up the side of a human head, as seen in symbol *b*. The short protrusions on these steps represent *little,* and by incorporating them into the steps, the idea of *a little way up* is conveyed. The head denotes direction, and the line on top of the head indicates *on top.* This complete unit says, "Go up a little way in this direction until you are on top." This panel (a very ancient one as evidenced by the dark patination) locates a waterhole on the topmost point of a sandstone dome near Jackson, Utah, reached a short way upward in this same direction from the location of the panel.

This sign for *little* can be conveniently and clearly incorporated into steps, as shown, but it cannot be as readily incorporated into a pointing finger. However, a very short pointing finger (figure 12, symbol *e*) is much more suggestive of "a little way in this direction" than other methods. Such short pointing fingers are

35

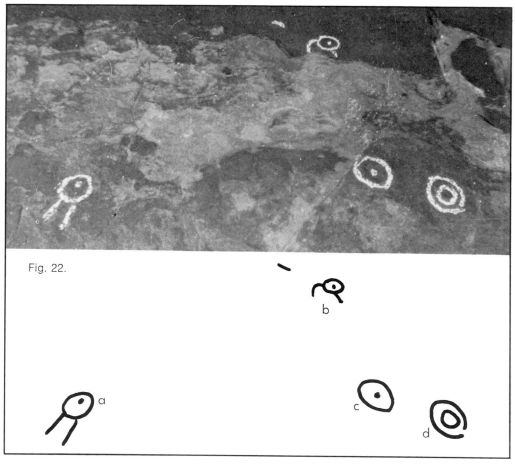

Fig. 22.

quite common. Another simple and suggestive way of saying *little*, without using the sign-language method, is by making the symbol very small in size—a technique which was very useful in drawing figures of people and animals. Many symbols thus have their own unique methods for indicating the same idea, not using any one standard symbol. This is equally true in the sign language.

Fig. 23. The personal name symbol *Searching Cloud* from an Ogallala Sioux roster denotes direction of vision (Mallery). The two lines point upward —just as the spread index and second fingers denote direction of vision in the sign language.

Fremont River,
Utah

The symbols of eyes, or *looking,* is another good example of the existence of various methods for saying the same thing. In the sign language, *looking* is very clearly expressed by spreading the index and second fingers of the right hand, with thumb and other fingers closed, and then placing these two spread fingers in front of the eyes. This sign at the same time appropriately denotes vision in any particular direction. In the form of a pictographic symbol it conveys these ideas just as clearly.

For example, in symbol *a,* figure 22, the circle with a dot in it represents the top view of a waterhole, and the two lines represent the two spread fingers of the sign language. This symbol therefore represents *looking at a waterhole,* and points directly at one which is located just a few feet away.

The conventional locator—eyes lining up and pointing at this waterhole—is not used for several reasons. If this type of symbol had been placed on the inside of the circle, it would indicate looking *inside* a waterhole. If eyes were placed on the outside, they would indicate looking at the *edge* of a waterhole. The simplest way to get the message across, in this case, was by using the two spread fingers pointing directly *at* the waterhole. Pointing at the waterhole itself eliminated any ambiguity, since common sense tells us the waterhole cannot "look."

From this example, we can see that depictions of eyes are sometimes more appropriate in other usages, especially on faces. Even so, in some instances of eyes placed on a face, the two fingers of the sign-language symbol are used at the same time to denote direction (figure 23). The necessity in a pictography for having several methods of saying the same thing is obvious.

These examples of eyes also show why symbols derived from the sign language are not always used—in many cases the pictures of the eyes themselves are much more descriptive than the two fingers!

Figure 22 emphasizes another important principle which is practiced in the sign language as well as in almost all hieroglyphic systems of the world. This is the principle of extending the meaning of a basic sign or symbol into a much broader range of meaning. For example, the concept of the circle and dot is *held in one place.* The dot indicates a fixed position, or *here;* the circle comes from the sign-language symbol *holding,* made by encircling arms. The basic concept of the circle and dot is very simple, and can be extended to mean many other things —*waterhole, unable to get out, corraled, out of reach, within, a good place, pinned down,* and other ideas based on its suggestive concept. Whenever this symbol is used, the author normally distinguishes the extended sense for which it is intended by its context in the panel or by certain symbols (determinatives) with which it is used. In figure 22 it clearly indicates a waterhole, simply by pointing and *looking* at one, and its use throughout the panel is thus established.

If one does *not* know the actual concept or idea behind the circle and dot, its extended meaning would not be so apparent. This brings up one of the most important prerequisites to understanding both the sign language and pictography —knowledge of the concept or actual idea behind the basic meaning of each and every symbol. Once these are mastered, the understanding of extensions will follow. **It is not always the concept itself that must be read into a translation; more commonly it is some meaning extended from that concept.**

It is this principle of extension that greatly simplifies Indian pictography and the sign language. It also keeps to a minimum the number of basic symbols and signs to be memorized. The large number of extensions possible to derive from a basic concept is common to this type of system. The sign language itself has many basic signs commonly extended into numerous other meanings.

The rest of the panel in figure 22 is now translated in order to show the reader the consistency of this extended meaning throughout the panel. This translation is supported by accompanying geographic evidence.

Symbol *b*, the *holding* symbol, extended to mean *waterhole,* is placed on the side of a symbol for a *large rock.* The pointing finger above and to the left of this incorporation indicates the only practical position from which this particular waterhole can be seen: This additional waterhole can be spotted only by lookng down from off the top of a higher section of this rock dome to the left of the waterhole. The direction in which this finger is pointing is apparent at the site, since in the opposite direction it would point at the sky. The intended direction of most "fingers" is similarly evident.

Symbol *c* represents a waterhole again. It is placed beside a symbol (*d*) with opposite meaning—a *hollow place,* or *nothing in it,* which in this case is extended to indicate an *empty waterhole.* The meaning *empty* is clarified by the opening left in the lower side of the outer circle from which the water "ran out."

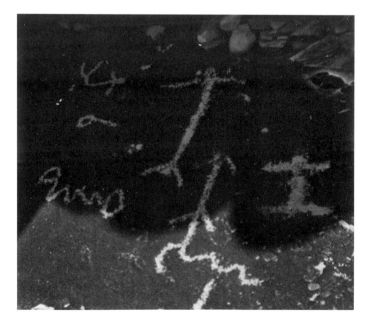

Fig. 24. Two long stick figures from Clark County, Nevada, utilize a symbol positioning identical to the sign-language finger positions for *behind, interior,* and similar meanings.

38

Pocatello, Idaho

The conjunction of symbols *c* and *d* seems to express an idea which would be quite difficult to portray in any pictography: "At times these waterholes have something (water) in them, and at other times they are empty." This is actually the case—their only source of supply is rain. The idea of different times for the same waterhole is expressed by placing symbols *c* and *d* on the same level, conveying the idea *same*. In Indian pictography, drawings done on different levels normally represent different people, events, times or objects; while symbols placed on the same level indicate the same or identical objects, people, time, or other similar meanings.

This is a very difficult idea to express, but is one that has been handled well by the author of this panel, a fact which becomes evident when it is read at the site in conjunction with the waterholes themselves. Plurality is intended but is not indicated by symbols *c* and *d*. It is, however, indicated by symbols *a* and *b,* which locate two separate waterholes. Plurality is often implied in such a manner in the sign language. Once it has been established it is unnecessarily cumbersome to apply it to each sign.

This very ancient panel comes from Jackson, Utah, and, in conjunction with figure 21, locates three large waterholes or pockets situated on a large sandstone dome. The position of these waterpockets aided greatly in this translation while at the same time offering supporting geographic evidence.

This panel is an excellent example of many of the problems encountered in reading Indian pictography. This panel could not have been clearly understood from a photograph alone, even though the basic concepts of all these symbols might have been known. It could not have been translated anywhere but at the site itself since much of its meaning depends upon adjacent geography.

This panel also serves to point out that certain types of positioning—such as positioning at different levels—often have a very useful purpose, in that the realm of possible expression is thus enlarged. For example, the placing of one man or animal symbol above, behind, or to the side of another indicates the meaning suggested by that positioning.

One of the more common positioning devices employed in Indian pictography is exemplified in figure 24. One figure is a little to the right, to denote a different individual, and is also lower, hence *inferior* to the other. This positioning may also denote that the lower figure was *last* in whatever was being discussed, or it may denote future tense. If the lower right-hand figure had been raised or placed to the right front of the figure on the left, it then would have denoted the opposite—*superior, ahead, first,* or the past tense. (Most symbols, just as in the sign language, are meant to be read in the present tense unless their positioning indicates otherwise.) These symbols are derived from the sign-language signs for these same meanings, made by positioning the index fingers of the hands in these

Fig. 25. Symbols *a* from the *Walum Olum* depict the succession of Indian chiefs. *Big Owl* (upper left-hand symbol) was succeeded, or followed, by *White Bird* (lower right-hand symbol). The sign language utilizes the same method to convey the same idea (*b*).

relative positions (figure 25, *b*). This sign is used so frequently in the sign language that it could hardly be omitted in a pictography needing to express the same ideas.

This symbol for *later* also occurs in the *Walum Olum* in denoting the order of succession of certain chiefs, thus substantiating the authenticity of that record (figure 25, *a*). (For more information on the *Walum Olum,* see the chapter, "The Red Man's Trampled Pencil.") This type of positioning was one of the early clues leading to the recognition of a relationship between pictography and the sign language. It must always be considered and included in the reading of any panel.

Another type of positioning is that of certain superimposed symbols (one drawn over another). The superimposition of symbols is a very common, practical, and integral feature of rock writing and was used to indicate such ideas as *behind, in front, association,* and other self-suggesting meanings. It is also probable that some authors of panels with long stories resorted to superimposition because of the lack of available rock space. This applies only to those superimposed symbols

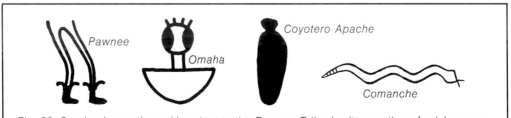

Fig. 26. Cornhusks on the ankles denote the Pawnee Tribe by its practice of raising corn (Mallery). The Omaha Tribe was noted for cropped hair and painted cheeks (Mallery). Rawhide extensions curling up on the moccasin toes of the Coyotero Apache identify them (Arizona-New Mexico example). The Comanche were known as "Snakes" (Texas example).

Iron Co.,
Utah

which show no age differentiation. (This can be determined on petroglyphs by comparing the different degrees of patination, and on pictographs by noting the greater degree of dimness on the older, underlying symbols.)

Indian pictography was capable of saying or implying anything which the author desired to communicate. If no basic symbol existed with which to convey a certain idea, then it could be *explained* by several symbols—improvising, just as the sign language does on similar occasions. As shown repeatedly, abstract words present no problem to the Indian; in fact, the sign language itself is the greatest witness to its own ability to express all abstract words of spoken Indian languages. **If it can be said in signs, it can also be said in symbols.**

Personal, tribal, and village names are easily depicted, since they almost always were descriptive words simple to transfer into picture form: "Red Cloud," "Sitting Bull," "Cutthroats" (Sioux), "Snakes" (Comanche), "Sunrise Hill Place," "Rocky River"—a few of the names so typical of Indian nomenclature. Indian names can, however, throw a monkey wrench into the mechanism of symbol affinity, since their meanings very often have no affinity to surrounding symbols. If this variance is thoroughly understood, however, it can be used advantageously in distinguishing names.

Tribal names were highly susceptible to change because of the unending migrations of the numerous tribes of America throughout the past centuries. History shows that they constantly picked up new names applied to them by other tribes, and the older ones were subsequently forgotten. This makes it difficult to trace a tribe by its tribal name alone very far back into history.

Tribal names are often inconspicuous and, if not understood, can be easily confused with the text itself. For example, the tribal name *Pawnee* is two bent leaves from a cornstalk drawn on the feet of a man (figure 26). This stands simply for the Pawnee Tribe, and is derived from its custom of raising corn, hence *walking* in it. It should not be confused with or read in any other context, such as "walking through a cornfield."

Pictures of realistic animals also often stand for tribal names, especially for clans having animals for their totems. Tanner explains a picture-writing example wherein the handle of a knife touches a snake and the point of the same knife touches a bear. This meant that someone of the Snake totem had killed one of the Bear totem (Tanner 1830, p. 165). Thus it is apparent that symbols of this type cannot be interpreted as dealing with the animals themselves.

Many of America's tribes had no clans, and therefore had no clan symbols. Nevertheless, they did have tribal symbols and symbols for the different bands of that tribe, based on some distinguishing feature of each group. These symbols were not always animals.

41

Another point to remember regarding the meaning of an animal form is that it may either represent that animal, or stand for any of its qualities, attributes, habits, or environments. Likewise, a picture of an object may either represent that object or stand for any use or idea associated with it.

In rock writing, contrary to what might be assumed, there is no order or direction in which symbols were meant to be read. Indeed, there *can* be no word order in many of the combinations and incorporations devised basically for the sake of clarity. Word order would place stringent limitations on clarity in trying to compose symbols into understandable phrases. **Clarity is the rule—not symbol order.**

A predetermined pattern of symbol order would also limit the use of this pictography to one Indian language only, since word order varies from tribe to tribe. If any particular order were followed, then this system could not be used except by a limited few. We know this is not the case. **It is essentially this lack of word order that enabled rock writing to be so widely used by all tribes.**

The symbols in rock writings were arranged in a cluster method. The placing of each symbol was predicated upon clarity and the meanings assigned to certain relative positions. In reading any panel, all symbols are first studied individually, until the whole story falls into place. The topic must first be distinguished. It is often revealed by certain key symbols in a panel (such as the arrowhead on the buttocks of the old man at The Dalles). These may often appear inconspicuous and unimportant, but are nevertheless the reading foundation of the entire panel. If the topic is not identified, then the panel cannot be fully read, even though most of the symbols in it are known.

Large panels in which a story has a definite beginning are studied until the topic is isolated and the beginning of the story located. It was the responsibility of the author to separate or distinguish anything that might appear confusing to the reader, and by context to keep the story in its proper chronological order.

Some panels might initially deceive the reader by appearing to be completely foreign to anything ever seen, but closer examination by the experienced student will show that they are not so different after all. In such cases, well-known symbols may only seem strange because they appear in rare and unusual phrases which necessitate unusual arrangements, combinations, or incorporations to get

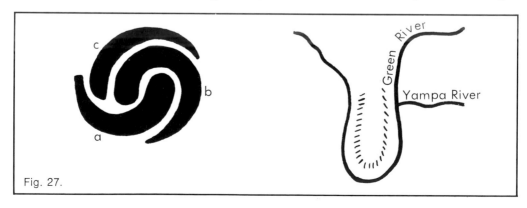

Fig. 27.

42

Pennsylvania

the intended meanings across. It is more often the phrase and its arrangement that are rare—not the symbols themselves.

This principle can be carried too far in some panels where, say, a large face or abstract body is not first recognized as such. When this is the case, attempts to break these symbols down can only result in disappointment. A good example of one of these phrases appears in figure 27. This arrangement is unusual only because of the rarity of what it describes. Panels such as this are exceptional, and should not discourage the student of rock writing.

THE CONFLUENCE OF THE GREEN AND YAMPA RIVERS

This unit comes from the vicinity of the juncture of the Yampa River with the Green River in the northeastern corner of Utah. At the point of this river confluence, the Green River is revolving in an almost complete circle in a canyon (shown in the sketch map in figure 27). This type of river junction is a unique occurrence, and any symbol describing it would be equally as rare and would therefore look strange.

The three revolving, eye-like symbols (*a, b,* and *c*) tell of this unique confluence. In reading this symbol unit, keep in mind that it merely tells *of* it — it is not a map to be viewed and therefore does not resemble one. This is important to remember in reading many panels containing geographic information and in the reading of maps.

A *darkened-eye* symbol represents a canyon. This eye is covered or blackened to indicate *dark*. This refers to traveling in the dark and is appropriately extended to mean *canyon*. The steep walls of a canyon make it difficult to tell where one is in relation to the rest of the country, or to see what lies ahead. "Traveling through an unknown country" is similarly expressed in the sign language by describing travel in the dark (Clark 1885, p. 417). In this unit, two of these canyon symbols (*a* and *b*) are revolving about themselves just as the canyon itself does. Symbol *a* has its end chopped off to indicate that it is not a complete revolution. (*Chopped off* or *unfinished* is indicated in the sign language by pretending to chop off the tips of the left fingers with the downward stroke of the right hand as if it were a hatchet.) This uncompleted revolution is an accurate description of the canyon bend.

Symbol *c* represents the canyon of the Yampa River as it comes in from the east and joins the Green in this revolution. (East is indicated, since the top of most panels is assigned the meaning of *top* or *north* when direction is to be implied.)

This unit reveals why many combinations, incorporations, and units are rare to non-existent in many parts of the country. This is to be expected because of the almost infinite number of phrases possible in Indian pictography. Rare phrases might run through a great number of topics, depending on what subjects were being discussed in any one area at the time; they must be studied in this light.

This example also points to the danger which exists in viewing pictography for its appearance alone, a tendency most apt to occur in viewing samples from an unusually attractive picture-writing system — Egyptian hieroglyphics, for example. The reader may be hypnotized into seeing its artistic merits only, and thus ignore its message. Just viewing them from an artistic standpiont alone obscures their basic purposes and reveals nothing of intended importance. **All symbols in all picture-writing systems were intended to be read and not just viewed.**

Combinations, incorporations, and units are usually the most attractive symbols in Indian pictography, but they must be broken down into individual concepts before each can be read as a whole. In figure 27, for example, the symbols in and of themselves depict only words of such varied meanings as *crooked, canyon, revolving,* and *chopped off.* This apparent jumble must be read as a whole in the proper linguistic order of the language of the reader. This unit might, then, be loosely read in English, "at a place where a crooked canyon coming in from the east meets a revolving canyon that almost, but not entirely, rotates about itself."

Logic and common sense play an intrinsic role in the reading of Indian pictography. It was assumed by the Indian authors that readers would employ their mental talents in obtaining the message. This pictography is not a system devised for the mentally lazy, nor is it something to be learned or read by rote as easily as an alphabetical system. Indian pictography, with its thousands of phrase possibilities which can be constructed from a few hundred basic symbols, necessarily and consistently demands the effort and logic of the human mind. Out of its limitless possibilities, many phrases are bound to be new to any reader and thus require his mental application to decipher them.

The rules of logic and mental exercise apply to the sign language as well. Many sign-language "phrases" and "sentences" may appear to the uninitiated to be as jumbled as a pictographic phrase. However, after acquiring a little familiarity with use, it will be seen that this apparent lack of order has a definite design conducive to clarity.

Washington Co.,
Utah

The value of having no set rules of organization in these two systems was demonstrated unintentionally by the Abbe Secard in his unsuccessful attempt to improve upon the sign language of deaf mutes—a language similarly without any apparent organization. He devised a method in which many new signs were created to distinguish the parts of speech for each sign. This method included tense, inflection, and plurality, and was constructed to follow the exact word order of a spoken language. Practical application proved the system too cumbersome and unwieldy, and after a life span of only eighteen years (1817 to 1835) it had to be abandoned (Mallery 1881).

This experiment did provide proof for the worth of the priority of clarity which exists in the Indian and deaf-mute sign languages and in Indian pictography — all of which have endured the practical test of use throughout the ages.

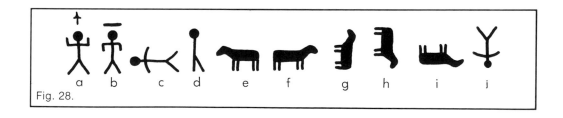

Fig. 28.

46

4.

On Behalf of
the Versatile Goat

ONE OF THE MOST USEFUL and versatile symbols of the entire Indian picture-writing system is the goat, and it is one which is really quite simple to understand. Perhaps one of the best ways for this symbol to be truly appreciated is for a person to attempt, by himself, the construction of a complete and understandable pictography. In the course of such a project, many conflicts in symbol meaning would surely arise as one attempted to depict certain expressions.

This may be better understood by using actual examples in Indian pictography to illustrate such points of conflict. For example, the figure of a man (figure 28, symbol *a*) often—but not always—stands for *movement straight ahead* in the direction shown by the arrow above the head. The fact that this symbol is often used to portray a direction straight ahead is evidenced by the existence of a great many examples of figures with bars (or other symbols) above the head, indicating the movement is *blocked* or *barred* in this direction (*b*).

A figure lying down (*c*) stands for exactly that—*lying down*. The conflict in symbol usage occurs when one tries to portray lateral movement with a human figure. A prone figure cannot be used for this purpose since it would be confused with the concept of lying down. The conflict could be partly resolved by drawing a profile of a person; however, this would require the depiction of a figure large enough to add profile features (such as the nose). Thus another conflict develops—that of adding the unwanted meaning assigned to such features. If a profile figure is used in which one leg is projected to indicate lateral movement (*d*), then there is a conflict with the meaning already assigned to the symbol—that of *starting off*, or *departing*.

At a time far back in antiquity, the Indian devised a much simpler method of bridging these conflicts. The answer lay in the use of the quadruped symbol. This particular device provided a very useful method of depicting a profile body. (In fact, the quadruped is quite difficult to draw in a facing view, as one might

47

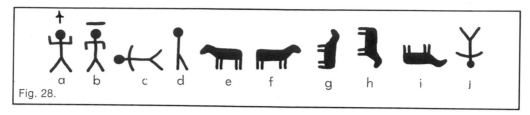

Fig. 28.

with the human body, and such portrayals are almost non-existent in Indian pictography).

The quadruped therefore solves the problem of depicting lateral action—to the left (*e*) or to the right (*f*). In addition, it can depict movement uphill (*g*) or downhill (*h*). The use of quadruped symbols to depict lateral movement accounts for the low frequency of profile human figures in Indian pictography. Conversely, the quadruped symbols are very frequent, as required for complete expression in a pictography. (The concept of death, however, can be demonstrated equally as well by the human form [*j*] as it can by the quadruped [*i*].)

These illustrations demonstrate the versatility of the quadruped. It allows the use of very simple symbols to portray and impart life to the various directions of movement so basic to and used so frequently in a complete pictography. It is also very useful in composing animated phrases (as opposed to pictorial renderings).

Because of their unique, neutral pictographic function, quadruped symbols, in almost all cases, fail to fully and correctly fulfill the requirements of a realistic depiction of any one particular animal. They have been called mountain sheep, dogs or coyotes (when horns are not applied), and occasionally deer. In reality they are only appropriate methods of expressing certain phrases—phrases which always refer to the actions of people and not to animals (unless animals are the topic under discussion). In reading rock writings, then, it is very important not to confuse *quadruped action* with *actual quadrupeds*.

Because of their strictly pictographic use in this sense, goat symbols often take on a highly abstract appearance, such as those in figure 7. Many basic symbols of Indian pictography are often incorporated into the body of a quadruped or are added to it as some significant appendage, resulting in the creation of countless abstract forms. These are simple to understand if the concept of each incorporated or combined symbol is understood individually and then interpreted as a whole.

The horns of the common goat symbol were the most difficult symbols in

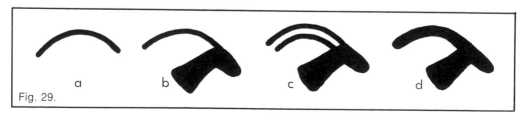

Fig. 29.

48

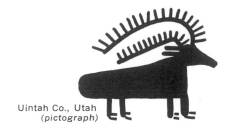

Uintah Co., Utah
(pictograph)

Indian pictography to crack. Figure 7 presents only a few of the great variety of forms in which they exist. The key to deciphering these forms was found when recognizable and independent symbols — such as various angles and canes—were first deciphered in their basic form, unattached to a body. After such an independent symbol was deciphered, it became a simple matter to add its meaning to the meaning of the goat's head (normally denoting either direction of travel or something pertaining to the head) to which it may be attached, and thus read the entire unit as a whole.

Symbol *c* of figure 29 was one of the most common styles of goat horns encountered, and yet was the most difficult to decipher. Many guesses assigned to this symbol always failed to withstand stringent cryptanalytic tests. It was not until the meanings of double-lined (open), and widened symbols were determined that the purpose of this particular horn became obvious. Open, or double-lined symbols (such as the empty waterhole in figure 22, symbol *d*) indicate empty space, and by extension *nothing there, taken off,* and other related meanings. This comes from the sign-language sign *wiped off,* in which the right palm sweeps the left in a motion as if to wipe it off. Symbols purposely widened, or bodies and open symbols pecked solid throughout indicate just the opposite: *something there,* hence *bad, encumbered, dirty,* or any other meaning which can be extended from this basic concept.

In picture-writing examples of the Dakota, documented by Mallery in 1893, meanings identical to those given here for doubled and widened lines were used. Dakota examples suggest even a much wider range of extension. They used doubled lines or open bodies (since there is *nothing on them*) to mean *clean, good* and *white.* Solidly pecked bodies similarly often represented *black.* (To the Indian, however, *white* and *black* do not represent *good* and *evil* in the sense used among white men.)

A single arc conforms to two different signs in the sign language — a *completed movement* and a *covering* (figure 29, symbol *a*). To show a *completed movement* in the sign language, the hand is pushed out away from the body in a sweeping arc. *Covering* is shown by the hand, cupped with palm down, held still. (This is also used to mean *hidden.*) In pictography, however, both arcs are indistinguishable from each other. Therefore, to show that movement is intended, the arc is attached to a head (*b*), which normally shows *direction,* hence *movement.*

When the arc which depicts movement (*b*) is doubled, as in symbol *c*, the combination indicates that something has been either *taken, wiped,* or *knocked off,* or that *nothing was there* to hinder this movement, or journey. Symbol *d* consequently represents an *encumbered movement,* clearly depicted by the widened

49

line, which indicates *something on it,* hence *encumbered,* and other related meanings. (This symbol should not be confused with the wavy or wiggly line which depicts an *uncompleted movement*—something in the *act* of moving.) A doubled covering symbol, of course, indicates that the covering was *taken off,* or *uncovered.*

An arc, the sign-language method of representing a specific completed movement, is very appropriate and indeed necessary in a pictography, and is ingeniously used to portray numerous ideas. These various uses of arcs on heads are the very reasons why such symbols coincidentally resemble goats or mountain sheep.

It must be remembered that the numerous variations in which horns occur do not all mean the same thing. Each must be studied in relation to its shape and the symbols used in conjunction with it.

Fig. 30. This panel contains symbols from both old and modern cultures. It was inscribed by Hunkup, a Southern Paiute, to record impressions of his train trip back East.

Fig. 31. Hunkup, in his Indian evaluation of the white man's peculiar ways, was as amused by the fact that they built houses for their horses (barns) as he was by the toilet facilities on their "fire wagon."

50

San Juan Co., Utah

HUNKUP TAKES A JOURNEY

A good example of how the goat may be used to convey a specific idea appears in figure 30. This panel, located about 20 miles south of Kanosh, Utah, was written by a Paiute named Hunkup, from Kanosh. For the benefit of other Indian readers, he depicted the things that impressed and amused him (figure 31) on his train trip to the East at some forgotten date (Beckwith 1947). There can be no question about the authenticity of the goat symbol in this panel, since it was clearly done with the same metal chisel which inscribed the trains and buildings, all of which show noticeable patination of the same degree.

Symbol *a*, appearing directly below the goat and again on top of the engine, is the same symbol-doubling used on horns to denote *nothing there, taking it off,* and other similar meanings. Here it is used to say that the train cars and engine could be *taken off* (disconnected). This usage is apparent in that these lines are not realistic features of the train. The goat helps to clarify the concept of disconnecting cars by its position directly over symbol *a*. This symbol, minus the horns, resembles a horse more nearly than a goat because of its arched neck. It might have been meant as a reference to the "iron horse" (train), a term popular in those days (not of Paiute or Ute origin).

Both ends of the lower horn are connected to this quadruped—one end to the head and the other end to the neck. This refers to the fact that the engine (head) is *connected* to the first car (neck) as depicted below the quadruped. The top horn adds the meaning implied by doubling and does not touch the neck, therefore indicating *taking off*. In other words, when the engineer *changed* or *reversed his mind* (reversed goat), he could take off or disconnect the cars.

This Indian used the idea of *reversed* direction to also mean a "change of mind." This is an excellent example of an Indian idiom, so basic to Indian pictography. The English language is equally replete with idioms, e.g. "a chip off the old block," "on his high horse," and thousands of other expressions so puzzling to Indians or non-English-speaking peoples, just as this one may be to non-Indians. Without knowing what this idiom means, one might naturally conclude that, since the goat and the train are pointed in opposite directions, they refer to the journey "to" and the return "from," but the meaning of these unique horns and the relationship of his goat to symbol *a* rule out this idea.

The man on top of the engine with his arms hanging down inactively means that the train *ran by itself*. The middle figure pictures the arm in the straighter *negation* position to indicate that Hunkup *did not like the long wait* (bar above the head). Note the tracks above this bar made by the passengers who changed trains, hence the purpose of depicting two trains. The last figure is in the act of urinating, to show that this train *had toilet facilities*. This fact is portrayed by the suggestive position of the left arm, and is clarified even more by the right hand, which is shown pointed at the ground—the sign-language sign for this act.

This panel, because of the depictions of trains and buildings, naturally does not resemble older panels, but there can be no dispute about whether Hunkup had a working knowledge of the pictographic writing system. The symbols he used—the goat, human figures "riding the train," and doubled lines—all came from the old system.

The practice of pictography among the Indians of central Utah is confirmed by Father Escalante in his journal entry of September 25, 1776. He describes and explains the meaning of symbols painted on a piece of buckskin—a very sacred token given to him by the Indians of this vicinity (Auerbach 1943). John W. Gunnison, who was killed by the very band of Indians to which Hunkup belonged, also attests to the practice of pictography among them (Gunnison 1857).

Many other panels in which trains or "fire wagons" appear in company with older symbols may be found near old Ute and Paiute encampments and reservation sites. They are vivid evidence of the recent use of pictography among these people. Several living Southern Paiute informants claim that some of the panels in central and southern Utah were made by their ancestors. Other panels they ascribe to the Hopi and invading Plains tribes. Those which are too high up on the rocks to be reached by human hands are ascribed to supernatural beings, or to God.

Fig. 32. Indians with packs in quest of wives

Puerco River, Ariz.

AN ANCIENT COURTING EPISODE

An example of a unique use of goat horns may be found in figure 32. This example proves conclusively that these horns do not depict mountain sheep: They are used here upon the heads of men—and also upon their packs!

The men in this panel are all carrying packs containing either their belongings or some precious item such as tanned hides. They can thus clearly depict lateral action without any conflicting meaning. Symbol *c* is phallic, showing that the intent of these men was to trade these packs for wives. This was a very common Indian practice among the more sedentary tribes, who—because of their farming activities and the probable lack of larger game in their dry climate—did not have an overabundance of hides; thus they were a valued item for barter.

Whenever the figure of a packman with a flute is encountered today, it is usually erroneously labeled *Kokopelli,* the hunchbacked Hopi deity known for his flute playing. The symbol of flute playing, however, was an almost universal method of depicting courting activities; flutes were commonly used in playing love songs in the hope of enticing a pretty girl into marriage. An affinity check on many flute-playing examples supports the "wife purchasing" and "girl seducing" intent of this symbol by producing numerous examples depicting a phallus, often erect; a small pack (indicating they did not have enough trade goods to make a suitable trade); figures lying prone (to induce a girl to lie with them); and figures having rabbit ears (denoting prolificacy). Therefore, flute-playing men with packs upon their backs portray a journey to a different tribe for the purposes of courting and purchasing wives. A similar meaning for the flute-player symbol is affirmed by the Hopi (Wellmann 1970) and by a few other Pueblo tribes.

The packmen in figure 32, shown journeying through Wayne County, Utah (the location of this panel), at a time in the past when a puebloid people such as the Fremont Culture existed there, are *not,* however, playing flutes. The courting intent, indicated by the hanging penis, is already apparent. Besides, the depiction of flutes would have interfered with the right-angled symbols in front of these men.

Note that the men stand erect, and that their packs are drawn to fit the full length of their backs to show their big load. (This is contrary to the bent-over condition and the concentration of a hump on the *upper* back which the writer would have depicted had he intended to portray Kokopelli.) Evidence clinching the argument that such figures normally depict men with packs appears in figure 33. This Paiute panel from near Las Vegas, Nevada, shows a white man or Spaniard (hat) with a rifle over his shoulders and a pack on his back, heading down the Spanish trail to California. This was surely not Kokopelli; he is not even known among the Paitues.

The right-angled symbols (*b, c,* and *d*) in figure 32 indicate that these

53

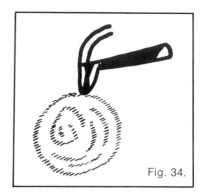

Fig. 34.

Fig. 33. A Paiute depiction of an early traveler, with rifle and pack, heading to California on the Spanish trail

men would *not turn aside* or abandon their course. They had come from a long way off—indicated by the gradual diminishing in size. The smallness of symbol *e* represents the size of things viewed at a distance—hence *a journey from afar*. This little figure's hands are reaching out, as are those of symbol *c,* to show that they are *going after something* (women).

The horns on the packs of *a, b,* and *c* do not refer to a pack full of mountain-sheep horns, due to the presence of the phallic symbol and the reaching arms, and since similar horns also occur on the head of symbol *a.* The horns on the pack of packman *a* curve out from under themselves. Coupled with the double-line meaning *nothing there* or *off,* they indicate removing and coming out from beneath

Fig. 35. This ancient panel recounts a journey into the depths of the Grand Canyon. (The arrow refers to the direction faced in looking at the panel. It also serves as a scale, since it is one foot in length.)

Los Alamos, N. Mex.

the packs—or, more simply, *taking them off*, proving conclusively that they were packs.

The *turned aside* symbol in front of this man, and his reversed direction indicate that he *abandoned* his pack and quest for women and *returned home*. (The reason for this has not yet been fully determined.)

The horns on the packs of *b* and *c* appear in the form of a journeying, doubled arc to say that the packs *completed a safe journey* at this stage of the trip. However, as they are not attached to a head, they might mean that a covering was taken off. This could have various connotations—the head appendages of these two packmen are not fully understood. Adjacent panels are obviously related to this panel and may give additional details, once they have been deciphered. But in the meantime, these packmen serve as excellent examples of the various ways in which horns can be used to convey information.

A Goat Symbol Among the Plains Indians

A symbol which may have puzzled the reader is that which is shown in figure 8, appearing again in figure 34. It is the Dakota personal name *Flat Iron*, just as it appears on Red Cloud's census record of about 1880. This combination shows a horned head and a circle in a manner that, to the uninitiated, seems completely foreign to the expression "flat iron." It is, however, very appropriate, and its relationship becomes clear once the proper symbol concepts are understood.

This goat's head facilitates an extremely simple way of saying *flat* by the use of doubled horns, which indicate *off*. These horns are placed at the extreme left end of the head and long flat neck, as if to say that everything was taken off the top of this area. In other words, this area was leveled, or *made flat*. The circle touching the mouth represents an iron plate, from which the Indian began to eat at about this period in history. This plate conforms to the sign-language method of saying *iron*, which is accomplished by pointing at anything made of iron. It can therefore be seen how the meanings *flat* and *iron* are portrayed in this unique example.

A Descent Into the Grand Canyon

The panel in figure 35, from near Tuweap, Arizona, on the North Rim of the Grand Canyon, is an excellent example of how horns and quadrupeds may be used together to express a concept.

Because of the extreme age and consequent lack of contrast afforded by this panel, it had to be heavily chalked in order to take a distinct photograph. The goats with incomplete legs were not fully chalked because of the difficulty in distinguishing their forms, but the rest of the panel can be readily discerned.

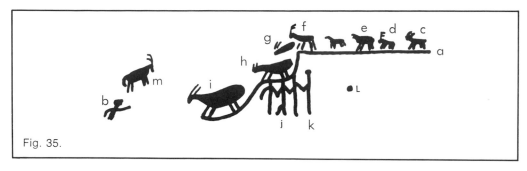

Fig. 35.

Symbol *a* depicts the *rim* and the *depths* of the Grand Canyon. Because of the supplementary aid given by this symbol in depicting this cross-section of the Grand Canyon, the goat symbols are more readily comprehended. The location of this panel on the canyon rim also lends supporting geographic evidence to the accuracy of this translation.

The string of goats following each other off the canyon rim and down into the bottom represents *many people* traveling down into the canyon. The fact that these goats on the rim are of many sizes indicates that the group was composed of entire families—men, women, and children.

Symbol *b* represents a figure beckoning this tribe to *come and stay*. This is indicated by the position of the arms—one is beckoning, and the other is pointing to the ground. That he is *across the canyon* is shown by rock incorporation (the ridge and depression in front of goat *m*).

The horns—those which can be fully discerned—in this string of visiting or migrating quadrupeds all have meanings appropriate to their positions. Goats *c, d,* and *f* all speak of leaving the rim. The horns of goat *d* show an *up* symbol, with the top line doubled to indicate *off from up*. Goat *f* uses the *distant* symbol pointing upward to say *far up*. The top of this symbol is also doubled to complete the meaning *off from far up,* or, in other words, "off from the high rim," indicated further by the positioning of this goat on the rim itself.

Goat *i* has horns with only a slight curve that are but a continuation of the angle of the head. In other words, the horns represent a deep bowl with the head down at the bottom of this bowl to indicate *going way down into*. The goat's head resembles a deep bowl with just a little liquid in the bottom of it (symbol *a,* figure 36). Symbol *b* of this figure shows this same bowl, slightly

Fig. 36.

56

Wayne Co., Utah

curved to add movement to its meaning, thus making it automatically resemble a head (for which it is commonly used when such meaning is appropriate). In this example the bowl shape is too crudely depicted to decipher as such, but from better examples studied in this area, some confidence is felt in assuming the foregoing meaning.

The bodies of goats *g, h,* and *i* all incorporate the *darkened-eye* symbol as the shape of their bodies. These canyon symbols thus indicate that the Indians are now *traveling within a canyon.*

The goats on the rim utilize different body shapes appropriate to their positions. The bodies of goats *g, h,* and *i* also become increasingly larger to indicate that this group is *getting closer* to its destination, as is the case when one appears larger as he approaches from a distance.

At a certain point in this journey goat *h* is "chopped off" at its tail to indicate that the journey was prematurely *ended,* at least by part of the group. The author resorted to human figures at this point in order to clarify and elaborate upon this section of the story. The heads of all four of these *migrating* or "traveling together" human figures form part of the path of the goats to indicate that they are *one and the same people,* and that they were already *within* the canyon. (Figure 37 provides another more recent example of "hand-holding" symbols.) The position of these figures below the canyon line (*a*) indicates the meaning of *beneath,* and hence *within,* and also clarifies the idea that symbol *a* is a profile view of the canyon and not the top view of a trail.

Symbol *k* is a human form for *gone* (since it lacks legs), and indicates that the people had already begun their journey. This is further indicated by the dot, or *here* symbol (*l*), designating the point of their departure, which was not too far behind. *Gone* is a combination of the symbol *here* (dot) and a finger pointing away from it, as if something had "fallen off the dot" (gone away). The figure with one advancing leg (*j*), meaning *departing,* together with the other symbols indicates that this group had just departed and had not gone far into the canyon when they *halted* their journey (probably temporarily). The hind legs of symbol *i* are purposely placed toward the center of the body to also indicate that this party had put some of the canyon behind them.

Goat *m* is positioned above and to the right of symbol *b* to indicate *first, superior,* or *before.* Symbol *m* seems to refer to something that happened *ahead* or *before,* and probably refers to a scout who visited the other side and then went *off the top* (horns) and back down into the *canyon* (goat body), while the remainder of the group waited for him in the canyon. It is not yet clear whether it is the scout beckoning the tribe to come on ahead (*b*), or whether this figure represents an invitation by another tribe already living there to *come and stay.*

The rest of this story and the clarification of this point is contained in adjacent panels which are related to this ancient account, but have not yet been fully deciphered.

This particular panel is an extremely useful and descriptive lesson in the value of both quadrupeds and horns in pictography. Many of these symbols appear with identical meanings in other panels having different topics; examples will come later.

Fig. 37. This Southern Paiute panel located in the vicinity of Las Vegas, Nevada, was painted with charcoal. It depicts entire families on their way to California after 1849. This example provides an important clue to the meaning of similar hand-holding figures in many older panels *(everyone doing the same thing, following each other, or migrating)*.

ON BEHALF OF THE VERSATILE GOAT

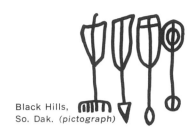

Black Hills,
So. Dak. (pictograph)

THE HORSE IS GIVEN A VOICE

Sometime after the arrival of the horse upon this continent, some Indian tribes who had become familiar with this animal adopted its form into their picture writing as a partial replacement for the goat. This was probably done for several reasons. One might have been that the goat did not actually represent any one animal and therefore little artistic pride could be taken in its depiction. However, the Indian (whose artistic talents are undisputed) could exercise his skill in the use of the horse symbol without interfering with what was being said in the writing itself. All that Indian pictography required for many expressions was a quadruped figure. The horse fulfilled this requirement and at the same time gave the Indian writer some artistic elbow room.

Indian pictography has always had a certain aesthetic appeal stemming from the unlimited choice and nature of its symbols. Although art was not the fundamental purpose of pictography, it nevertheless had the side benefits of artistic merit and appeal. With the recent adoption of the horse symbol into its structure, Indian pictography became more decorative while at the same time remaining true to its basic pictographic function.

THE UTES ARE EXPELLED

The Dakota Indians are well known for the skillful renderings of their battles with the white man and with other red men. Few people realize, however, that the Utes—one of the traditional enemies of the Sioux, and the tribe most feared by the Plains Indians (according to Cheyenne informants)— also practiced this artistic record-keeping. They, unlike the Dakota, made their entries upon the eternal rocks rather than upon paper and hides.

The following account comes from one of the many recent Ute panels in Uintah County, Utah. It is a graphic illustration of the pride in artistic skill which has recently crept into Indian pictography. It also shows many examples of how horse animations replaced those of the goat, and may give the reader a clearer insight into how goat and horse symbols can function so well in a pictography. The selection of this panel, telling of the Ute war in Colorado and the subsequent removal of that tribe to Utah, was influenced by the fact that its contents, or message, can be documented from our own history books. This panel was inscribed sometime after 1880, when the event took place.

The removal of the Utes was a result of an uprising known as the Meeker Massacre, in which the White River Utes killed their agent (Meeker) and others. A force of 190 soldiers was then sent to the land of the Utes to frighten them. The plan backfired, however, and the Utes surrounded the soldiers, killing their commanding officer and many of the men. The remaining soldiers were then pinned down under siege for several days.

Fig. 38. A Ute record of the tribe's expulsion from Colorado

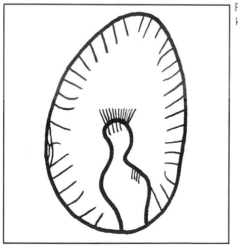

Fig. 39. A Dakota symbol tells of the surrounding and killing of ten Crow Indians (Mallery).

Clallam Co., Wash.

While this siege was underway, Chief Ouray of the Uncompahgre Utes used his influence to urge the Utes to withdraw the siege and sign a peace treaty. This was eventually accomplished. Although the Utes were the victors in this battle, they nevertheless lost the war when they signed the treaty which ended in their expulsion from Colorado. Figures 38, 40 and 41 of panels in Uintah County, Utah, give a simplified and condensed Ute version of this battle and the resultant removal to Utah.

Figure 38 shows an egg-shaped circle with a white man in its center (*a*). The pointed circle represents *end*, while the lines radiating inward describe a *compressing inward* into a small area. The entire symbol therefore describes the *siege* (compressing) of the group of soldiers sent to frighten the Utes. It further indicates that this siege had *ended,* shown by the incorporation of the symbol for *end* into the circle. (Compare this symbol with the Dakota symbol found in Cloud Shield's winter count (figure 39). This symbol tells that the Dakota surrounded and killed ten Crows [Mallery 1893]. The only difference in these symbols is the depiction of the people being surrounded.)

The head with open mouth facing the circle (*b*) represents the *talk* which brought the battle to an end. The two facing horses (*c* and *d*) indicate that, because of the talk, one party in the negotiations (the Utes) became *bound* or *held back,* and were no longer free to roam at will—shown by the tethered horse (*d*).

Symbol *e* is a horse whose unusual length represents a *long journey* (from Colorado to the Uintah Basin in Utah). A man and his wife have dismounted. They are placed in front of this horse to indicate that the *completed journey* was made by the men *with their women and families* (*f*). The man (*g*) is holding a gun and is pushing his chest out to show that he is *brave* and *has been at war,* shown also by the positioning of symbols of the war and the peace talk behind the horse, man and woman.

This Ute is reaching forward to grasp the peace pipe of a friendly tribe, the Uintah Utes (symbol *h*, figure 40). That they live at the place just arrived at is indicated by the sitting position of the man. (*Sit* is extended in the sign language to mean *living there.*) The sitting man is shown with his wife behind him (*i*) to indicate that their *families* were also there.

Symbols *j* and *k* continue the story. Both figures are sitting, showing that the White River Utes were granted permission by the Uintah Utes to *live* on Uintah land. The figure representing the Uintah Utes (*k*) is handing the peace pipe to the figure representing the White River Utes (*j*), who is accepting the pipe and is now sitting (*living there*).

Symbols *j* and *g,* the White River Utes, show the hands solidly pecked,

61

Fig. 40. The Ute record continues.

Fig. 41. Horses portray Ute action in this battle account.

THE ROCKS BEGIN TO SPEAK

ON BEHALF OF THE VERSATILE GOAT

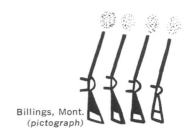

Billings, Mont.
(pictograph)

to indicate *something on it,* the sign-language method of indicating *Indian.* (The back of one hand is rubbed back and forth with the fingers of the other hand.) In this panel the solid-pecked hand shows that the people who came to live here were Indians—or of the same tribe. (The expression *Indian* among most American tribes is normally applied by a tribal member to only those Indians who are members of his own tribe. All others are referred to by their tribal names.)

Note that nearly all symbols of men and women are shown with only one arm. Artistic depiction could not have been the intent of this panel; some appeal was deliberately sacrificed in order to stick to the message. Second arms and hands would perhaps have made the figure more attractive, but they also would have included their unwanted meanings.

The continuation of this story is shown in the panel in figure 41. It elaborates upon the battle and siege of the soldiers in Colorado. The shield figure with a lance (*a*) represents the *soldiers* on foot, protecting themselves *behind* a hastily built rock *fortification.* The shield is a very old universal symbol representing defense behind protective fortification. This shield figure is purposely pecked wide to add the meaning *bad.* It therefore indicates that the soldiers' defensive fortifications were not the best.

The line on the head of this shielded figure means that something (the Utes) was on *top of them* (above them or higher), and that the soldiers were down in a ravine of some kind. The belt line with divided lines represents the placement of objects (rocks) side by side, idicating the type of fortification. The lance represents *preparedness to fight.* The picture of the white man with hat and mustache (*b*) indicates that it was the soldiers who were peeking out from behind the shield and defending themselves. (*Peeking out* is indicated by the X-ray view of the head beneath the hat.)

The two smaller horses (*c* and *d*) represent the Utes on both sides of, or *surrounding,* the soldiers. The horses' heads face the belt line or rock fortification to show what they were up against. The legs of horse *c* are backing away, and the forepart of the horse is pecked only lightly to indicate *lightly covered* (the same symbol used to denote *wet*), or *slightly bad.* In this example, it indicates that it was *bad* to get too close. The Utes kept their distance and did not charge the soldiers. This is indicated again by the standing position of the horses; only one hind leg (*d*) ventures a little forward.

The ears of horse *e* are in the path of the lance, indicating *danger in looking and exposing oneself.* This horse is pecked solid or *bad* to emphasize this danger, and it is also depicted looking over the back of horse *d* to add the idea of *exposure.* Symbol *f* of a human head (Ute) behind a horse elaborates by saying, "It was dangerous to peek out, so we kept our heads down."

63

Fig. 42. The Utes' unhappiness in their changed way of life is eloquently expressed.

64

THE ROCKS BEGIN TO SPEAK

ON BEHALF OF THE VERSATILE GOAT

Clark Co., Nev.

The foregoing story agrees in every detail with the American version available on the subject (*The Last War Trail,* Emmitt 1954).

This particular Indian author, besides adding the innovation of the horse symbol to his talents, has practiced his skill upon the figures of the Utes in a manner similar to the artistic records of the Dakota. It is even possible that he was influenced by the Dakota style. The addition of artistic expression to Indian pictography, however, is recent to both Ute and Dakota, and does not exist in their older rock-writing forms. This artistic keynote, therefore, cannot be relied upon in identifying their older records.

THE UTES REBEL

Recent Ute recorders could not always conveniently use the horse symbol to replace symbols of goats and other quadrupeds. Figure 42 of a panel from the Duchesne River on the Ute reservation in Utah illustrates this. The panel is a Ute account explaining why their people ceased the old, equestrian, nomadic way of life and were placed on a reservation. It tells how this reservation was divided among white settlers, leading to the Utes' flight to South Dakota in 1906. This panel unintentionally overlaps and continues the history of the Utes from the time of the Ute story related earlier.

Symbol *a* is a mounted Ute on the warpath—the *old way* of life. The Ute riding or depending upon the buffalo (*b*) also denotes the old way. (Note that this Ute is shooting an arrow at the animal he rides.) The horns on this Ute's head are formed by two quarter-moon symbols, conveying two meanings: *strength* (the horns themselves) and *happiness derived from the buffalo.* The concept of happiness comes from the sign-language idea of *sunshine* or *light in the heart,* but since this would be hard to express on this small figure, an equivalent idea for happiness—moonlight shining on the head—is substituted. Note the small arc on top of this Ute's head, denoting a *white* area or the "light of these once shining moons." This buffalo and rider are tilted to say, "The way of life which gave the Utes strength and happiness has *ceased.*"

Symbol *c* represents the arrival of the white man upon a horned quadruped. The ramming horns of this symbol have "knocked the war-bonneted and mounted Ute off his land and caused him to cease his equestrian way of life." These horns use the meaning *off* or *nothing on it,* by being doubled, helping to clarify this *ramming* or *knocking off* idea.

The buffalo skull or head on the tail of this goat implies that the buffalo is *behind* (a thing of the past) as a result of its massacre by the white man.

The figure riding this horned quadruped represents a white man riding and depending upon *force,* in this case symbolized by the ramming horns. This Ute author, however, refused to use the standard "hat" symbol in referring to the

Fig. 42.

white man. Instead, this angered author uses the nearest thing there is to swearing in the sign language. He equates the white man with the sexual organs of a diseased woman (*d*) because he *turned aside* (*e*). (That is, he did not honor his treaties with the Utes.)

Symbol *f*—two *holding* circles and a dot widened to say a *bad place* represent the Ute reservation (held or owned by many).

Symbol *g* is a Ute behind a shield, defending himself and his reservation. (Note the horse's foot *standing* [living] on the reservation symbol.) His braced lance, however, has the *nothing there* (doubled lines) symbol on its tip to show that this defense was *without a lance head* (any effective weapon) as they defiantly attempted to keep their reservation from being opened to white settlement. (Compare this tipless lance with the pointed lance on the mounted Ute just above the goat symbol. Note also that both lances have the *T* or *holding firm* symbol attached to them.)

The reservation symbol (*f*) is divided by many short, doubled lines, like the spokes of a wheel (barely visible in this photo), to show that their reservation was being divided into many pieces, with nothing left for the Utes. This actually occurred in 1898, and again in 1905 when the Uintah and Ouray Reservation was opened to settlement by the white man.

When this happened without their consent, 400 of the Utes under the leadership of Red Cap journeyed to South Dakota to create an alliance with the

Hot Springs Co., Wyo.

Sioux. They made it to South Dakota, but their alliance failed. After two years they returned to Utah and to what was left of their reservation (O'Neil 1968).

The location of this bullet-ridden panel spells out the ultimate irony in this tale of the unfortunate Utes: The Ute land on which this panel was situated is now owned by a white rancher.

The examples presented in this chapter of quadruped forms and their versatility aptly illustrate their necessity and function in Indian pictography as expressions of lateral action and other appropriate meanings or animation. Their purpose, which has puzzled many, is quite simple and actually quite obvious. It more than adequately accounts for the hundreds of thousands of abstract quadruped forms scattered throughout this country.

Quadruped forms are appropriate in almost all topics wherein any lateral action must be portrayed; therefore their seemingly excessive use is justified. A true understanding of their meanings accounts for the frequent occurrence of these quadruped symbols in fishing, buffalo, and deer areas, and for their occurrence in numerous panels of topics unrelated to each other.

These facts are far removed from the shallow theories offered so far that quadruped forms represent hunting accounts or hunting magic. This evidence also conforms to the emphasis placed by Indians upon such tribal matters as war, history, migrations, and notable deeds—events which to them far outweighed in importance the more common and everyday affairs of hunting. (For further reading on this subject, see the chapter, "The Red Man's Trampled Pencil.")

From the examples presented, we have seen the facility with which quadruped symbols were used to express numerous animated actions and phrases. These concepts would be much more troublesome, if not impossible, to express in any other pictorial method. It is not difficult to see why these quadruped symbols were so popular in pictographies in this country and all over the world.

5.

America's Rosetta Stones

THE HOPEFUL DREAM rarely realized by individuals attempting to decipher an unknown writing system is the finding of a key in the form of a "Rosetta Stone" upon which undeciphered characters exist side by side with the same message in a known system of communication.

The Rosetta Stone was found in 1799 near Rosetta, a village on the Nile River in Egypt. It contained information in the unknown Egyptian hieroglyphic and demotic methods of writing, together with the same information in known Greek letters. It was from this bilingual key that the unknown systems were eventually deciphered and our knowledge of Egyptian writing and history expanded to what it is today.

The hope of finding such a useful key to aid in the decipherment of Indian rock writings was not considered even remotely probable—that is, until several actually *were* found. And even these did not, at first, seem to be of much use. These panels often consisted, for example, only of a white man on horseback amidst some of the more ancient symbols, and were thought to be merely artistic depictions of the Indians' early view of the white man.

But later, after quite a few symbols had been deciphered and their meanings applied, it was found that these panels contained stories familiar in tone to recent Indian histories. It was then that the realization of their importance struck: Some of these panels containing symbols of the white man were actually Indian versions of well known, documented events and battles between the two races! (The Ute account in the preceding chapter is a good example.) These panels are, in effect, *bilinguals*. The only difference is that the English version appears in our own history books rather than upon the same rock!

If both parties related these stories factually, then the most important features should be nearly identical, giving due consideration to the viewpoints and cultures of the authors. They *did* prove to substantiate each other, in most

Fig. 43. A Mexican-Kiowa battle, El Paso, Texas, 1839

instances. As a result, these Indian "Rosetta stones" aided greatly in deciphering many new symbols. They also provided evidence that existing deciphered symbols from these and similar panels were accurate and could be reliably used as a basis for further translations.

The panels presented in this work are but a few of the most interesting and useful examples of "Rosetta stones" encountered in the long and painstaking process of deciphering rock writings. Space limitation prevents consideration here of every concept behind each symbol translated, but the most important ones are presented as each symbol is translated. Many which are not fully explained here will be examined thoroughly in later readings.

KONATE'S ORDEAL

A unique geological formation of boulder outcroppings exists in the middle of the barren desert east of El Paso, Texas, forming a striking contrast to its surroundings. One of these outcroppings is known as Hueco Tanks, a favorite stop for the Butterfield Overland Mail route of the past century. Archeological evidence indicates that this site, because of its refreshing tanks of rain water

caught and held in natural basins, was a favorite oasis for traveling Indians throughout the ages. Evidence of this is seen in the many painted panels found beneath the protected overhangs and caves of Hueco Tanks. (The panels at this site were painted rather than pecked, probably because the rock was very hard, and its color provided little contrast when pecked.)

One of the most interesting events portrayed upon these rocks actually took place, in part, at this very site, in the year 1839. It concerns a battle between the Mexicans and a group of about twenty Kiowa who rested here in the course of a raiding trip to nearby El Paso.

The English version of this story appears in the *Seventeenth Annual Report of the Bureau of American Ethnology*. A Kiowa told the story to James Mooney, to whom we are indebted for recording and thus preserving it for posterity (and for providing us with an invaluable aid in the process of deciphering). The panels at Hueco Tanks which relate the same story told to Mooney were probably written upon these rocks some time after this battle took place—perhaps when the Kiowa returned to raid this same area or to collect the bones of their dead, as custom dictated.

Other documents verify a battle at this site between the Mexicans of El Paso and the Indians in the same year, but these accounts greatly exaggerate the number of Indians killed (100 to 150) and refer to them erroneously as Apache.

The master panel at Hueco Tanks which relates the Kiowa version of the story appears in figure 43. It was necessary to reconstruct part of this actual rock painting because of the extreme damage it had suffered at the hands of vandals (figure 44). Little did this Indian author dream he was placing his masterwork only a few feet from a future state park picnic area!

This reproduction and the one in figure 45 do not include any unrecognizable symbols that might require guesswork in reconstructing.

In 1939 Forrest Kirkland reproduced these same panels in watercolor. The University of Texas published them in 1967. It was this publication, *The Rock Art of the Texas Indians,* that led to the recognition of this panel as a depiction of the Kiowa story told to Mooney. A trip made to this site for first-hand study confirmed the discovery.

The first clues to the topic of the panel were the symbols of the Mexicans dressed in the clothing of the early 1800's (symbols *28, 30* and *32* — page 78), and the sign-language symbol for *Kiowa* (*18* and *19*). The latter is conveyed by placing the bunched fingers of the right hand near the side of the head and shaking, or rotating, them. Some tribes explain this to mean "crazy heads" (Mallery 1881). Note the similarity between this sign-language movement and the two symbols in this panel.

Some initiative was shown by Royal A. Prentice in his attempt to locate this story of the Kiowa, Konate, at the similar-sounding Conant Springs, Quay County, New Mexico. This correlation was published in *El Palacio* (Vol. 58, No. 3, March 1951). A quick perusal of the panel at that site, however, shows a fort or church, a tipi, fighting men on horseback, and other symbols completely foreign to the events as related by Mooney's Kiowa informant. Also, Prentice's is the wrong geographic location, considering where the events took place and where the Indians were living at the time.

A striking similarity is apparent in the detail and thoroughness of Mooney's information and the story as told upon the rocks. This is in keeping with the traditional Indian way of relating stories wholly, truthfully, and without unwarranted color.

This, then, is the story as related to James Mooney (parentheses added):

While resting there (at Hueco Tanks) they (the Kiowa) were surrounded by a large force of Mexican soldiers, who killed several of their horses and forced them to take refuge in the cave. . . .

On being driven into the cave the Kiowa found themselves cut off from both food and water. They were watched so closely by the Mexicans that they could only venture out to the edge of the water under cover of darkness to get a hasty drink or cut from the dead horses a few strips of putrefying flesh, which they had to eat raw. One man was shot in the leg while thus endeavoring to obtain water. From the stench of the dead horses, and the hunger, thirst, and watchfulness, they were soon reduced to a terrible condition of suffering.

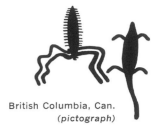

British Columbia, Can.
(pictograph)

. . . It was evident that the Mexicans were afraid to attack the Indians and were determined to keep them penned up until they were starved. To add to their distress, the decaying carcasses of the horses soon made the water unfit to drink. After ten days of suffering they realized that a longer stay meant dying in the cave, and it was resolved to make a desperate attempt to escape that night.

The sides of the well were steep and difficult, but they had noticed a cedar growing from a crevice in the rock, the top of which reached nearly to the height of the cliff, and it seemed just possible that by its means they might be able to climb out. That night, after dark, they made the attempt and succeeded in gaining the top without being discovered by the soldiers on guard. One only, the man who had been shot in the leg, was unable to climb. . . .

As they emerged they saw the fires of their enemies burning in various directions about the mouth of the cave. The Indians were sheltered by the darkness, but some of the soldiers heard a slight noise and fired at random in that direction, and seriously wounded Konate, who was shot through the body. The Kiowa succeeded in making their escape, probably helping themselves to some of the Mexican horses, and carried with them their wounded comrade until they reached a noted spring. . . . By this time Konate's wounds were in such condition that it seemed only a question of a few hours when he would die. Finding themselves unable to carry him in his helpless condition across the desolate plains, his friends reluctantly decided to leave him to his fate. Placing him within reach of the water, they raised over him an arbor of branches to shield him from the sun, and rode away, intending on reaching home to send back a party, in accordance with their custom, to bring back his bones for burial.

Deserted by his companions, his wounds putrefying under the hot sun, Konate lay stretched out by the spring silently awaiting the end. The sun went down and day faded into night, when far off on the hillside he heard the cry of a wolf; . . . despair seized him as he realized that the coyotes had scented their prey and were gathering to the feast, and now he heard the patter of the light feet and the sniffing of the animal as a wolf prowled around him; but instead of springing upon the helpless man and tearing him in pieces, the wolf came up and gently licked his wounds, then quietly lay down beside him.

Now he heard another sound in the distance, the *tso dal-tem,* or eaglebone whistle of the sun dance; it approached, and he heard the song of the *k'ado,* and at last the spirit of the *taime* stood before him and said: "I pity you, and shall not let you die, but you shall see your home and friends again." The *taime* then sent a heavy rain to clear out his wounds and afterward talked long with him. . . . Then the spirit left him, saying, "Help is near." The Kiowa insist that all this was not a dream or vision, but an actual waking occurrence. . . .

The story goes on to tell how Konate's comrades met six Comanche traveling in the opposite direction. The Kiowa asked them to cover his body. However, when the Comanche arrived at the spring they found Konate much improved, whereupon they abandoned their trip and took him home to his tribe. He recovered completely from his wounds and lived for many years.

The rock-written version, at Hueco Tanks, appears, in part, on the master panel in figure 43. After the complete panel was deciphered, it was **found that**

Fig. 43.

the story began with symbol *1*—a horse with its tail up (to show that it was alive when it arrived there). It had just been killed, shown by a red line piercing the horse through the heart. The *dead* symbol (an upside-down man) forms part of this piercing line.

It is obvious from the rest of the panel that the ambushed riders were Kiowa, so the author did not give the Kiowa sign here. The story also reveals that there were more than one Kiowa, so plurality is to be assumed.

The very small animal (*2*) represents the Mexicans in ambush, with their ears laid back, as a rabbit does when it hides, indicating that they did not want to be seen. The smallness of the body reveals that the two parties were some distance apart.

The story continues with symbol *3* of a Mexican (note the hat) "having a firm grip on the Kiowa's ability to get around them." The curved line means *veering around,* and the clutching hand indicates the *firm grip.* The left hand of this Mexican is holding his stomach in the sign-language *hungry,* to show that he is trying to starve the Kiowa out. This is apparent: The Mexican is fat, and the Kiowa (*4*)—holding his own stomach to show that he is hungry—is thin. The feet of the Kiowa are in the position *arriving,* to indicate that the Mexicans believed the Kiowa would "come to them" when they got hungry enough to end the siege. This never happened.

Symbol *5* represents the Mexicans "lying down and waiting behind the Kiowa's back," in the hope of ambushing them as they came out.

Symbol *6* shows the Kiowa being severely punished (the "cut-off" head), and in much pain from *hunger and thirst,* indicated by the squeezing in of the

74

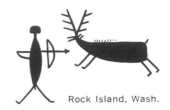

Rock Island, Wash.

body at the middle, so that it is nearly "cut in two," and by the hand shown clutching this area of pain.

The right hand of this Kiowa is reaching for water. The snake-like symbol (*7*) represents *water*. It has no head; it therefore cannot be confused with an actual snake. What appear to be rattles (*8*) is instead the symbol for *often* or *repeat*, communicated in the sign language by touching the left forearm several times with the index finger of the right hand, beginning from the wrist and working up. This symbol, together with the two *passed through* dots at the end of the tail, indicate that the Kiowa came out and attempted to get water many times, but they were *pushed back* in their attempts, shown by the legs appearing as though one is falling backward (*6*).

If this snake-like symbol *had* been intended by the author to represent a rattlesnake, the meaning would still not essentially change. The rattlesnake would show that the Kiowa, because of their hunger and thirst, were reaching out for something very dangerous.

The little man with the relaxed ears (*9*) shows that the Kiowa eventually became so hungry and thirsty that they *no longer cared,* hence they "relaxed their ears" (vigil) and made a desperate dash to water and the dead horses. The steps of this dash (*10*) are far apart and appear in two's to indicate *running* and then *stopping* (behind rocks).

The red rectangles on horse *11* (with its tail down to indicate that it is dead) are *bloody places* where the hungry Kiowa cut out pieces of decayed meat to eat. Symbol *12* of a dead man (upside down) is superimposed over the water to indicate that the *dead* horses were *lying in the water*. They had been dead for a long time and were consequently putrefied.

The long legs of this dead man utilize the symbol *distant,* which is made in the sign language by bending the flat hand slightly inward at the wrist and then pointing this hand in the direction being discussed. This symbol, in conjunction with the unusually long body, helps to convey the idea *a long time*—in this case, *a long time dead* or "stinking." The left arm of this dead man is flexing, hence *doing*, and it also is touching the water to help clarify the idea of a decaying process.

The two men holding hands (*13*) indicate that the Mexicans were *doing*, or "working together" in keeping the fires going outside the Kiowa cave refuge so that they could spot them as they came out. The rising white column with a black line in its center is the sign-language *ascending*, or *smoke*, and is made by lifting the spread fingers and palm of the right hand high above the head, after the sign *fire* has been made.

This smoke column is now so faint on this panel that its exact shape—and

75

Fig. 43.

Fig. 44. This valuable panel was badly damaged by unthinking people who wrote their names upon it. An attempt to cover the names with spray paint resulted in further damage.

Superstition Mt., Ariz.

even its existence—is questioned, so the above meaning may be in some doubt. Kirkland, however, portrays it vividly.

Symbol *14* represents the crowded cave in which the Kiowa were confined and hidden. (Kirkland's reproduction shows a hungry Kiowa in this square, but the panel itself is now too faded to distinguish accurately.)

Symbol *15* represents the *bloody path* of a man crawling (steps close together) back to the cave after he was shot in an attempt to reach water. Symbol *16* of an arrowhead pointing down from above indicates that he was *shot* before he made it to the water. Symbol *17* says the same thing, but uses rock incorporation to do so. The hole beneath this figure's feet indicates that he had *left the cave,* and the crack above him indicates that he headed *back* into the cave. The arm of this figure is shown holding an arrowhead (bullet) which has hit him in the leg, thus making him one-legged.

Symbol *18* is a Kiowa with a "furry tail" to indicate *limp,* hence *ready to die.* Symbol *19* elaborates by indicating this was because the Kiowa were *still waiting for water.* A tilted body indicates *stopped* or *waiting,* and the right hand is held in the sign Kiowa, as already explained. These two symbols together indicate that if the Kiowa waited any longer for water they would be in danger of perishing.

Symbol *20* reveals the escape route. The front legs of this climbing horse are in a *cave* (hole), and its head faces another crack to show the *crevice* before them which they could follow. The hump on the horse's back represents the top of a *hill.* The symbol *distant* placed on top of this hump indicates that the top of the hill was *far up,* and is placed below the feet of a "contented, fat white guard" *stationed above them* (*21*).

Symbol *22,* of the Kiowa actually climbing, has an arrowhead on its knee to show the *danger before them* in this climb. Symbol 23 shows the Kiowa secretly (note the *hidden* symbol above the head) climbing hand over hand up a tree (*24*). The head is higher than the raised arm to show their *caution* in "peeking over" as they proceeded upward. Note the bird tracks used as hands to indicate that one arm is reaching *up,* and the other is hanging *down.* These bird tracks might also represent the *safety* the Kiowa were seeking by escaping. Symbol *21* (the fat guard) is shown with his legs in a *knocked back* position to indicate that he was taken by *surprise.*

The line passing behind the man's neck (*25*) indicates that the Kiowa *passed* (forced their way) behind the bonds of the Mexicans. The Mexicans were *holding onto them,* indicated by the right hand clutching this line. The line passes through the grip of the other hand (*26*), revealing that the Kiowa forced their way through this "grip" and escaped.

Symbol *27* of the large Mexican indicates by its size that they were *larger* (more numerous) than the Kiowa.

Fig. 43.

Pueblo Co., Colo.

Symbol *28* to the far right is a Mexican with his coat covering his body and most of his legs. This indicates that he was *afraid* to show himself. He is holding a Kiowa by the neck to indicate that he is *holding* them, or has them *bound* in this hunger siege. However, the Kiowa (*29*), with his left arm hanging down to show his idleness, *revives* himself (recovers), indicated by the raising of the right arm.

Symbol *30* is a Mexican, tilted (*waiting*), loosely holding a *movement* symbol in his right hand. This movement symbol is combined with a circle, which is the sign language *holding,* as if to say, "loosely holding them from passing in front" (getting away). (A line in front of a circle indicates *passing in front.*) This Mexican is holding the movement line near its end to indicate the *siege was near the end,* since the Kiowa should be about starved by now.

The meaning of these two Mexican symbols (*28* and *30*), in conjunction with the reviving Kiowa (*29*), indicates that the fearful Mexicans were *mistaken* when they thought the Kiowa were at the "end of their stick." Their *grip* (siege) *was loose,* and the Kiowa were not as weak as thought; in fact, they were capable of escaping.

Symbol *31* (a line passing out between two curved lines) indicate this *escape* or "going out from an objectionable area after dark." The black between the curves indicates that this escape occurred at *night,* while the curves themselves indicate *an objectionable place.* These two veering curves normally touch to form the pointed oval which designates *an objectionable area.* In this case, however, they have been placed apart to illustrate their escape, or "passing out" from such a place.

Symbol *32* depicts a *fearful* Mexican (hat covering the face) in the typical clothing of 1839. This Mexican has just "let go of a bent stick," as indicated by the arms in the negation position *not wanting it,* and by the falling stick itself. This long, bent stick is in front of the Mexican's left foot, representing the *escape* of the Kiowa and showing that they were *in front* of the Mexicans, who now *no longer wanted* them, since they were *no good* (bent), or not worth chasing. The negated arms, hat, and stick therefore indicate that the Mexicans were afraid, and did not want to pursue the escaped Kiowa.

The panel relating Konate's abandonment and subsequent blessing on his homeward journey appears in figure 45.

Symbol *a* shows Konate, weak and lying down. Horns that curve naturally inward, like a bull's, indicate *strength*. Opposite horns, like these, indicate *weakness*. The bird track on one of them means that he had to lie down because of his weakness. His two hands are clutching the area of his wound. The lines extending from his ears indicate that he *heard* something while lying there. The two marks on his chest are the marks made by piercing the chest (part of the Sun Dance ceremony). These marks evidently allude to what he heard.

Symbol *b* clarifies and elaborates upon what Konate heard in his weakened condition. The lines from the ears indicate that he *listened,* while the mouth of the face is contracted inward to symbolize the puckered lips made when one *whistles.* As he was lying there, near death, Konate heard the whistle of the Sun Dance.

Symbol *c* is the spirit of the taime reaching out with "something on his hands" to give Konate. The mouth of the taime indicates the *good* words or *wiping clean* blessing that he is also giving.

Symbol *d* is Konate with his right arm stretching toward the sky, praying for *something good.* This indicates that the taime came in answer to his prayer. Konate's left hand forms the identical sign-language sign *he told me,* or *I was told.* The little mound in this hand represents *words* (*e*). The drawing of the arm toward the mouth indicates that he *received* these words. The symbol of a leg above this "mound" of words says, "One who is lying down arises again." The three upward lines at the knee of this leg represent a broad, upward movement, and therefore indicate that this prone leg would *arise.* Simply said, the mound of words and the leg together mean, "I was told that I would arise again."

Fig. 45. Konate faces his ordeal and, with divine aid, survives.

These same broad movement lines extend both upward and downward from the eyes to indicate they were *open*, and that this was no mere dream.

The kilt-like clothing on symbols *a* and *d* are actually the tail feathers of a bird which forms this same fan-like shape. They are used here to denote the fan of a medicine man placed over the procreative area (area of life) to *heal* Konate. This is one of the basic functions of fans among Indians. They are still used in this manner by medicine men today. (Many examples of this fan symbol actually show the narrow handle of the fan as part of the body itself.)

This fan, or *healing* symbol, is used on Konate to show that he is being healed. The tassels on the corners of the fan on symbol *a* represent the back-and-forth movement that tassels make. They therefore represent a *fanning*, as is customary in such ceremonies in order to fan the sickness away. The arrowhead tassels on symbol *d* represent the *bullet* lodged in Konate which has been "fanned" away. These attachments are not tassels, but are nevertheless used as such because of their relationship to the idea of moving back and forth, and of fanning sickness away.

The diamond-like symbols on the fans are alternated in open and solid spaces to indicate that parts of the wound were *good* (*nothing on it*), and parts were *bad* (*something on it*). This indicates *healing*. The short lines on Konate's body and arm represent the *rain* which came and washed his wounds.

Symbol *f* is the wolf who came up to Konate. His hind leg is the *not turning aside* symbol, indicating that the animal stayed close to him. Symbol *g* is the *going around* (veering) symbol, and is doubled to add the meaning *good*, or *wiping clean*. It shows that the coyote "walked around Konate licking his wounds clean."

This panel also utilized unrealistic and poor art in three examples to convey

81

the seriousness of Konate's condition. In symbol *d* the legs are off center, and the right arm protrudes from the neck rather than the body. This is all done purposely to show that Konate was very much "out of shape" (so to speak).

Figure 46 shows the rocky outcropping of the Hueco Tanks themselves. The outer line of this symbol represents the *siege* around the entire area. This idea comes from the circle, the *holding* symbol, which in this case is made to hug or conform to the shape of the mountain to show a "close siege around the entire area."

The two curved lines inside this symbol represent the *cave* or "hollow place" (*nothing there*) where the Kiowa were holed up. The red area at the top and on the right side represents the *blood* spilled upon the rocks (Konate's and another Kiowa's) while climbing to the top. (One corner of the symbol is raised upward to indicate *climbing*, or *going up*.)

The colors used in all of the foregoing panels have additional meaning in and of themselves. Red signifies *blood*, or *danger*. For example, in figure 43, the red of symbols *18* and *19* indicate the "danger of dying if they waited any longer for water" (*limp* [*18*]; *waiting for water* [*19*]; *and dangerous* [*red*]). Also, in symbol *15*, bloody footsteps back to the cave are shown in red.

White in these panels denotes *unhappiness* and *mourning*. Note the many examples in figure 43 where this color clarifies the meaning: white horses (*1*, *11*), unhappiness about the death of the horses; white cave (*14*), the unhappiness being experienced in the confines of the cave; the white *distant* symbol (*20*), the unhappiness about the distance to go to the top; and the Mexican—unhappy because the Kiowa wouldn't come out (*3*).

Black is the symbol for *rejoicing*, and also for *night*. Note that it is used for conveying the idea that the Mexicans rejoiced over the siege of the Kiowa, and to show that the Kiowa escape occurred at night.

Fig. 46. This representation of the "piled up" rocks at Hueco Tanks, Texas, rather than being an attempt at art, is an important paragraph in Konate's story.

82

Lewis & Clark Co.,
Mont. *(pictograph)*

The author did not intend that the symbols be read in any particular order. The sequence used here was chosen for convenience in simplifying the explanations. After gaining more experience in reading large panels, the reader should go back to the master panel in figure 43 and read it by clusters. It will be found that the complete story is very comprehensible when read in this manner. It really doesn't matter where one might begin.

This same principle applies to all panels. There is *no standard order* in which symbols must be read. Symbol incorporation and positioning do not allow for any formal sequence in reading Indian pictographic panels.

This Kiowa story, as translated from the three foregoing panels, is only part of a long story. The remainder, told verbally to Mooney, exists upon other panels strung out close to the panel in figure 43. They, however, are so deteriorated and have been so vandalized that they are now very difficult to distinguish, let alone photograph.

What has been presented should suffice to show the ability of the American Indian to communicate, in picture-writing form, all the details and aspects of a long historical battle account which was cherished and handed down in oral form for many generations.

6.

Indian Versions of American History

THE CATHOLIC FATHERS, Francisco A. Dominguez and Silvestre Velez de Escalante, in company with a handful of men, were the first recorded Spanish party to pass through what is now Washington County, Utah.

The details of this historical event may be found in *Father Escalante's Journal* (*1776-1777*), an English translation prepared by Herbert S. Auerbach, printed in the *Utah Historical Quarterly* (Volume XI, 1943). It appears here in a condensed and simplified account:

After crossing the Virgin River, a few of the men in Father Escalante's party were hailed down by some "Pahrusis" Indians. These Indians, after overcoming much of their initial distrust, accompanied the Spaniards in catching up with the rest of the party, which had gone ahead and was some distance in front of them. The two groups joined, and then a halt was called in which the Spaniards sought to persuade the Indians to guide them to the Colorado River. The Indians were reluctant to go, complaining that they were "barefoot, and could not walk much."

After two or three hours' discussion, in which the Spaniards offered gifts as an inducement (knives, strings of glass beads, and sole leather), two of the Indians finally consented to take them a little way and put them on "a good straight road."

There was some disagreement about the route to be taken. The Spaniards were determined to continue south; but such a course would take them to the Grand Canyon, which the Indians knew they would not be able to cross. The route proposed by the Indians was up a canyon through the Hurricane fault, leading to the flat, easily traveled land to the southeast. From this position, or "good road," the Indians knew the Spaniards could eventually reach the two best fords for horses in this area, now known as Lees Ferry and Crossing of the Fathers. This was the course finally agreed upon.

85

Fig. 47. An Indian version of the 1776-77 Dominguez-Escalante expedition (See sketch on page 88)

Mohave Co., Ariz.

After proceeding up this canyon for a few miles, they encountered a narrow place. More than half an hour's effort did not produce much headway; only three of the saddle horses could be induced to pass through. This frightened the Indian guides, who thought they might be blamed and punished, and they fled to the top of the canyon. The Spaniards turned around and went back down the canyon to continue southward as they had originally intended to do.

Father Escalante was not the only one to record the details of this encounter. The Indians thought it just as important. They recorded all the events just related upon a cliff about twenty miles away!

These Indian guides were probably not Paiute, since the interpreter, a Ute, could not understand them. (All dialects of Ute and Southern Paiute, including Chemehuevi, are mutually intelligible; not too many words differ.) The interpreter had to converse with the guides by means of the sign language and by the few words which were interchangeable in their related languages.

These particular Indians may have been remnants of the linguistically related Hopi, or *Anasazi*, who were once so populous in this area. Most of the Hopi had left the area by the time of the event related here.

These Indians were wearing turquoise necklaces, a further indication that they may have been Hopi. (Father Escalante in his journal wrote that these necklaces "looked like rosaries" from a distance.) The Paiute, furthermore, were not known to have made these.

Father Escalante also mentions that these Indians lived along the river and planted gardens there. This is where most of the Anasazi ruins are found. The straggling Hopi to which the guides may have belonged probably left to join the rest of the tribe sometime between 1776 and the time of the Mormon settlement of the area. Their departure at this relatively recent time would also account for the fact that the Paiute vividly remember the "Mookweetch" — as they call the Hopi — who once lived throughout southern Utah, and who the Paiutes claim authored many of these panels. (*Moqui* is the term applied to the Hopi by the white man—a corruption of the Paiute word *Mookweetch*.)

The large panel shown in figure 47, written sometime after 1776, tells the same story found in Father Escalante's journal, this time from the Indian viewpoint. This encounter was probably the Indians' first glimpse of the white man and his unusual trinkets, and must have impressed them greatly. At any rate, it sufficiently motivated them—whether Hopi or Paiute—to record the event in painstaking detail alongside other ancient tribal histories contained in one of the many stone libraries nearby.

This story is a little jumbled in the arrangement of certain of its sections. Each cluster, however, is self-contained and presents no serious problem.

87

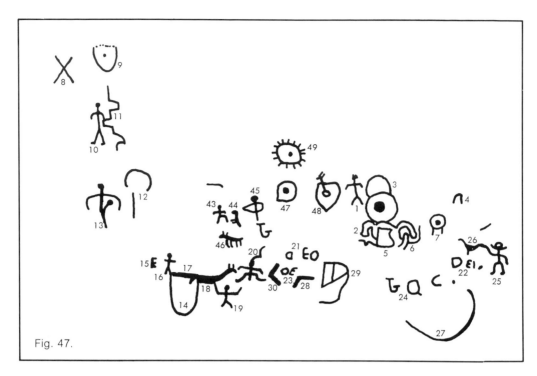

Fig. 47.

For convenience we begin the story with symbol *1*, a man with the *distant* symbol used on both arms to mean "keeping someone at a distance." This figure represents the Indians and shows their initial distrust of the Spaniards.

Symbol *2* is a man with right arm and doubled fist pointing down at the ground. This is the sign-language *sit*, and is commonly used as an invitation to *come and sit*. This arm and fist are open, or unpecked, to show that the Spaniards' invitation was *good* (*nothing there*).

Symbol *3* is a portion of a circle above and behind the head of the same figure. This circle means *beyond*, or "on the other side of the horizon," as suggested by its placement on the other side of the head. It is used here to indicate that a few of the party had gone ahead and were some distance away. The head with the large dot in it, below this partial circle, is the symbol *holding* (something) *in one place,* and indicates that the parties joined each other and then called a halt in their journey (staying in one place).

Symbol *4* clarifies this. It is positioned ahead and to the right of symbol *7* to indicate *first*. This symbol for *side, beside,* and hence *with,* incorporates the *distant* symbol into its right side to indicate *with* and *distance,* or *first caught up with.*

Symbol *5* is a picture of a high-topped moccasin. Extending from its heel is a piece of sole leather, given to the Indians by the Spaniards in trade for guide service.

Symbol *6* depicts the index finger of the right hand as it is poked through the "hole" formed by the curved index finger and thumb of the left hand. This

88

Yellowstone Co., Mont.

indicates the manner in which the Spaniards *laced* (poked) the sole leather on.

Symbol *7* clarifies this lacing process by showing two-finger extensions representing the path of vision of both eyes (indicated in the sign language by spreading the index and second fingers, with the others closed). These lines, or fingers, are attached to the bottom of a circle to indicate *looking down*. The entire symbol says, "holding something (sole leather) in place while looking down," and refers to the lacing process. The symbol *4* therefore indicates "a catching up with before the soles were laced on." This entire unit (*3-7*) indicates that after the two parties joined, a halt was called, and moccasin soles were laced on.

Symbol *8* is the sign-language *trade,* in which a similar *X* is formed by crossing the two forearms. Symbol *9* represents a necklace. The dot inside, *holding in place*, helps clarify the idea that it was something that draped around the neck.

Symbol *10* is a man leading someone up the bottom of a canyon. The meandering line containing many right-angled turns is an *easy trail,* or "shortcut." The man holding it is *leading* (someone) up this trail. The wide-terraced opening sitting on end (*11*) in this trail represents a *rocky* (terraced) canyon.

Symbol *12* is the sign-language *knife*. This sign is made by pretending to stretch a piece of meat between the teeth and the fingers of the left hand. A cutting motion is made with the right hand on the imaginary meat to portray cutting, hence *knife*. In this symbol, the inverted *U*-shaped sign represents an *opening* (mouth), and the lower line is the *cut meat* protruding from this mouth.

This *knife* meaning is clarified by symbol *13,* which has the *gone* symbol (a fixed-position dot with a crooked finger pointing away from it) in the area of the stomach to indicate "the cleaning of an animal in which the intestines are removed and thrown away." This was an important purpose for which the Indians used knives, and therefore helps explain the entire *knife* concept.

The Indians were probably intrigued by the appearance of the cutlasses of the Spaniards, which differed greatly from their own stone knives. This might account for the lengthy description on this panel.

The combined meaning of this cluster of symbols (*8-13*) indicates that necklaces and knives were exchanged for guidance up a canyon.

Symbol *14* represents a deep, steep-walled bowl, used here to represent the Grand Canyon. In this section of the panel, this Indian author tells how they tried to dissuade the Spaniards from going south toward this huge canyon, difficult and arduous to cross, especially with horses.

Symbol *15* is the letter *E,* used here to say *Spaniard*. (In this panel the strange-looking symbols [alphabetical letters], which the Indians may have noted on the Spaniards' equipment, are used in this unique sense.) Symbol *16,* an Indian

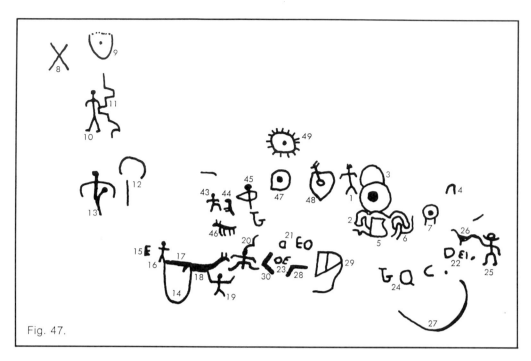

Fig. 47.

with outstretched arms, is *barring* (trying to stop) the Spaniards (indicated by the
E) from going across this great, deep canyon.

The broad line (*17*) across the top of the canyon represents a *bad trail*
(*something there*). Symbol *18*, a horse, clarifies the idea that the steep sides
or "cliffs" in this canyon would be very difficult for horses to climb. This is why
the horse's hind leg is incorporated to form part of the canyon wall or cliff on
the opposite side. It is also why the man (*19*) is touching the horse's front hoof—
to indicate that the horses could not make it across this great canyon. (Note the
horse's tail *turning aside* from this bad trail across the canyon.)

Symbol *20* elaborates by the symbol *crack,* positioning this crevice-like symbol
on a man's head. It thus means *going in the direction of a crevice.* The arms of
this figure are stretched way out to illustrate that this is a *wide* canyon. This idea

90

Pahrump, Nev.

is strengthened by the use of the *distant* symbol as a part of each arm to show *a long way in both directions* (wide). This arm symbol is distinguishable from the arms of symbol *1* by its extreme measuring length. The legs of this figure form a cross with the body—referring to the *crossing over* to the other side of the canyon.

Symbol *21*—the alphabetical letters *DEO* (the *D* is backward)—is the Latin for *to God;* while *DEI* (*22*), further to the right, means *of God.* The presence of these two Latin words substantiate that this was indeed the Dominguez-Escalante expedition. It is logical that such religious Latin phrases would have been used by these early, adventurous missionaries; it is not easy to believe they would have been used by other less religiously-motivated expeditions.

These Latin words and alphabetical letters are shown on this panel by the Indian author to indicate to other Indians the peculiar manner in which the Spaniards wrote. (Note the other letters, *DE* [*23*] and *JQC* [*24*], and the symbol resembling a comma after the *C.*)

Symbol *25* clearly proves that the Indians are describing the writing of these Spaniards. It is a figure in the act of forming the letters to its left with the aid of the tail feather (quill pen) of a bird (*26*). His right arm in is a writing position. The circle on this man's head means *holding* extended in the sign language to also mean *remember*), and the bowl-like curve below this circle is the sign-language *fast.* The author was evidently very much impressed at the speed with which the Spaniards "quickly remembered" and wrote their letters. The same *fast* symbol appears (*27*) below the alphabetical letters *JQC* to again illustrate the speed with which these symbols were written.

Symbol *28* represents *something written upon a cliff.* The shape of the symbol represents the top and slope of a cliff. The lines of this symbol are broadened to indicate that there is *something on it* (rock writing). However, since the symbol is placed in the midst of alphabetical letters, it represents the writing of the Spaniards—not that of the Indians.

Symbol *29* is evidently an Indian rock-writing tool, a pointed rock with a line extending from the point to indicate *that which has been written.* The line passing through this tool means *in front*, and is used here to convey the idea that this tool is "in front of one," as it is when one writes. This complete symbol helps to show that the alphabetical letters presented are the writings of the Spaniards.

Symbol *30* is the symbol *closing*, or *getting dark*, extended to mean *dim*, or *hard to see.* The lines are broadened to mean *something there*, and the context in which this symbol is used makes it evident that it refers to the Spanish writing. This symbol therefore indicates that the writing of the Spaniards was "hard to see." In other words, the Indians could not understand or read it.

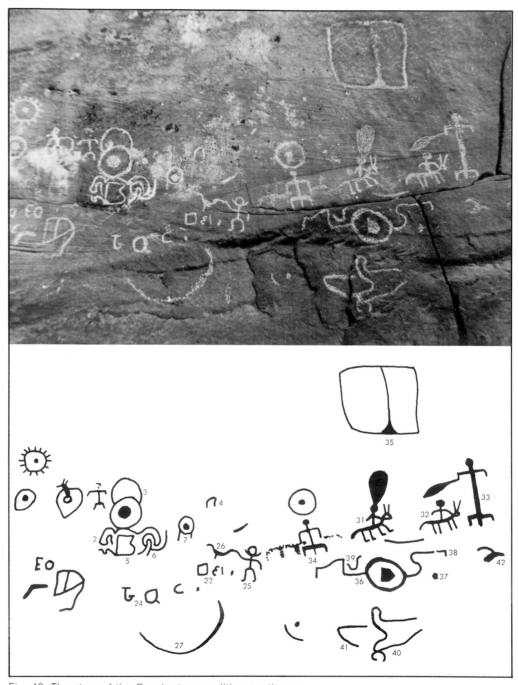

Fig. 48. The story of the Escalante expedition continues.

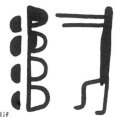

San Bernardino Co., Calif.

Symbol *31* in figure 48 shows a Spaniard on horseback *not turning aside* (horse's feet) as he heads up a canyon. The *darkened eye* (canyon) symbol is placed on his head to indicate *going into a canyon*. Rock incorporation also indicates this by the placing of the horse's hooves near a crack. Symbol *32* shows the lead horseman being blocked by a tall, human figure (*33*), indicating that they were held up for a long time. This tall figure holds the symbol for a *bad, narrow, objectionable place* over the rider's head to further say that it was a "bad" geographic feature (a narrow place in the canyon) which blocked the rider's journey.

A close examination reveals that the arms and legs of this long figure are squared on one side and rounded on the other (*not turning aside* and *turning aside*). This figure depicts a "long," hopeful attempt at "trying to cross something," since they both cross the body. The legs, however, do not connect evenly with each other (not very distinct in this photo), and thus reveal that they failed in this attempt. This figure's right leg is also widened to show that it was *bad on this side and not on the other*, and they were hindered in crossing over. Note how this long figure's left leg touches a wide crack at its narrowest point to clarify the idea that they were in a narrow place in a canyon.

Symbol 34 represents a man with a *holding* (something) *in one place* symbol positioned above his head to show that he could go no further in his journey. The right arm of this figure is leading a horse (lightly pecked). His legs are in the *not turning aside* position, and are widened at the top to say *bad*.

Symbol *35*, a square (representing a place) with a line in front or in the middle of it, represents a *narrow* place in front or ahead. The triangular-shaped symbol on the bottom of the *in front* line conveys the idea of narrowing.

Symbols *36* to *41* help explain everything that has been said regarding the difficulty encountered in this canyon, and add a few new details to the story of how the riders failed to pass through this narrow place and had to change course.

The circle (*36*) represents a *bead*, and the two lines to either side of it represent drilling a way through. These two lines, however, are offset to indicate the riders *failed* to pass through. The dot (*37*) represents a *destination*, and the line curving up away from it indicates that they *turned away* from this course. The right angle at the end of this line (*38*) tells that they did *not turn aside* however from their ultimate destination which lay across the Colorado.

The pointed square in the center of the circle, or bead, is incorporated to mean *being held in a closing* (narrow place). Symbol *39* is a long-handled ladle used to indicate that the canyon was *deep* (reaching way down in for water).

Symbol *40* is one hand with two fingers, *separating and going in two different directions*, similarly indicated in the sign language. The Indian guides split from

93

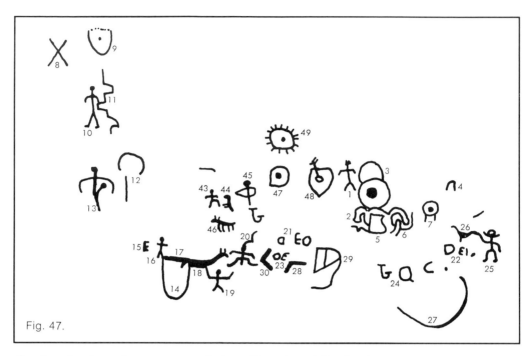

Fig. 47.

the Spaniards and went upward (top finger), while the Spaniards went the other way, or back down (lower finger). This lower finger also forms an incomplete figure *8*, which means *to return by the same way* (crossing over one's own path). The top of this lower finger does not complete the circle, revealing that they had to return by the same route, and did not complete their trip. The abbreviated symbol *top* (*41*) placed in front of the diverging fingers clarifies this and shows that the Indians and Spaniards separated before reaching the top.

The curved line and dot to the left of symbol *41* indicate that the Spaniards *veered around something*, clarifying the idea of the change of course around this canyon.

The symbol *beside*, or *with*, is incorporated into the squared, meandering line immediately to the left of the water ladle (*39*), to indicate that the Indian guides were still *with* the party prior to their failure to pass through the narrow place in the canyon.

The goat's head with widened horns (*something on it*) symbol *42* tells that the Spaniards headed on a *bad* route southward after leaving the canyon. (*South* is indicated by the direction in which this head is facing.)

Symbols *43-46* back on figure 47 retell this part of the story and add a few details which could not be clearly incorporated into the symbols just read. Symbol *43* is a figure running uphill (the Indians), with its arms showing *distrust* (keeping someone at a distance). Symbol *44* is another figure looking upward and reaching out for the Indians. These reveal that the Indians *fled*, fearing that the Spaniards would *pursue* them—perhaps to punish or blame them for their difficulties.

Symbol *45* is a *gone* symbol passing in front of a "chopped off" *canyon*

94

Taos Co., N. Mex.

symbol to indicate that the Indians had left the canyon before they had completed their journey through it, leaving the Spaniards below (the *J* below this figure). A horse (*46*) is also shown going back down the canyon.

Symbols *47-49* elaborate upon this short-lived guide service. Symbol *47* means *being held in one place*, referring to the canyon difficulty. Symbol *48* shows the guides leaving the canyon. The outer circle is the *canyon* symbol. The inner circle, formed by the legs, combines with the outer circle to make a doubled circle—hence, *nothing in it*. The head protruding from the outer circle tells that the Indians went to the *top* and *outside* the canyon. The circle is flattened on top to indicate the top of the canyon. The two lines on the head of this figure represent a *nothing* blow. (They were not "hit on the head," or harmed, by the Spaniards.)

The *held in one place* symbol (*49*) has radiating lines to convey the idea that this *holding* outer circle moved outward to thus *release* the dot. In other words, the Spaniards let the Indians go and did not follow them.

This panel is an excellent example of how an Indian recorder might inscribe sections of a story two or three times by using different pictographic symbols, in an effort to make his points perfectly clear to the reader. This definitely reveals that Indians recorded important events in full for the benefit of future readers, and not as merely personal, memory-aiding devices.

KIT CARSON'S NAVAJO CAMPAIGN OF 1863-64

This story is right out of the pages of America's west, and has been extensively documented in history books and early diaries. This translation comes directly from the walls of Largo Canyon, New Mexico, the early homeland of the Navajo, where part of the story took place.

The Navajo had for many years made raids throughout New Mexico and Arizona. The United States Government assigned Kit Carson the tasks of stopping these raids and of sending the Navajo to a distant reservation at Fort Summer in eastern New Mexico.

The Navajo version of this story, in substance, is as follows:

The white soldiers came into the land of the Navajo, and sought to make us believe them and go with them to another land. In order to accomplish this they made their camps in our cornfields, piled the corn up, and burned it. They also killed most of our sheep. Instead of submitting to surrender, however, we closed our ears to their words and would not believe them. We relied upon our strength and retreated to a rough canyon (Canyon de Chelly) wherein we could hide and fight.

The soldiers entered this canyon in the midst of winter to punish us and make us believe what they said. They had difficulty in passing through the canyon, and some soldiers broke through the ice and hurt (froze) their feet.

95

Fig. 49. The Navajo record of Kit Carson's 1863-64 campaign

Those of our people who were in the bottom of the canyon at this time fled to the tops of the cliffs where they could have a better hold, and could fight from above. But we were suffering from hunger and could not fight as effectively as the soldiers below. Thus we showed little resistance.

Many of our people who were watching from their hiding places later left these places to surrender to the soldiers in order to obtain blankets, get food to heal their hunger, and warm themselves by the fires. We thus sought the safety of the soldiers.

San Juan Co., N. Mex.

Those who had made a defiant stand were captured and confined to prison. Those who escaped were pursued. Those who refused to leave the canyon were killed and multilated.

Because of our hunger, the killing of most of our sheep, the war upon the corn, and the pursuit of those who fled, the hand of death was placed in our path. In our weakened condition, and in order to heal our hunger, we surrendered. Thus we left the dangerous path of fighting behind us, and this war upon us and our corn—so harmful to both our land and ourselves—ended.

After our surrender, we journeyed across a large river (Rio Grande). Here some of our people drowned and were carried away by the current. This journey took us to a flat land upon which the soldiers lived and where we were to stay.

The master panel which contains all the generalities of the foregoing story appears in figure 49. It was apparently not intended by the author that the story begin with any specific symbol, since the entire panel must first be read to fully understand it. However, symbol *1* is a convenient place to start. It shows two different methods of inscribing symbols. The outline is a canyon (Canyon de Chelly), roughly pecked to indicate that it was also a *rough* or uneven place. This rough pecking has been smoothed, or rubbed over, to add the meaning *smooth*, or *good*. In other words, this *rough* canyon was a *good* place where the Navajo could hide and fight.

The fact that one or more symbols in a panel were inscribed in a manner unlike others appearing in the same panel does not necessarily suggest that they were written by different authors. **Different methods or techniques of inscribing symbols were intentionally used in order to add the meaning suggested by the technique itself.**

Symbol *2* is a soldier wielding a club or sword with which to punish the Navajo. The line across his head is sign-language for *white man* (hat). This horse incorporates the *canyon* symbol into the shape of its body. The horse's back runs along the same crack which the canyon symbol (*1*) touches, to indicate that the soldiers were coming through this canyon. One of the front legs of this horse passes through a diamond-like symbol, indicating a *forcing through* (breaking through the ice). The arrowhead between these two front feet shows that they were *hurt* (frozen) from this breaking through.

Symbol *3* is used in this panel to represent *winter*. It is a "second suit of clothing" for warmth. It helps to clarify the concept of horses breaking through ice. The front feet of the other horse (*4*) are hobbled to show the *difficulty* the horses had while proceeding through the canyon in the winter.

Symbol *5* is a retreating Navajo "cut in two" from *hunger*. He is attempting to fight, indicated by the *war* symbol (*6*)—two arrowheads pointing at each other —superimposed over a corner of his hungry body. The top arrowhead is poorly and indistinctly made, to indicate the lessened ability of the Navajo to fight due to

Fig. 49.

their hunger. The lower arrowhead—that of the soldiers—is much more distinct, and sharper; their fighting ability was much better.

The short line passing through this Navajo's head is sign-language for *believing* and *obeying* (words "passing" clear through the head). This symbol is distinct from the pointed crowns of the soldiers' hats. It is used here to show that the Navajo were beginning to believe the soldiers. The legs also show this change in attitude: They are in profile, while the body is a front view. This therefore indicates a *turning aside* (change of course from fighting). The line along the base of this Navajo's kilt-like body also indicates that they *followed* the soldiers' *trail*.

The arms of this figure are flexing to indicate *doing with the hands*. This flexing is commonly used to indicate the speaker, or *one talking with his hands*, as one might do—especially Indians using the sign language. This symbol can therefore be extended to say *I*, *me*, or *myself*. Since the story concerns many people, it means *we*.

The deer tracks (*7*) represent the Navajo *fleeing* up the cliffs when the soldiers entered the canyon. The concept behind this symbol is based on the fact that the dew claws of a deer never make an imprint except when the animal is running or "fleeing." One set of the deer tracks (lower right-hand) indicates the *suddenness* of this flight, since the dew claws (two dots) are *not* shown as part of this track. Together with the tracks showing dew claws, they tell that the unsuspecting Navajo (walking deer) were surprised by the soldiers, and fled (running deer). Symbol *8* indicates that the Navajo fled upward because the bottom of the canyon was a *bad position* for a defense (a *position* symbol enlarged to show *bad*).

Symbol *9* is the *war* symbol again, used here to indicate that the Navajo fought from the rim. The bottom arrowhead has a *trail* symbol (horizontal line) on it to represent the trail below which the soldiers were following.

Oregon
(pictograph)

Symbol *10* shows steps going up a very *steep* slope. (The right triangle forms a part of these steps, indicating this steepness.) The horizontal *T* at the base of the steps depicts a hand holding a stick *for a long time,* and is used to mean *holding on* (firm grip). This entire unit tells that the Navajo held their position on the steep cliffs for some time.

Symbol *11* depicts the Navajo in their show of strength before surrendering. The horns represent *strength*, and the single ear with a square on it indicates that they placed something (hands) over their ears and would not listen to nor accept the white soldiers' words. The eyes and mouth reveal that this was a *retreating* show of strength—in other words, they were "backing up," as is often indicated when such facial features are shown.

The rough-pecked square forming the base of the neck represents the *rough land* on which they were fighting. This square rests at the base of the rock, thus using rock incorporation to imply *land*.

Symbol *12* comes from the Ute sign-language method of describing the Navajo—hair folded and wrapped up in a bun behind the head. This symbol also touches the base of the rock to say *Navajo land*.

The crooked arrow (*13*) stemming from the base of the rock, touching the square below the head and then the head itself, indicates that because they (the Navajo) refused to listen, this defense of Navajo land was a *careless* or "crooked" arrow which *hurt* only their land and themselves.

Symbol *14* is a *hidden* head watching the soldiers. On this head are several *gone* symbols to indicate that these people later left their hiding places to go to the soldiers. This meaning is conveyed by the superimposition of one of these *gone* symbols over an arrow being surrendered (*15*), and by the *healing* feathers on this pack.

Symbol *16* provides further clarification. It is a moccasin track heading toward the soldier on horseback, revealing that the Navajo sought the protection of the soldiers.

Symbol *17* is the *strong* and defiant Navajo who had to be *captured* (horns of strength bound together). Both arms of this figure touch cracks in the rock to show that this capture took place in Canyon de Chelly. These arms are also in the *negation* position to show that they did not want to go. The two lines on top of the head mean *compressed*, to imply that they were destined for imprisonment (confinement). The mountain lion track coming off the shoulder (*18*) and pursuing the deer track above it indicates that those who *escaped* and fled were *pursued*. (Reluctant captives often had to be carried on the shoulders of the victors; therefore any symbol leaving a shoulder indicates *escape*.)

Symbol *19* appears to represent a body, upside down to indicate *death*.

Fig. 49.

One arm and the head are missing to imply *punishment* and *mutilation* of the dead by the soldiers. Symbol *20* is another upside-down body with one arm and the head cut off. The single arm is in the *negation* position and continues on down, following a crack, to hold its own foot. It thus indicates *not wanting to leave the canyon*. This body incorporates the symbol for *side*, or *with* (near the neck line). This entire symbol says that those who refused to leave the canyon and go with the others were killed and their dead bodies mutilated.

Symbol *21* is a Navajo handing over his arrows. This *surrender* is indicated by the arrowhead with a *gone* line below it to infer *gave*. His horns denote *weakness,* and his pack contains but a few seeds, or *food* (scattered dots). This pack also utilizes a doubled line (*nothing there*) to indicate it is *empty*. The feathers on this pack are *healing* symbols, and indicate that they surrendered in order to fill their empty packs, or to *heal their hunger* (receive rations from the soldiers). These feathers have the same connotation as the feather fan on Konate in the Kiowa account. This Navajo is also warming himself with a blanket obtained as part of these rations.

Ganaskidi, a figure very similar to this surrendering figure, appears in the sandpaintings of the Navajo. He is credited as the god of harvest and seeds. *If* this symbol represents this Navajo deity here, then it is apparent that his pack of seeds is now empty and he has nothing to offer his people. This is academic, however, since he would be completely out of context here and would show little affinity to the surrounding symbols.

Symbol *15* is similar, but the horns, pack and body are all different: The pack is almost full; the horns are *M*-shaped to denote *squatting,* probably by a fire, and this time the arms are still clinging to (touching) the arrows, to show that they hoped to give them up only temporarily in order to get rations. However, the hands in symbol *21* have actually *let go,* in a more earnest and sincere surrender. This definitely shows that **these figures are being used in varying**

100

Washington Co.,
Utah

linguistic contexts, rather than as merely different methods of depicting a mythological being.

The bloody hand (*22*) above this figure's head denotes the *death* which blocks them from continuing on their old paths. The hand is solidly pecked to indicate *something on it*, referring to *blood*. It is the bloody hand of one who would kill them (the soldiers).

Symbol *23* is again the symbol *fleeing*, and symbol *24* is the track of a *pursuing* mountain lion. These two symbols indicate that if the Navajo fled they would be pursued.

Symbol *25* is many circles (*holding*), all bunched into one to indicate *many holding*. It refers to the large flocks of sheep the Navajo owned. Note the sheep track below (*26*). This sheep track is cut (not pecked) with many diagonal lines to show that many sheep were *killed*. The line passing through part of symbol *25* is the symbol *gone* (a line descending from a dot). In this example it descends from the second circle from the inside, and points at the sheep tracks as if to say "many sheep once owned are now gone" (*killed*, as indicated by the track). One circle is not included in this *gone* symbol, thus showing that a few were left.

Symbol *27* is again the *war* symbol. It is tilted here to show that the war had *ended*. Symbol *28* is yet another *war* symbol, but the points are offset to indicate that the Indians had *failed* to put up a good fight. The track (*29*) behind the Navajo figure means that they turned their backs on the dangerous path of fighting for their land.

Symbol *30*, a terraced mound, represents a *pile* of corn which the soldiers burned. Symbol *31* is the *war* symbol again, attached to the corn to show that *war was made upon the corn*. It is also tilted to show that this war later *stopped*.

Symbol *32* is a soldier's tent in the cornfield. It is rubbed out to indicate *ruined, destroyed,* or *burned*. Symbol *33* is a bird track used to help clarify the idea that *damage* was done to the corn; birds are known to be very destructive in this way.

Symbol *34* represents the Rio Grande River, and the line down its center means *passing through* or *floating down*. This line refers to the Navajo who drowned. In symbol *35* the short vertical lines placed above the horizontal line represent the *people above the water*; those placed below the horizontal line represent the *going under,* or *drowning* of these Navajo.

Symbol *36* represents the *flat land* (Fort Sumner). The numerous scattered dots (*something there*) above this line (*37*) indicate *many people* living there. These many scattered dots, the plural deer tracks (*7*), and other symbols establish that the entire story refers to many people, not just one or a few. Symbol *38* is a soldier's tent, to show where the soldiers lived.

101

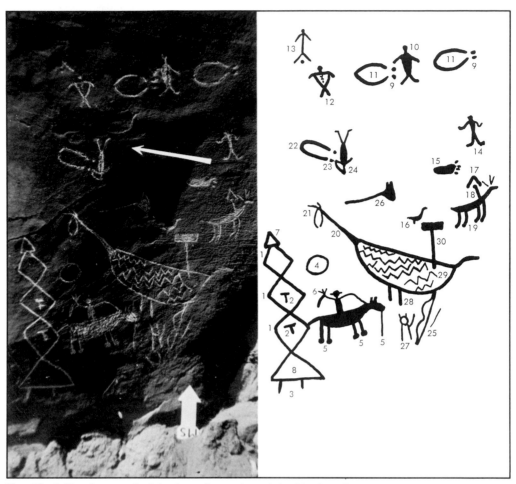

Fig. 50. A Navajo record of the forced crossing of the Rio Grande

The next two panels will be translated in a manner designed to help the reader interpret and understand rock writing without having each symbol fully explained in sequence. One of these panels (figure 50) tells of the drowning of some Navajos while they attempted to cross the deep Rio Grande River on the long walk to Fort Sumner. This panel is located just to the right of the panel

Kane Co., Utah

in figure 49, and is an elaboration of the story of the Rio Grande crossing, only touched upon in the master panel.

As this panel is read, a numeral in parentheses will follow each phrase. These numerals locate the symbols in the panel from which that phrase is translated. It may be helpful for the reader to remember that the ridge (indicated here by an arrow) represents the bank of the river, and that the hollow to the right of this ridge represents the river channel itself. Remember also that the quadrupeds represent people and not animals! They are pointed in the direction being discussed.

An Indian who had been there may have told the story in this way:

At the river bank we were lined up together (1) *waiting to enter the river* (2). *Some of our people did not want to get too close to the river. They stood back away from it* (3—legs to one side of arrowhead). *However, we were held so that we could not escape* (4). *Many Navajo refused to move from where they were standing* (5), *and were therefore whipped* (6) *and forced into the water. We had danger* (arrowheads of 7 and 8) *before us* (7—the water) *and danger behind us* (8—the soldiers). *Our people were afraid and wanted to flee* (9—dew claws). *They did not want* (negated arms of 10) *to pass through this objectionable place* (11—the river ford).

Some of our people knew that if they entered the river they would later (lower position of 12) *swallow water* (12) *and drown. So they did not want* (unchalked arms of 13) *to cross this place* (dot between legs of 13) *where the water was very deep* (14—ladles on arms), *and dangerous to pass through* (15—a barefoot track denoting *unprotected* or *dangerous*).

Some of those who did venture into the water (16—a wading bird) *had the water close over them* (inverted V—17). *They then had to be rescued* (18—carried) *to the opposite shore by another swimmer* (body and legs of 19). *If our people turned around to come back upon the shore* (20—position and heading), *they were not allowed there* (21—an objectionable heading). *If they returned* (22) *in fear* (23) *of the water, they would be hit on the head and killed* (24).

They were prodded on with weapons (25) *and had to turn around and head back toward the bad river* (26—heading and solid pecking). *Meanwhile the onlooking soldiers* (ears of 27) *laughed and joked about this.* (The upraised arm is the sign-language sign for *joke.*)

While their legs were yet far from reaching shore (28), *the bodies of some of our people filled with water* (29) *and they were gone from sight* (30—went under).

Fig. 51.

Fig. 52.

104

Largo Canyon, N. Mex.

Figure 51 from this same site gives additional details of this long walk to Fort Sumner.

This panel depicts the Navajo walking together in the "Great March" (*a*) to Fort Sumner. The upraised hands (in the attitude of carrying a heavy load) indicates the great burden placed upon the Indians by this march. The lines around the neck of the large head (*b*) tell of their *capture*. The large *holding circle* (*c*), or *pen*, represents Fort Sumner, which lies ahead.

The "horns of strength" on the head are worn down, indicating the *weariness* of those who failed to finish this long walk (died). The half-pecked head equals this *unfinished heading*, a detail further clarified in the head "missing" its destination (*c*), and in the cross on the face "missing" the eye (*not crossing over and seeing*). The positions of the circle (*c*) and eye of the head (*b*) — offset to the left—indicate *missing*.

The phallic symbols (*d*) represent those who arrived first in this long walk consisting of several different groups arriving at different times.

The arrowhead "hurting" the feet of the quadruped (*e*) who is pointing in the general direction of Fort Sumner represents the sore feet suffered by many of the women (indicated by the natural hole under the tail of this quadruped).

The panel in figure 52 is also located near the master panel. It elaborates upon the Navajo surrender, and is very simple for the reader to understand.

Our warriers feared (a) *to follow the path* (b) *of war* (c) *that lay ahead (position of war symbols above the deer track), so they (plural bows) unstrung the bows* (d) *that they had once held firmly (short horizontal line on bow strings). The fighting therefore ended (e—tilted war symbols). A few others had already unstrung their bows at an earlier time* (f).

Compare these war symbols with a more artistic examples from Three Rivers, New Mexico (figure 53), definitely proving that this type of symbol consists of two opposing arrowheads, the sign-language concept for *war*.

The numerous panels relating to the Kit Carson campaign are strung out in quite a few sections along the base of a cliff. Only four (figures 49-52) of these panels are presented here.

This example of relating a story in many different panels reveals an important procedure in the reading of rock writing. This procedure is very similar to the modern practice of adding footnotes, so as not to confuse the reader and to keep from cluttering the main text.

In Indian rock writing this is accomplished by recording the crux of the message in one large master panel, such as figure 49, and then elaborating upon

the story by giving details in other panels located nearby (figures 50-52).

This is a very common practice in the recording of long stories. It was often done out of necessity, since one rock large enough to tell the entire story could not always be found. Another reason for recording the story in this way is that, by keeping a long story spread out in several panels, it could be written (and read) much more clearly.

This practice, however, often required a master panel which tied the meanings of all subordinate panels together. Subordinate panels relating only specific details of a story are somewhat difficult to understand unless one first reads the master panel containing the generalities of the story.

7.

Pages Out of the Past

THE ROCK WRITINGS OF EASTERN UTAH are unusual in that many panels found in the area depict live snakes. This is a feature found only rarely in rock writings. Texas also boasts an abundance of snake symbols, but this is to be expected since it is the homeland of the Comanche Indians, well known in the sign language as "Snakes."

Symbols intended to depict realistic snakes should not be confused with similar wavy lines that denote various types of movement. Realistic snakes can almost always be distinguished from movement symbols in that they are shown with rattles, tapered bodies, head, tongue, open mouth, or some other physical characteristic.

THE ORIGIN OF THE HOPI SNAKE DANCE

Why is there such a concentration of snake symbols in eastern Utah? The answer reveals itself in the content of the numerous panels found there. Many not only bear out an interesting Hopi migration tale, but also indicate an early use, if not the possible origin, of the Hopi Snake Dance.

This particular dance is exclusive to the Snake and related clans of the Hopi tribe. It is performed in the late fall in the hope of bringing rain to mature the crops for harvest. In this ceremony, which is still performed today, many live snakes are carried in the four cardinal directions and turned loose, from whence it is believed they carry, on behalf of the Hopi, messages to their deities to send forth crop-saving rain.

This Snake Dance was brought to the present Hopi location by the Snake Clan, who claim to have once settled in Utah in their long migrations over much of this continent — travels undertaken in obedience to a divine command.

A panel from near Castledale in Emery County, Utah, illustrates this Hopi tradition and presents a good argument that the Fremont culture of eastern Utah

107

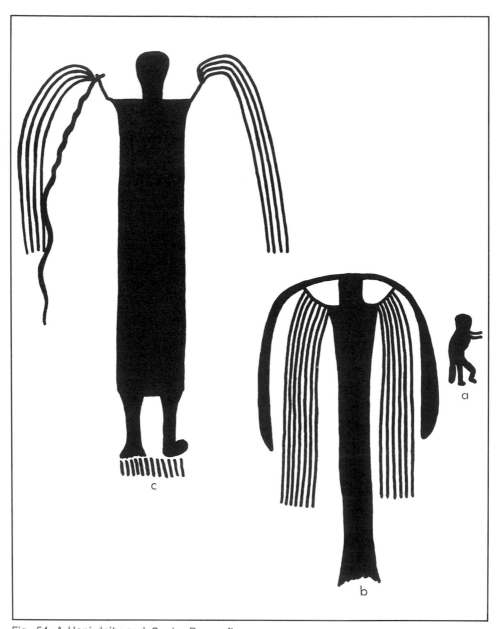

Fig. 54. A Hopi deity and Snake Dance figures

Wayne Co., Utah

was the ancestor of the present-day Hopi Snake Clan. The panel is known as the "Buckhorn Indian Writings," and is one of the largest paintings to be found in the country. Because of its size, only a few pertinent elements can be explored here. This, again, is a panel which points out the necessity for having the cultural information with which to understand and read it.

Figure 54 is a reproduction of three key symbols from this extensive panel. Symbol *a* represents the profile of a dancing Indian, "reaching out" for something. Note the body leaning forward, the flexing legs, what appears to be a foxtail (commonly used in such ceremonies) hanging at his rear, and the loose hair on his head. This costume in profile is identical to that worn by the Hopi in some dances today, especially in the Snake Dance.

This dancing figure has his back turned to one of the Hopi deities (b), dwelling in his abode (represented by the wide line, *something on it,* over his head). This figure of a deity has the symbol *safety,* or *salvation,* streaming down from his arms, which he is keeping to himself within his abode. (This figure is not to be confused with a bird, since it has a human head and body. Deities are normally depicted in human form among the Hopi.)

The head of this deity is protruding partially through the roof of his abode to show either that this being is a spirit, or that he refused to come all the way out of his dwelling place. Symbols *a* and *b* in conjunction with each other say that the Indian dances had not been effective in bringing this deity out of his abode and securing his help. More distinctly, they *had not seen him,* indicated by the fact that the back of *a* is turned toward the deity.

Symbols *a* and *b* are also lower than symbol *c*, hence *inferior,* to imply that the rain dances the Indians were then performing were not sufficient to bring the god out of his abode.

Symbol *c* is higher, and shows the *correct,* or *superior,* method of communication with the deity — that is, the pacifying of live snakes. Symbol *c* is also larger, hence *closer* to the deity than symbol *a* (made small to denote that it is dancing at a distance). Symbol *c* is holding a live snake in his hand, and long movement lines — extensions of the fingers — are running down along the snake's back to represent *rubbing* or *stroking.* This stroking is still an actual part of the Hopi Snake Ceremony, now performed with feathers. It is done to befriend and pacify the snake, who is believed to have an influence with certain deities in obtaining water. After all, in the words of Hopi informants: "It can survive in the driest deserts throughout the hottest summers."

This particular section of the panel seems to imply the actual origin of the use of live snakes in a dance to bring rain.

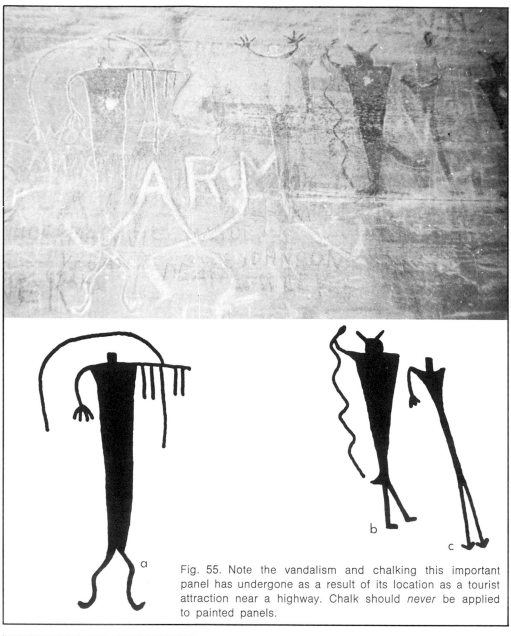

Fig. 55. Note the vandalism and chalking this important panel has undergone as a result of its location as a tourist attraction near a highway. Chalk should *never* be applied to painted panels.

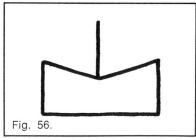

Fig. 56.

110

Las Vegas, Nev.

Figure 55 shows the Hopi deity (*a*), this time reaching out of his abode and giving of his *safety,* or *good fortune* (rain), to the people now that they have *completed* their dance (flexing legs and "stopped" feet). His right hand is reaching downward to say that the people can now *gather* their harvest.

The reason for this god's benevolence in this section of the panel is evident from the symbol of a man holding a live snake in his hand (*b*) and taking an *initial step* (note the feet) in using snakes. The ears of this figure are relaxed, to indicate that he *isn't worried* about the fact that he is holding a live snake.

Symbol *c* is a man who is standing in mud, indicated by the *opening up* symbols placed beneath his feet. This implies the mud spreading when walking after a rain. These *open* symbols therefore are the *rain* which came as a result of the Snake Dance. Compare these feet with the symbol *coming rain* (figure 56) obtained from the Hopi by Thomas V. Keam and published by Mallery in 1893. The only difference in the meaning of these two symbols, in the light of recent translations, is that Keam's symbol actually represents *coming rain at a specific place,* such as a garden, indicated by the rectangle used to show geographic limits.

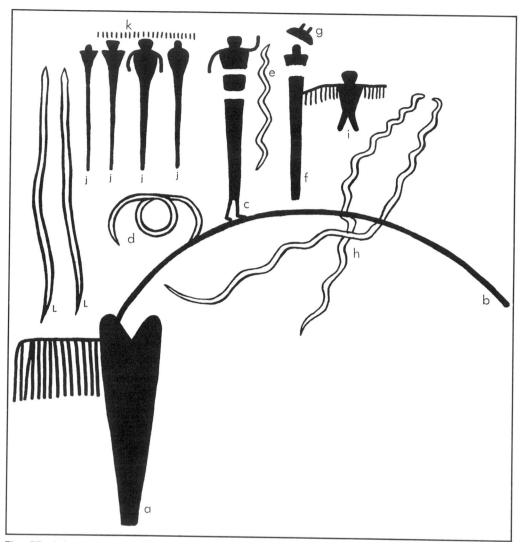

Fig. 57. A few of the distinguishable symbols in a large panel depicting the Snake Dance

Figure 57 depicts the actual Snake Dance itself. Symbol *a* is a deity reaching out of his dwelling and saving the crops. The *V*-shaped symbol *opening* exists where his head should be. The arc formed by symbol *b* is a *covering* of this opening in the neck of the deity. This is the *sipapu* — the spirit entrance to the underworld, which to the Hopi is heaven and the abode of some deities.

The sipapu is very common in Hopi ceremonies, and is still used in the Snake Dance, where it is represented by a hole dug in the dance arena and covered with a sounding board. The dancers stomp on this board each time they circle the arena with a different snake.

Symbols *a* and *b* clearly indicate the sipapu. Symbol *a* is *the spirit coming out,* indicated by its body and arm protruding outside the covering, as if in the act of emerging.

Nev.- N. Mex.

Symbol *c* is a man *stomping* on the sounding board over the sipapu, and symbol *d* represents the *circuit* made around the arena with each snake before it is freed (*e*). This circuit also incorporates into its shape the symbol *covering*, and touches the actual covering of the sipapu to indicate that the dancer *returned* to it after each circuit (to get another snake). This is as it is still performed among the Hopi today.

Symbol *f* is an accompanying dancer who makes this circuit each time to help guide the one holding the snake.

Symbol *g* is a mound above this dancer's head, tilted to say *stopped*. It refers to a part of the ceremony which takes place after the dancing has ceased. At this time a section of the ground is covered with cornmeal and all the snakes are placed in a pile on top of it. The mound in symbol *g* represents this pile of snakes. The two lines extending above the mound (*nothing there*, or *off from*) say that after the snakes had been piled up, they were *taken off* the pile. This is exactly as it is in the present ceremony. The snakes piled upon the cornmeal are immediately grabbed and taken in the four cardinal directions to be turned loose to carry to the deity their messages appealing for rain.

Symbol *h* (two snakes crossed to form a swastika — the *four cardinal directions*) indicates this very thing. They are shown here coming out from the covering, indicating they have been danced with and are proceeding to the four directions. Note that the heads of these two snakes face each other to show that they *talked*, or *delivered their messages*. Symbol *i* is the *salvation* or *saving rain* with which the Indians were blessed as a result of this message.

Symbols *j* are the young children brought to this ceremony to be initiated into the Snake Clan. The size of these figures and their triangular-shaped chests indicate they are *young*, or *new*. The numerous digits above their heads (*k*) indicate there are *many* of them.

That these children were made members of the Snake Clan is indicated by the two *good* snakes (*l*)—made *open* or *wiped clean*. These snakes constitute part of the same line in which the children are taking their places as members of the clan. Initiation of children into the Snake Clan is still performed as one of the numerous ceremonies preceding the dance itself.

Symbol *a*, a deity coming out of the underworld via the sipapu, strongly suggests its identity — *Alosaka* (Muyingwa), one of the few Hopi deities who actually makes his home in the underworld. He is the god of reproduction of man, animals and plants — a kind and gentle god but often aloof (Colton 1959). The long (16-day) snake ceremony seeks divine aid for these reproductive blessings, so it is more than likely that it is Alosaka, the germ god, who is reaching out of his underworld home in an act of benevolence to the Hopi.

Fig. 58. Rain and crops are sent to reward the Snake Clan, as shown in this panel from eastern Utah.

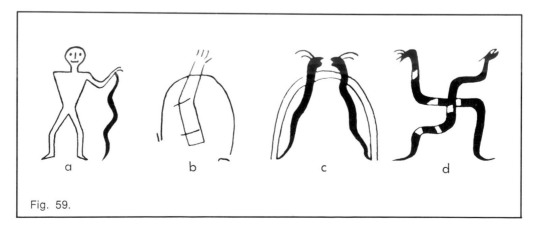

Fig. 59.

114

Ontario, Can.

Figure 58 from Horseshoe Canyon, Utah, a considerable distance from the site just discussed, substantiates the translation given here. It also indicates that the Snake Clan once settled in eastern Utah.

The man in this panel (*a*) is holding a *snake* in one hand and in the other his *plucked crops* which grew as a result of the *falling rain* (*b*) brought through the intervention of the snake. The cloud above the falling rain is in rectangular shape to illustrate a *dance ground,* and the projections hanging below this incorporated cloud and dance ground have little feet attached to them (*c*) to indicate *dancing* (the Snake Dance). This panel is excellent in that it actually portrays the rain and crops produced as a result of this dance.

Compare the symbols translated in the foregoing panels with similar symbols of the Ojibwa and other eastern Indians (figure 59) documented by Schoolcraft, Hoffman, and Tanner. These tribes did not have to use the snake to bring rain in their already wet climate; they did, however, use them in other significant ways. Symbol *a* is a man walking with a serpent; *b* is a spirit having the ability to *reach through* the walls of his dwelling; spirits (*c*) are *looking into heaven* (note the goat-like horns); and *d* denotes *wariness* — the swastika formed by these snakes indicates *looking in all four directions,* hence the need for caution.

These symbols, identical in meaning to the Snake Dance panels but in different context, substantiate the accuracy of these translations. They also provide an example of the consistency of Indian pictography throughout the country.

THE HOPI LIFE PLAN

The panel in figure 60 is perhaps one of the last panels which can be read in its entirety by living Hopi. It plays a very important part in the life of the traditional Hopi and its translation has been handed down through the years.

This particular petroglyph is called "The Hopi Life Plan" by the Hopi themselves, and the following legend and translation were provided by the Hotevilla faction. Nothing has been added or changed, and the wording appears just as approved by traditional Hopi leaders. It should be noted, however, that there are several personal Hopi interpretations of this panel, just as Biblical scriptures are disputed among white men.

> When the Hopis first arrived upon this land the Creator was the only one living here at the time. When the Hopis met their Creator here, they asked him to be their leader. The Creator refused and said that there were yet many evil intentions in their hearts that they must first fulfill before he could be their leader. Those who managed to survive and live through all their evil intentions would meet the Creator after all was over and he would then be their leader. The Creator is therefore the "first" and the "last" because of this meeting arrangement.

> One of the many instructions given to the Hopis by the Creator at this time

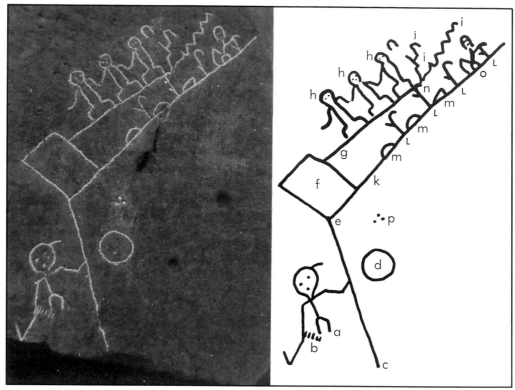

Fig. 60. The Hopi "life plan"

was that they should migrate all over this continent and, while doing so, they should leave their picture writing and clan symbols upon the rocks near their ruins as a sign that the Hopis were here first and were rightfully holding this entire continent in trust for the Creator. In regard to this they were told by the Creator that a time would come when another race would come upon this land and claim it all, but that these Hopi writings upon the rocks would justly retain and hold the ownership of this land by the Hopis in trust for the Creator.

Many aspects of the story will be recognized in the following Hopi translation. Symbol *a* in figure 60 represents the Creator pointing down to the "opening" from where the Hopi claim to have come. The short vertical lines near the Creator's hand (*b*) thus represent the Hopi people. The Creator is holding in his left hand the *life plan* or *trail* (*c*) upon which the Hopi are to embark. Near this hand is a circle (*d*) which represents the *holding* of the entire continent in trust for the Creator as he had instructed (Since this photo was taken, viewers of this panel have added a bow to the right of the Creator in the process of chalking and scratching the panel for purposes of photographing.)

Point *e* on the trail or life plan represents a time when it was predicted by the Creator that the Hopi would *digress* from the true path given to them and pursue another way. The square (*f*) is said to represent *Oraibi,* and the line or path (*g*) stemming from this square represents the *false path* of the wicked of Oraibi — the Hopi who are always trying to outdo and hold themselves *above* others, without the help of God. (This line is above the true path.)

116

Chihuahua, Mex.   (pictograph)

The three figures (*h*) standing upon the false path represent the *wicked* themselves. Older Hopi claim that heads have recently been added to these symbols, for they remember a time when no heads existed on these figures. The absence of heads would represent the *punishment* or *death* that the wicked must undergo as a result of following this false path.

The two zigzag lines (*i*) stemming from the false path represent the *careless* and *different paths to permanent destruction* pursued by the wicked. Each zigzag is the pursuit of a careless and wicked intention that will eventually come to a *dead end* when all evil intentions have been exhausted. This "dead end" is shown by the symbol *turning around* or *sagging down* (*j*). The upper zigzag line has recently been scratched and marred to such an extent that it resembles a fourth figure, which the Hopi say was not there originally. Whether it was or was not does not seriously affect this translation.

Symbol *k* is the *true path* to everlasting life, symbol *l*, which is shown at four points along this true path. The incorporation of the symbol *old age* (a cane) with *life* (a branching corn leaf) represents everlasting life.

This true path to everlasting life is bisected at three different points by three half circles (*m*), which might have been complete circles at one time. (This panel has been scratched over so often that it is difficult to distinguish the correct form of these symbols.) The Hopi say they are gourds which are shaken, thus representing three great *wars* or *shakings* that will transpire before everlasting life is reached. The last circle represents the "final war of purification in which all evil will be destroyed."

At point *n* on this panel the false path connects with an everlasting-life symbol, showing that some may *return* to the true path and to everlasting life. The two zigzag lines which extend beyond this point of possible return to the path of everlasting life thus truly indicate permanent destruction, since the wicked *have gone beyond the point of no return*. Symbol *o*, at the end of the true path, is the *great spirit* holding an everlasting-life symbol in his hand. He is shown waiting here at the end of the trail just as he was shown at the beginning of it. For this reason he is called the *first* and the *last*.

Symbol *p* is difficult to distinguish, again because of the panel having been repeatedly scratched instead of chalked. It more closely resembles three dots, but the Hopi claim it is a Catholic cross added to the panel after a bad experience with the Catholics in the seventeenth century. This symbol was placed there by the Creator's instructions, to show that the Hopi Way and the Catholic Church *should not combine*.

The actual age of this panel is not known. The oldest living Hopi claim it was there when they were young. This would have been prior to the 1906 religious

Fig. 61. A refuge into the depths of the Grand Canyon (see sketch on page 120)

Fig. 62. Note the faint symbol *movement down under* (top center) positioned just above the entrance to this large cavern.

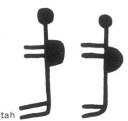

Washington Co., Utah

split between the Oraibi and Hotevilla factions — an event which the Hopi claim fulfilled part of this prophecy.

The subject matter and prophetic elements of this translation are not a part of this study, nor does it matter whether this panel is ancient or quite recent. What really counts is the fact that it is of definite Hopi origin and, as such, substantiates the Hopi use of symbols identical in meaning to symbols used by other American Indian tribes.

That this panel is of genuine Hopi origin is evident from its close tie to Hopi tradition and because of the many symbols derived from the sign language: *many people* and *close* (*b*); *path* (*c*); *holding* (*d*); *forks in a trail* or *two* (*e*); *going back and forth* (*i*); *turned around* (*j*); and *old* (*l*). Furthermore, the symbol *area* (*f*) and the concept of having heads cut off to denote punishment (*h*) are identical to pictographic symbols for the same meaning throughout much of North America. This panel therefore definitely reveals that the Hopi practiced the same sign-language-derived pictography used by other tribes. It also shows that an understanding of a portion of this system persisted right down into the midst of our space age. The ability of the Hopi to retain these fragments of antiquity when other tribes have lost so much is undoubtedly due to their refusal to accept many of the advances of civilization and the influences of Christianity. They have maintained this stoic resistance from Coronado's time into the present and thus remain a lingering refuge of Indian culture and religion. Traditional Hopi stoutly maintain it was their ancestors who wrote upon the rocks throughout the country, and that such writings tell of their migrations, histories, disputes, and land claims. This panel presents ample evidence of the truth of such claims.

A REFUGE IN THE DEPTHS OF THE GRAND CANYON

The panel appearing in figure 61 is located in an alcove high in the cliffs of Mule Canyon, Arizona, one of the canyons leading into the Grand Canyon. Completely hidden from sight behind a rock in this alcove is an entrance (figure 62) to a large and lengthy underground cavern. Few artifacts have ever been found in this cave; however, evidence of fires reveals that the cave was used for some purpose.

This cavern forms an impenetrable haven—a natural place of refuge for women and children in time of war. The entrance is long and narrow; an enemy crawling through this passage could easily be dispatched by unseen guards hiding in the dark recesses. The cavern also provides a protected window overlooking the approach up the talus to the inconspicuous cave entrance, from which a great length of the canyon can be viewed. The Indian painting (figure 61) found in this overhang indicates that this was precisely the purpose for which this cave was used.

119

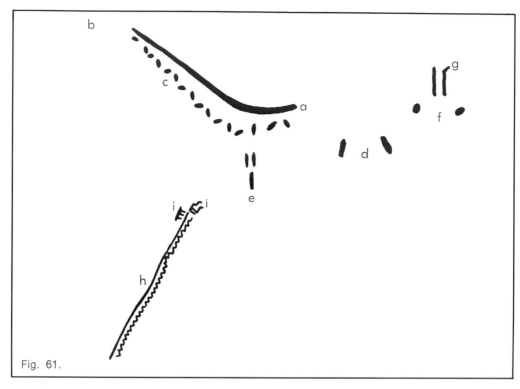

Fig. 61.

Symbol *a* represents a widened, hence *bad*, trail upward to a *high cave* or *alcove*, indicated by the line extending and pointing at a similar rock feature (*b*). The moccasin tracks (*c*) below this line represent someone seeking the safety of the cavern. The tracks are placed under this line to indicate that the people in flight are *down under*, or *within* the canyon. The tracks diverge in such a manner that the toes always point outward in an extreme, unnatural angle. This represents a *separating* or *splitting up*, indicated in the sign language with similar finger movements.

Symbol *d* is the opposite of *diverge*. These lines are two fingers spread far apart, both pointing inward. This is the sign for *meeting*, or *coming together*, as would be the case if imaginary lines were extended beyond the fingers until they met. These two fingers are purposely placed far apart to show that this meeting was to be at some distance, indicating that after the people split up they were to meet at the cave.

Symbol *e* is a finger, or person going upward to either a *good* place or an *entrance*, indicated by the two parallel lines. This symbol clarifies the meaning of the moccasin tracks and trail up to the cave.

Symbol *f*, two dots, is commonly used in this manner to imply something that is to be *passed through*. The two lines above it show that this passing through has already been accomplished and that the people are now in a *good place high up*. *Far*, or *high up*, is incorporated into the right side (*g*) of the two lines that indicate *nothing there*, or *good*.

Clark Co., Nev.

Symbol *h* is the ceiling of this hidden underground tunnel. The zigzag line beneath it suggests that the cavern is *crooked* and extends far beneath the surface, indicated by its length. The dome-like curve in the center of this line represents a *room* or large cavern with the tunnel extending far beyond it.

But this, curiously, is *not* a true description of the cavern. The cavern actually extends perhaps only twenty-five yards to the large room itself. It would appear that the author hoped to discourage his enemy, who would naturally be skilled enough to track the fleeing Indians, by making him believe that the cave was much deeper and longer than it really was. The intended deception reveals that the author was a member of the tribe using this place as a refuge, and uncovers his motive in drawing the panel.

Symbol *i* is placed above the entrance to this cavern. The three lines indicate *movement down between;* since it has a long surface line for its top, the meaning *down under* is added. This same symbol is painted over the actual entrance, as shown in figure 62. The placing of this symbol over the man crawling in (*j*) is clear evidence that it represents the *entrance* into the cavern.

The figure of a man with his two legs sticking out as he goes down headfirst into this cavern (*j*) completes and clarifies the unit. All the symbols of this panel, when read as a whole, show that this cave was used as a place of refuge when danger was imminent.

MAJOR POWELL'S COLORADO RIVER EXPEDITION

A brief Paiute account of Major Powell's Colorado River Expedition of 1869-70 appears in figure 63. This panel, and many others describing Paiute encounters with the white man, were inscribed in an area near Las Vegas, Nevada.

The Southern Paiutes occupied much of the Colorado River area, including the Grand Canyon. The area was shared with their neighbors, the Hualapai and Havasupai, the river itself forming somewhat of a boundary line between the tribes.

In the course of exploring the Grand Canyon (on August 26, 1870, to be exact), Major Powell chanced upon and helped himself to a Paiute garden below Lava Falls. On the final day of his trip, August 30, just before reaching the mouth of the Virgin River, he encountered several groups of Paiutes (Powell 1957). Some members were probably from the Las Vegas area and may have been responsible for later recording these events in that location.

Major Powell's feat of traveling through the Grand Canyon by boat was an important historical event. Such a feat would surely have impressed the Paiutes, who were intimately acquainted with this area and its rugged nature. It seems natural, then, that one of their number would be inspired to record this event in the picture writing of his race, to take its place with other historical documents.

121

Fig. 63. A Paiute record of Major Powell's exploration of the Colorado River in 1869-70

The author of this panel probably lived at the springs where it is inscribed. This site is about forty miles west of the Colorado River at present-day Hoover Dam, and about sixty miles west of the junction of the Virgin River and the Colorado, the point at which Powell himself culminated his portion of the river trip. (Some of his men continued on down the river with the boats.) This Paiute author may have witnessed part of the expedition at some point on the Colorado — most likely near the Virgin River. Or he could have been living on Cottonwood Island, which was inhabited by Paiutes at the time this expedition passed by.

The key symbol in this panel, revealing its subject, is the white man wearing boots and hat standing within a boat pointed at both bow and stern (*a*). This was similar to the type boat used by Major Powell. Also, the boat symbol is solidly pecked at both ends to denote that the ends of the boat were *covered* or *enclosed*. Powell's boats were designed in this manner, so as to make them watertight.

The hands of the white man pictured within the boat are *covered* or *hidden,* indicated by the use of the *something on it* process; his left hand is done in the *wet* technique. This seems to imply that the white men were hiding their true purpose for being on the river. Hands imply *doing,* but in conjunction with limp arms, they say *doing nothing.* The Paiutes, therefore, were suspicious of Major Powell's motives for exploration, knowing that their innocent or idle-looking hands were hiding their true purpose for exploring this river.

The Paiutes' suspicions were later justified when the Cottonwood Island Paiutes — the Shivwits and the Uincarets (Paiutes pronounce them *Seeveets* and *Yooveenkahduts*) bands — were required to leave their homelands along the Colo-

122

Kane Co., Utah

rado and move closer to civilization, thus giving the white man ownership of the land explored by Powell.

The boat's left side (to the right in this picture) parallels the contour of the rock, implying the following of a natural contour, or simply that the boat followed the natural route of the canyon.

Symbol *b* of a goat with four legs signifies *travel*. The highest horn incorporates with the goat's back to form a *V* on its side, meaning *open,* or *an opening* —in this case the opening of a canyon, the Grand Canyon itself. This highest horn is also crooked, denoting the *crookedness* of the canyon; it also forms the goat's head to denote *going* into a crooked canyon.

The other horn traversing the full length of this goat's back indicates a *journey the full length,* or *from one end to the other* of this canyon. This lower horn is a single one; a doubled horn would indicate a *safe* journey. This was obviously not the case, since the Paiutes killed three of Major Powell's men who had left the expedition, supposedly near Separation Rapids. (Note how this lower horn enters the *V* to its apex to denote *within* the canyon.)

Symbol *c* is a finger pointing in the direction of the Grand Canyon to the east. This demonstrates the importance of noting the direction faced when looking at any panel, since many are oriented to a specific direction. For instance, this rock was deliberately chosen so that the reader would have to stand facing the direction in which the Grand Canyon lies.

The shorter *wet* finger converging to the near left of this long pointing finger directs the attention of the reader to *something wet way over there,* or the Colorado itself. The left finger is small to denote *distance,* and converges to say *at* or *there.*

Symbol *d* is a small mound which represents a *mountain* of this shape situated a few miles ahead and to the left of this rock. It was included to help the reader orient himself, and to make him understand that the long finger points to the *right* of the mountain and thus toward the Grand Canyon area of the Colorado.

Symbols *e* are unique; they are two letters of the English alphabet, reversed and connected as they would be if reflected in the water. They of course denote the white men on the river, or *looking at themselves* in the water. In this case, alphabetical letters are used to represent white men, just as similar letters denote Spaniards in the Indian story of the Dominguez-Escalante expedition.

The Paiutes were not, of course, familiar with the English alphabet, and their rendering makes it uncertain just what the letters actually were. They could be a *TJ* or a *WJ*. They might even be backward — a *JW,* which could be John Wesley Powell's first two initials. This, however, is probably more wishful thinking than fact.

Fig. 64. A Ute depiction of the wreck of Consolidation No. 10

Duchesne Co., Utah

THE WRECK OF CONSOLIDATION NO. 10

The panel in figure 64 is unique in that it records an incident in the history of white men, and not of the Ute tribe of which this unknown author was a member. The event described, however, did occur on the Uintah Railway, which knifed deeply into land then part of the Uintah and Ouray Ute Reservation.

The birth of the Uintah Railway in 1903 was at a time when all mining claims on this reservation prior to January 1, 1891, were made valid. This railway was then formed to haul out the valuable uintaite (Gilsonite) deposits found in the area at an earlier time.

All the details of the building of this railway and of the wreck of Consolidation No. 10 (including actual photos of it), may be found in *Uintah Railway, the Gilsonite Route* (Bender 1970, p. 107).

This panel, devoid of any artistic frills, is located on the old Uncompahgre area of the Uintah and Ouray Reservation. It is extremely valuable in that it provides evidence substantiated by accepted historical authorities. Its translation documents the meaning of many symbols—*trail, footsteps off the trail, negation, crossed, leading, going down, wet, objects, nothing there, bad, little, failed to cross* —and various types of rock incorporation already presented in this work from older panels throughout the West.

Consolidation No. 10 is the engine (*a*) which has just crossed a bridge (*b*). This bridge symbol is a neck, meaning *narrow,* and a rectangular head meaning place or object, to represent the idea of a narrow bridge.

The engine and tender (*a*) are placed beyond the bridge to show that they have *crossed* it. The engine is indicated again (*c*) by the protruding smokestack — the rest of the engine having submerged in the mud (*something on it*) beneath the bridge. Compare this Ute depiction with an actual photograph of the wreck.

This bridge was located across Salt Wash about two miles west of Mack, Colorado. At the time that Consolidation No. 10 reached it—before sunrise on October 1, 1911—it was in a flood-weakened condition. As the train crossed it, part of the bridge collapsed, and the engine and tender rolled over into the raging flood. The remaining boxcar and combination passenger coach-baggage car were left stranded precariously on what was left of the weakened structure.

The four squares (*d*) represent the entire train, which consisted of four units. The smallest square is the tender. In the second square from the end a cross is placed to show that the last two units of the train (the boxcar and passenger coach) did not entirely cross over the bridge. This idea is clearly portrayed by the rider on horse *e* whose arms are in the *negation* position and whose head touches the cross. (Throughout this panel a horse and rider represent people riding the train.) This entire unit tells us that the last two cars and passengers *did not cross* the bridge.

Fig. 64.

Fig. 64. An actual photograph of the wreck   From *Uintah Railway, the Gilsonite Route* (Bender, 1970)

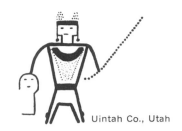

Uintah Co., Utah

This part of the story is repeated for clarification: Symbol *f* is the sign language *little,* already described in figure 21. This index finger and thumb also form part of a *trail* (*g*) — the railroad which crossed the collapsed bridge (*h*), *nothing there,* and then *goes down* (*i*) (descending birdtrack pointing to the last two cars). One toe of the birdtrack is longer and reaches down to point to a line protruding from the last car; this again says *little,* or a *little way.* The entire unit says, "The last two cars were only a little way from going down off the bridge."

Symbol *j* shows the plight of the passengers. Note the stationary or *stuck* horse (dots on the hooves), and the upraised *praying,* or *beseeching,* arms of the passenger. The placing of the feet of this horse on a little ledge uses rock incorporation to convey the idea of *on the bridge,* or *edge.* The forefeet of horse *e* are placed in like manner. The rock depression (*k*) represents the wash itself. The horse (*l*), pointing the opposite way, represents the passenger car *going back* off the bridge to where it would not be in danger of rolling over. The spiral (*m*) represents the idea *rolling over,* since its outer end forms a base line and since it is placed between the horse's legs. In the sign language a horizontal spiral, as opposed to an upward or downward spiral, represents *rolling over.*

This horse and rider are of a neutral stick-figure type to show that the car and passengers are *out of danger.* This is evident in the contrast of horse *l* to horses *j* and *e.* The latter two are widened and solidly pecked to say *bad* (in a dangerous position.) Horse *l* was not widened, and is therefore now *out of danger.*

The heads of both rider and horse (*e*) touch the last two cars and point in the opposite direction to clarify that these two cars *headed back* (eventually were pulled back to safety).

Rock incorporation is used again in symbol *n.* It is placed down over the edge of the rock to portray the idea *down.* The head of this upside-down (*dead*) man is indistinct. It might be a birdtrack *going down.* Two men, however, did die in this wreck. This may explain the author's intent, if indeed the symbol in question is actually a head.

Symbol *o* aptly demonstrates the versatility of Indian pictography. The mounted chief represents the engineer and engine, or *leader;* the trailing warbonnet represents his *followers,* or *those who trail behind* (the rest of the train). Note the rock incorporation: A natural hole is the head of this engineer. This says he *headed into a hole.* The arms also fail to meet in crossing his body, thus revealing that he *failed to stop* before reaching the hole.

Symbol *p* of a horse with tail tied to the front feet of another horse represents the equipment used to pull the wrecked engine out of the wash and back up on the trail. Note the *muddy* belly (*wet* technique) of the second horse. The tail of this horse is composed of dots to indicate that it went *off the beaten path* (footsteps only — not a trail).

Movement line *q* represents the traveling train, and symbol *r,* a falling man, indicates its *wreck*. Symbol *s* of a neutral stick horse *going up,* or *getting up,* indicates its *recovery*. These last two symbols are used to help resolve any doubt the reader might have concerning the meaning of certain sections of this panel, providing further proof that it was definitely inscribed for others to read, and that it was intended as a historical record among the Utes.

These purposes have been apparent in the many historical panels discussed in previous chapters. This panel adds to the growing proof that a widespread pictographic system existed among many Indian tribes and that it retained its ancient form right up into modern times. (We note the exception of the use of the horse in preference to the goat as a symbol.) One cannot help wondering and regretting that some interested and foresighted scholar did not record the meaning of this panel from the author's own lips. It is unmistakeable proof of the pictographic skill hidden in this Ute author's mind in this surprisingly late period of 1911.

128

8.

Many Tongues— One Ear

IT IS TOO EARLY TO DETERMINE the degree to which Indian picture writing may have existed throughout North America, but the evidence accumulated so far does definitely indicate the general use of this system throughout the United States, Canada, and much of Mexico. Similarities in Indian pictography prevail throughout the same vast area which comprises what is thought to be the geographical confines of the sign language (if, indeed, there actually *are* any boundaries — see Mallery's evidence upon the subject).

Some examples of panels throughout Central and South America appear to have a relationship to North American picture-writing, but so far the results of study initiated in this area are inconclusive. For the time being, then, our study will be limited to North America.

Perhaps one of the best examples of a symbol universal to this area is the bird symbol. It is unlikely that the meanings assigned to it—*taking flight, seeking safety,* and others—were thought up independently by different individuals throughout the country; it probably originated in one place and gradually spread. The concept behind this symbol evidently comes from the principle in military strategy of having an advantage in the added safety of height. To depict the idea of fleeing to the safety of a hilltop, a bird was used—either taking off, flying, or alighting. This symbol also enabled the picture writer to be specific regarding these different stages of flight.

The true thunderbird of Indian mythology, as distinguished from this bird symbol, is not known among all tribes of this continent; it was used only in a limited area. This thunderbird therefore cannot be the same as the widely used bird of pictography. Besides, the mythological counterpart is very different in appearance. The thunderbird can often be distinguished by the lightning radiating from its wings, or the lines denoting thunder streaming from its mouth, both of which show relationship to thunder and rain. The bird symbol in general use never possesses these features, and is depicted merely as an unspecified bird.

129

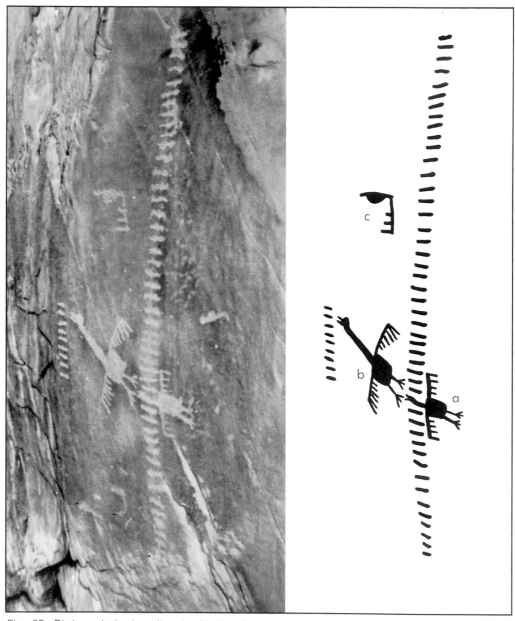

Fig. 65. Bird symbols describe the flights of some southwestern Indians to the safety of their cliff dwellings.

A great many panels found in many widespread areas contain this bird symbol used with identical meanings—*seeking,* or *reaching safety.* One excellent example has already been presented—that of the wings upon the deity of the Hopi Snake dancers, which symbolize *reaching safety, salvation,* or, more specifically, *good fortune* in being blessed by crop-saving rains.

Other similar examples of bird symbols used with identical meanings are to be found in panels adjacent to many of the cliff dwellings of the Southwest. Near

Alberta, Can.
(pictograph)

Tsegi, Arizona, for example, bird symbols clearly tell the story of a hasty flight to the safety of the high and protected cliff dwellings so common here (figure 65).

The short horizontal lines in this panel represent the number of times these flights to safety were necessary. The neck of bird *a* forms part of this enumeration in order to show that it was *part* of the upward flight to safety.

The squared bodies of these birds indicate *property,* or the cliff dwellings suggested by the upward flight of the birds and the location of the panel itself. Bird *b*, however, does not show as many flights to safety. The reason for this is found in comparing the sizes of the two birds. Bird *b* is larger (the bodies of many people incorporated into one) than bird *a*. It indicates that the people living in this cliff dwelling *outnumbered* those living on the cliffs depicted by bird *a*. The neck of bird *b* is longer than bird *a,* and reaches higher to say that their cliff refuge was *higher* and hence *more secure* from attack.

The feathers on the wings of bird *b* become longer at the wing tips to indicate that the Indians of the larger band would offer no help, nor would they share their refuge with the smaller band. The shorter feathers on the larger bird denote *far off* (explained in the wife-purchasing example in chapter 4), and are purposely placed next to the body to say that the people of the smaller, less fortunate group were *not allowed to come close* and share in the more secure refuge. This *angered* them — note that bird *a* is biting the heels of bird *b*.

Symbol *c* consists of a right angle used in conjunction with a bowl-shaped symbol pecked solid in the *something there* technique (under the top horizontal line). This combination indicates *something up and beneath*. The three horizontal bars which become smaller as one proceeds up this right angle clarify the idea *keeping others away*. This entire combination refers to the nearby cliff dwellings high up and beneath protective overhangs.

Such panels, besides containing examples of this particular symbol which affirm its widespread use, also provide evidence that these cliff dwellers were in fact the authors of many of these adjacent panels, since these stories tell of their dwellings and the events that transpired there.

Numerous examples of the bird symbol may also be found in the Great Lakes region and in many areas of Canada. One excellent example from Lake Superior shows a bird with outstretched wings, flying toward shore, placed in front of several fragile canoes crossing these large, dangerous waters. The protection implied by this bird appropriately indicates that the men occupying these canoes ultimately reached the safety of the distant shore.

Another bird, similar to the one depicting the Navajo wading into the Rio Grande, is also placed in front of these men in canoes to indicate that they *waded in the water* as they reached shore. The meaning of the wading-bird symbol has

131

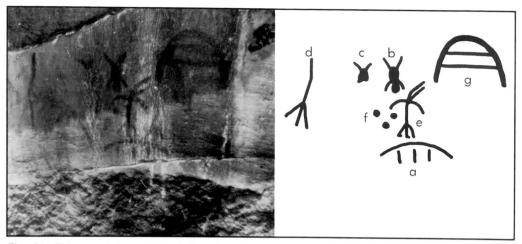

Fig. 66. This panel from Rainy Lake, Ontario, Canada, tells of the capsizing of a canoe with three men in it (*a*). The upside-down man (*b*) indicates that one man drowned. Symbol (*c*) may be a second drowned man, but it is too faded to discern accurately. The bird track *going down* (*d*) clarifies *sinking* or *drowning,* and the bend in this track indicates *distance* (sinking to the bottom of the deep lake).

A third man (*e*) has the mouth of a bird, pointing upward (as some birds are required to do when drinking) to indicate *swallowing.* This man has a penis long enough to reach the ground, thus indicating *reaching shore.* His legs are also in the *arriving* position. This figure, with its *seeking safety* wings (arms), says, "This person swallowed water while seeking the safety of the shore, but succeeded in reaching it."

Symbol *f* (three dots) represents the position of the three nearby islands where the canoe capsized; symbol *g* represents the island reached by the survivor. The two *nothing there* lines indicate that it is *deserted,* or barren.

The remainder of the panel is too faded to venture any further attempts at reading.

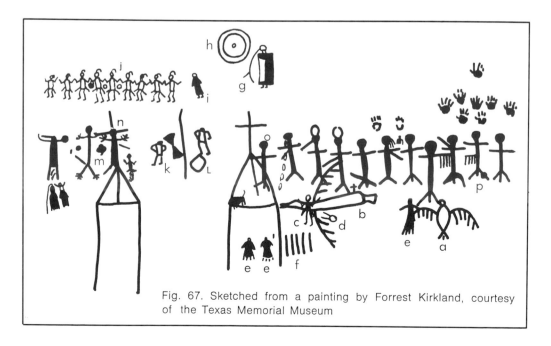

Fig. 67. Sketched from a painting by Forrest Kirkland, courtesy of the Texas Memorial Museum

132

Valencia Co., N. Mex.

been authenticated by an Abnaki Indian informant of Maine, who described it "just same as heron wading alongshore" (Mallery 1893). This wading-bird symbol substantiates by affinity the meaning of this flying bird, and greatly rules out any chance that these birds were either clan totems or personal names. Bird wings applied to a human figure on Rainy Lake in Ontario, Canada, denote this same *seeking safety* meaning in an episode of a capsized canoe (figure 66).

Another excellent example of the bird symbol — this time from a completely different cultural area — occurs at Meyers Springs, Texas (figure 67). This panel, probably of Lipan Apache origin, depicts an early Spanish priest holding *salvation* for the Indian in his hand (symbol *a,* a bird with outstretched wings). Bird *b* is shown flying toward a church, and is superimposed over a breech-clouted (*uncivilized*) Indian (*c*), as if to say, "The only way for the uncivilized Indian to obtain salvation is by going to church."

In order to show that these birds or *salvation* symbols are in proper affinity to the remainder of the panel, it is necessary to translate some of the more interesting and pertinent symbols: Non-believing Indian bystanders (*d*) are looking at the conversion of the other Indians. The three *e* symbols represent the long-robed priests. (The downward movement lines at the base of the robes are used to indicate the full length of their robes.) Six Spanish missions are indicated (*f*). A forked-tongue (*lieing*) priest (*g*) puts on a *good* front (open space in front of square body), but is really *bad*. Symbol *h* indicates that he *holds* the Indians in one place with *good,* or *nothing, talk.* A priest (*i*) is controlling a line of captured, uncivilized Indians (*j*) who, according to their flexing (*doing*) arms, are probably being used as slave labor. The *turning over* symbols on the heads signify their *deaths.* Symbol *k* is an admonition by the priests for the Indians to stop their *warring* (tilted arrowheads) and their *roaming around* (circle at the foot of *l*). Symbol *m* (a flower indicating *beautiful land*) and the man passing between this flower and the dot represent an Indian *going* through *to heaven* as a result of learning Christianity (a cross put into the head symbol *n*). Symbol *o* is an Indian crossing over a cross which he holds, and entering the church, thus indicating that he is *joining* and *holding to* this religion.

The eleven figures standing in a row represent an Apache version of the Ten Commandments (indicated by the *barring, restricting,* or "thou shalt not" arms). The eighth and ninth figures together represent one commandment — not undressing another, possibly referring to adultery, thus making ten commandments in all. These Indians thought the Christian requirement of wearing clothes was also one of these commandments (*p*) — note the leg forcing its way through a pant leg and the downward movement at the waist indicating *pants* or a *skirt.* More of this lengthy panel is understood, but the foregoing is sufficient to establish by affinity the *salvation* meaning of the two birds.

133

Fig. 68. One paragraph in the Navajo account of the Kit Carson campaign

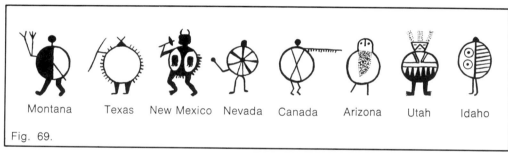

| Montana | Texas | New Mexico | Nevada | Canada | Arizona | Utah | Idaho |

Fig. 69.

Fig. 70. Note the affinity these goats have to the shield figure of a white man (center). Goat *a* is peeking up over the tail of goat *b*, which is going up behind, or is in back of, goat *c*.

134

Galisteo Basin, N. Mex.

One final example — this one from the dissimilar Navajo culture — appears in figure 68. A part of the series of panels relating the Kit Carson story, this picture shows birds identical in meaning to the foregoing bird examples, but which are, nevertheless, unique in the way they are used. These birds tell that the Navajo in Canyon de Chelly alighted safely on the cliff tops while the soldiers were passing through below. The tails of these birds are spread out to indicate *strutting* or *showing off* while *safely out of reach*. They are all tilted to indicate *waiting*, and two of these birds are blocked by a tilted (*stopped*) war symbol, as if to say the Navajo were really just *waiting for the war to stop* so they could *return* (indicated by the lone bird facing in the opposite direcion) to the bottom of the canyon or to their homes.

The usage of this bird symbol in identical meanings throughout North America cannot be questioned, since it has been shown to exist in different cultural areas in Utah, Arizona, New Mexico, Canada and Texas.

Evidence also shows that distinctive features of a bird — wings, a bird track going upward, or a beak (figure 42) — may be used to portray the appropriate meanings in lieu of an entire flying bird.

The shield figure — a man defending himself behind a large shield — is another example of a symbol having widespread use. The shield symbol itself is found with countless embellishments, each of which has an affinity to the defense theme.

Figure 69 illustrates several of these shield figures from various parts of the country. Similar figures are to be found in other scattered locations from Pennsylvania to California. They are more abundant, however, in areas where war-like tribes flourished, such as the Southern and Northern Plains, and in eastern Utah which, according to Ute and Paiute stories, has long been a bloody battleground.

Shield figures do not belong exclusively to Plains cultures. They are equally apropriate in the pictography of Pueblo and other cultures, some of which are known to have used shields, and some of which did not. In the latter case, shield symbols represent defended positions behind rock dwellings or any shielding fortification. This symbol therefore has a very appropriate universal application among all people of all tribes, thus accounting for its widespread use. See the example of the shield figure in the panel drawn by the Utes depicting a siege of soldiers in a protected gully in Colorado, figure 41 Another example of white-man shield figures appears in figure 70. This southern Paiute example from near Las Vegas, Nevada, accompanied by goat symbols, reveals an additional point of importance: Goat symbols were commonly used very recently, especially by Paiutes, and are not strictly an older symbol as might be supposed. This panel also closely resembles, in style, panels heavily coated with patina, possibly thousands of years older, thus showing the unchanging form of Indian pictography down through the ages.

Fig. 71.

Fig. 72. This panel from the Galisteo Basin in New Mexico is an excellent example of symbols having an affinity to warfare, on a shield figure. Note the stone war club in this figure's hand, and the many arrow points radiating from the shield. Also note the arrowheads coming from all four directions above this shield figure's left shoulder.

Pawnee Buffalo Robe

Yet another example of a historic shield figure exists in the account of the battle between the Kiowa and the Mexicans near El Paso, Texas, related in chapter 5. This shield figure is to be found in the midst of the string of panels that relate this story. It is a good example of how such figures are to be read.

The lone shield figure (71) depicts a shielded man with his lance braced for *battle* (symbol *a*). The typical hat reveals that he is *Mexican,* and it is tilted to signify that he is *waiting* to show himself. His shield is the rocks behind which he is hiding. One leg is in the act of *departing,* but the other is *not turning aside,* indicating that the Mexicans had pretended to depart in order to lure the Kiowa out of their stronghold. Symbol *b* — a lance trying to penetrate behind the shield of the Mexicans — is broadened to incorporate the meaning *bad,* or *difficult,* thus conveying the message, "It was difficult to hit the Mexicans."

Several other symbols are commonly used throughout the country as part of the make-up of a shield figure. These symbols include war clubs (the New Mexico example in figure 72), lances, bare legs shown in profile to indicate *turning aside,* bare feet to indicate *danger,* arrowheads, quadruped animations, *holding firm T's,* the symbol for *holding on loosely, alert* ears, and horns of *strength* or *weakness.* All of these show a decisive relationship to shield and warfare symbols, and thus establish the meaning of such symbols beyond any doubt.

The shield figure is, then, another excellent example of how one basic symbol had a universal meaning and use among many widely dispersed people. Further clues are present in numerous other symbols throughout the country, the meanings of which can be documented in the works of Schoolcraft, Hoffman, Mallery, Brinton, Denig, Dibble, and others. For example, all the symbols in chart 5, columns *B* through *G,* show a related meaning throughout a large area of North America and are identical to, or are based upon, the symbol concepts in column *A,* these having been deciphered through cryptanalysis.

By themselves columns *B* through *G* are documented examples presenting a very convincing case for the widespread use of Indian pictography. Comparisons with column *A* only substantiate and reinforce this case. The chart contains only a few examples selected from those available.

The picture-writing symbols of the Dakota, Ojibwa, and Delaware shown in this chart should be familiar to the average reader of Indian history, since some of the symbols from these tribes are readily available for study. Few readers, however, realize how many different tribes on this continent have been credited in various authoritative publications as having had a picture-writing system, or of having used some symbols derived from one. The following tribes, in addition to those mentioned, all used one form or another of picture writing. The length of this list (and it is far from complete) shows how extensive the practice was: From the eastern United States—Iroquois, Kickapoo, Passamaquoddy, Penobscot, Winnebago,

137

	A Rock Writings	B Dakota	C Ojibwa
1	War	Fight	
2	Dead		Dead
3	Talk	Talking	Intense Talk
4	Feather, Heal, Power		Power
5	Arrowhead	Arrow Point	Arrow Point
6	Fast		
7	Area or Object	House	Lodge
8	Medicine, Strong	Making Medicine	Shamen, Power
9	End		End
10	Sequence		Number of War Parties
11	Stopped, Waiting		Stop, Rest
12	White Man	White Man	White Man
13	Small Particles	Measles, Smallpox, Acorns	Small Objects
14	A Mound, Hill	Hill	Mountain
15	The Four Directions		The Four Directions
16	Broad Downward Movement	Blood Flowing Down	Sitting Down
17	Piled Up	Mountain	
18	Bloody Hand	Wounded or Killed	Death
19	Sheep That Have Been Killed		Own Tongue Kills You
20	River Movement	River	Stream
21	Nothing There, Good	Good Weasel	Garments Thrown Off
22	Something There	Dirt, Blood	

Chart 5.

D	E	F	G
Delaware	Hopi	Aztec	Other
War	Fighting	Warfare (Mixtec)	Campaign (Pima)
Killed Another		Dead	Dead (Iroquois)
Talking Together			
	Eagletail, Power		Power, Heal (Navajo)
Arrow Point	Arrow Point	Arrow Point	Arrow Point (British Columbia)
		Fast	
Village	Dwelling	Place	Enclosure (Hidatsa)
Strength			Strength (Apache)
Number of War Parties	Five Years	Sequence	Third (Hidatsa)
The Whites		Spaniard	White Man (Penn Wampum)
	Small Particles	Salt, Sand, Wet	
Hill, Land		Mountain, Hill	Rounded Hills (Blackfeet)
Hunting in Four Directions	The Four Directions	The Four Directions	Four Cardinal Points
	Terraced	Terraced	Heaped Up (British Columbia)
	Stained Hands		Bloody Hand (Arikara)
River	River	Stream Current	River (Assinaboine)
Pure, Virtue			Lean, Nothing There (Hidatsa)
			Something Being Held (Kiowa)

Ottawa, Potawatomie, Wyandot, Shawnee, Mingo; from the South — Natchez and Choctaw; from the Central States and Plains — Assiniboin, Omaha, Osage, Comanche, Arikara, Cheyenne, Crow, Hidatsa, Shoshone; from the West—Pima, Zuni, Coeur d'Alene; and from Canada — Sarcee, Cree, Micmac, Abnaki, and Malecite.

Consideration of this lengthy list including tribes from many of the major linguistic stocks throughout the country makes it very difficult to believe that all of these tribes used different, independent systems. This is all the more inconceivable since we know that almost all these tribes understood and practiced the same Indian sign language.

A system of picture writing based as far as possible on the universal sign language would be natural and logical, since the majority of symbols employed would have been based on hand signs, which, together with their numerous extensions, **were already understood and memorized.** The evidence already presented bears out this sign-language relationship by demonstrating many of the symbols which were thus derived.

The final percentage of sign-language-derived symbols, however, cannot be accurately determined until all symbols of Indian pictography are deciphered. Even then, a conclusive percentage would be difficult to determine, because many signs necessarily involve several signs, and thus *describe* a concept. Animals and other forms of life are similarly described. The relationship between signs and symbols in such cases is not as obvious.

Another point to be considered here is that the sign language and pictography both have built-in advantages and simplified methods of portraying some concepts, and thus, out of convenience, diverge in their relationship to each other. This, however, only applies to individual signs and symbols — not to the general relation-

Fig. 73. This painted panel from Mexico contains symbols similar to those found in the United States.

140

Galisteo Basin, N. Mex.

ship of both systems. A few difficult hand signs even seem to be based on pictographic symbols.

Another aspect in the discussion of the far-reaching implications of Indian pictography is the obvious differences in outward appearance of panels created by changes in topics, but this difference does not affect the argument. Recent panels from the pueblo areas of New Mexico and Arizona show a pronounced trend toward this distinction in appearance, and even some artistic expression is obvious (figures 19, 53, 60, and 72). In some areas the development of the unique pueblo panels can be traced. For example, on the top portion of a patina-blackened cliff face at Oraibi, Arizona, is an extensive, yet simple panel. This panel generally resembles the Great Basin panels. The talus at one time reached the base of this panel, but the centuries have eroded it away, exposing much more of the cliff face below. On this lower cliff face newer panels were inscribed, their more recent origin evidenced by the lighter patina. These panels show a gradual change toward pueblo-oriented symbols and apparent artistic expression.

This recent change in panel appearance, or topic, conforms to the trend of some tribes toward a highly developed pueblo system. For example, the Hopi, during their basketmaker stage, had a very simple culture similar to the desert culture of the Paiutes. But as they developed into a pueblo culture they automatically created many new traits, clans, ceremonies, and religious paraphernalia. To keep pace with this change the pictography of the Hopi, as would that of any progressive culture, continually added symbols in order to record events including these new elements. The addition of picturesque or personal touches, such as the Ute horse symbol, only augmented and embellished the basic system; it did not replace it.

This topic change and expansion does reveal a minor weakness in a pictographic system — that is, the difficulty a non-pueblo Indian would have had, for example, in interpreting symbols peculiar to a pueblo culture. This may be somewhat like a student of the arts reading a technical medical discourse for the first time. Although he could read it, much of the nomenclature would be completely unfamiliar, and the message consequently obscure. However, some idioms and the variance in cultural topics from area to area are the only basic difficulties so far encountered which may have affected the general understanding of Indian pictography. This is only the same variance that occurs within any language, and it in no way affects the question of whether the system had general use throughout the continent.

There is little doubt that many of the panels in northern Mexico were written in the same pictographic system as that used by the Indians of what is now the United States; many of these panels contain symbols identical to those in this country (figure 73). It must follow, then, that the pictographic system used in the

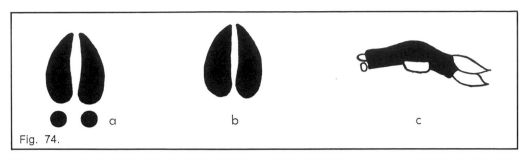

Fig. 74.

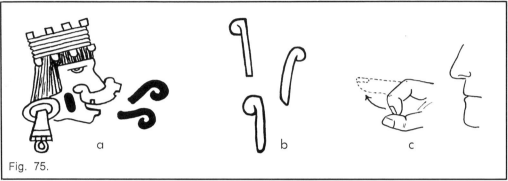

Fig. 75.

Fig. 76.

United States and Canada extended deep into Mexico. It may even have had some influence upon Aztec, Mayan, and other more civilized systems of picture writing (although the latter two systems are quite different in many respects). This is not surprising — these cultures and their antecedents existed in a highly civilized condition which had seen the evolution of a system of writing which had even introduced sounds. Nevertheless, mingled among and a part of these different writings are many pictographic symbols identical in meaning and concept to those of the Indians farther to the north. For example, in Aztec picture writing (very

Sierra Madre Mts., Mex.

pleasing to the eye, perhaps due in part to the soft Indian paper on which it was more easily painted), we are able to find evidence of symbols identical in meaning, suggesting that Aztec was derived from, or still used much of, this older, "parent" system.

One of the most obvious of these is the symbol of a deer hoof including the dew claws (figure 74). In the pictography found in the United States, the symbol of a deer track with the dew claws imprinted behind (*a*) represents *fleeing,* hence, by extension, *fear.* The concept behind this symbol is simple to understand: The dew claws of a deer never make an imprint unless the deer is running (*fleeing*). These dew-claw imprints are left on the ground when the ankle of the deer bends low enough to leave these marks—only when he runs. Symbol *b* shows the common track of a walking deer.

Examples of these symbols have already been shown in the petroglyph describing the flight of the Navajo from Kit Carson's soldiers (chapter 6). The Aztecs use these dew claws also to indicate *flee* (Dibble 1950), but they were more artistic in their depictions, and meticulously show the entire hoof and dew claws in profile (*c*).

Many other symbols suggest that the Aztec picture-writing, even though it is a distinct system, was probably derived from the same pictographic system used in the United States or that it still used many of its symbols. Some of these examples appear in chart 6 in the following chapter, "World Comparisons"; others appear in chart 5. These similarities reveal how deeply these symbols had penetrated into Mexico.

It is also evident that many of the symbols of Aztec picture writing are derived from the sign language. An example of this is the symbol for *speech* (symbol *a,* figure 75), which is also identical in some Mayan and Mixtec examples. This symbol evidently comes from the sign-language *talk,* made by snapping the index finger outward from the mouth several times (*c*). This same "snapping index" symbol is used by the Aztecs, meaning *to smoke* (*b*). To those who understand the relationship of smoking to talking in Indian cultures, the derivation of this symbol is quite obvious. Smoking was always a very ceremonial occasion, and the peace pipe was used extensively by numerous tribes in various councils or talks. According to many Indian informants who still revere this practice, the smoke that ascends from the pipe are the "words" of the council or meeting "ascending to God," to be witnessed by him.

One more example of the kinship of Mexican symbols to the sign language appears in figure 76. This panel appears on a rock near Mecamecan in southern Mexico. The man in this panel is holding the *speech* symbol (snapping index) in his hands, which are being drawn toward him. This is the sign-language method of saying, "I was told." A variety of phrases can be similarly said in the sign

Fig. 77. These pictographic components used in Mayan glyphs are identical in meaning to symbols of Indian pictography (after Seler).

language by moving the open hand palm upward, in various movements. The open palm represents a *handful of words,* or *much talk.*

If we can trust the accuracy of the sketching of this panel, which comes from Mallery's book, it depicts a man receiving a very important message or instruction from God, as indicated by the slant of the arms upward. (Compare this example with the Kiowa method of saying the same thing in figure 45, symbol *d*). These two examples reveal the relationship of this symbol, even though the Indians of Mexico resorted to a more picturesque and decorative style of writing.

Numerous examples of Mayan glyphs read strictly in a pictographic sense are also based upon this parent pictography. An example is the day sign for the word *caban,* a Mayan word meaning *that which is brought down.* The basic component of this and other related glyphs appears in figure 77, symbol *a*. The dot in Indian pictography means *here,* and the movement lines reaching up over the top of the position symbol clearly depict, in a pictographic manner, *brought down from above.* The arc over the dot indicates the palm of the hand *clutching* or *covering* the dot, and the wavy line pointing downward indicates that both the hand and the positioned object were *brought down.*

Symbol *b* confirms this meaning in a non-phonetic structure, by combining this symbol with a picture of an axe, thus portraying the felling of the tree. This same symbol *bringing down* appears on numerous other glyphs with appropriate meanings.

Symbol *c* is a glyph in which the sign-language *to eat* is used. The author of the work from which these examples are taken (Seler 1904) claims that the Indians of Huaxteca, Mexico, related to the Mayans, were still using this sign when he visited them. This gesture represents the bent hand being carried to the mouth as in the act of eating. It is identical to the sign *eat* as used in the United States. Note the two front teeth (two connected rectangles) near the center of this hand used to clarify this meaning. The entire glyph, then, shows a man holding food in his hand which he is either giving or receiving.

Symbol *d* indicates *cut up* or *divided,* and is very similar to examples in the United States for denoting this same concept.

The complete decipherment of Mayan hinges upon a thorough understanding of the pictographic concepts which form the foundation of the entire system. The

McKinley Co., N. Mex.
(pictograph)

majority of Mayan glyphs occur with great variation in form—the same problem originally encountered in Indian pictography which indeed is the first clue to be sought in establishing a system as a pictography. It follows, then, that Mayan is also based upon a pictographic foundation from which numerous phonetic constructions were devised, thus making it much more advanced than the parent system itself.

The sampling of evidence presented in this chapter and throughout this work in regard to the widespread use of the same pictographic system throughout North America proves beyond any doubt that many of the basic symbols of Indian pictography were at one time used universally throughout much of this extensive area.

9.

World Comparisons

ROCK WRITINGS ARE NOT UNIQUE TO NORTH AMERICA. They are to be found in pecked or painted form in almost every country of the world—from desolate Siberia to the lush islands of the Pacific. The listing of just a few of the countries where these writings have been found illustrates the variety of locations in which they occur: Israel, Egypt, Afghanistan, Algeria, Africa, Turkey, France, Spain, Italy, Sweden, Norway, England, Ireland, Fiji, Hawaii, Tahiti, China, Japan, India, Australia, the Canary Islands, and almost every country in South America.

The purpose that rock writings once served has disappeared with the vanished pages of time, especially true in such countries as Spain and France, where many of the writings are from a prehistoric age. The ages of the writings in these countries can be somewhat established by relating them to the objects and animals depicted. For example, illustrations of the bison and mastodon in Spain and France would place such writings at a time when such animals still existed there. One could not, of course, expect to find documented evidence establishing the purpose of these drawings.

On the other hand, in countries such as Australia, Hawaii, and New Zealand where the practice of rock writing persisted through part of the last century (in fact, it is occasionally practiced in Australia to this day), we are able to partially document the purpose of some writings. Information obtained from the natives of Australia reveals a topic list obviously very similar to that of the pictography of the American Indian—life and history, hunting, folklore, legendary characters, fishing, love affairs, chants, totemic maps, ritual, dream totems, and magic (McCarthy 1967). Australia, with its "outback" where the aborigines still retain much of their stone-age culture, is a natural location for finding such treasures—a place where the clock seems to have stopped.

The writings of Hawaii and New Zealand did not fare as well. Here the writing systems perished with the cultures of the people. Having suffered the same

147

PHOTO BY K. C. DEN DOOVEN

Fig. 78. A Hawaiian gene-
alogical record

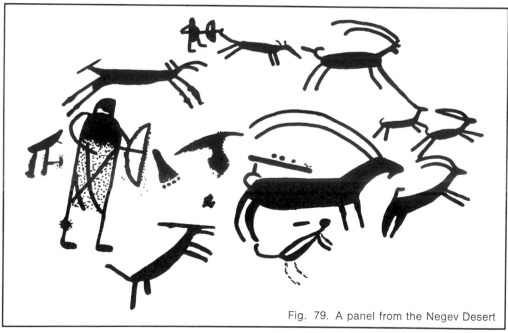

Fig. 79. A panel from the Negev Desert

Egypt

wanton neglect that American pictography underwent, they died out without ever having been systematically recorded, leaving the task of decipherment to the reviving hand of cryptanalysis. What little can be gleaned from the scant documents on the writings of these two countries, however, reveals an existing pictography in which communication seems to be the underlying purpose. For example, Hawaiian rock writings recorded trips, communication ritual, prophecies, histories, events, and legends (Cox 1970).

Genealogical records, for which Hawaiians are well known, may also be added to this list. Figure 78 is a long line of men, one man below another, with each head placed between the legs of the man before. This is the method used in the sign language to show birth and lineal descent (line 24, chart 6). This photograph therefore represents twenty-nine generations of one family.

Aside from bits of information like that above, and similar information from New Zealand, little is known of the pictographies of the Pacific. As a result of the neglect and lack of interest in rock writing in recent centuries, not one complete pictographic system can be found in the world that is still used or that can be fully understood as such.

American Indian pictography, under the scrutiny and the persistent eye of cryptanalysis, is the first rock-writing system, or pure pictography, to be at least partially deciphered. As a result, a considerable amount of structural understanding is now available by which to compare, study, and eventually decipher other similar, forgotten pictographies of the world. This study takes a first step in this direction by analyzing similarities in structural makeup among symbols throughout the world. It reveals that most world rock writings are strikingly similar to Indian pictography in their utilization of symbol combinations, incorporations, and the cluster method of arrangement.

This similarity can be recognized by any student who has a basic understanding of the structure of Indian pictography, simply by examining the photographs and sketches available. For example, study the panel from the Negev Desert in Israel (figure 79). Anyone familar with the rock writings of the Southwest, not told the location of this panel, might confidently tag it as a panel from Utah, Arizona, Nevada, or California. Such an error would be natural, since panels from these two widely separated areas bear amazing resemblances in appearance, topic, structure, and depiction of lateral action.

Another excellent example of one of the most popular of world-wide topics—warfare—appears on a rock in the Camonica Valley at Cemmo in northern Italy (figure 80). If we apply the now known symbols of Indian pictography to the reading of this panel, we come up with a very interesting result. Here again animals are used to represent lateral movement and people. Quadrupeds in this example represent two powerful opposing armies lined up and facing each other in attitudes

149

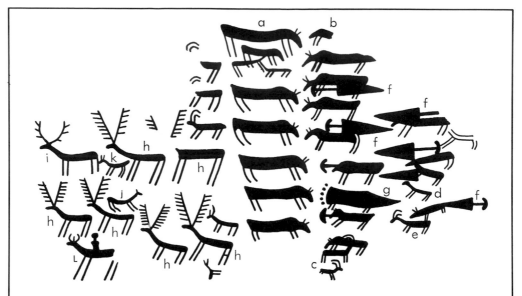

Fig. 80. This panel, reproduced from photographs, is located in northern Italy, and contains many symbols similar to Indian pictographic symbols

of combat, in the old-world style of fighting. That these quadrupeds represent powerful armies of warriors is indicated by the strong, bull-like necks and shoulders of the animals. The soldiers of side *a* outnumber those of side *b*, a fact communicated by their larger bodies. The quadrupeds or soldiers of both armies have their heads lowered in defiance and stubborn resistance, and the slant of their legs indicates that they are braced for battle.

In this fierce battle, side *a* made a successful flanking movement to the right and knocked side *b* off its position of defense (*c*). The horns of these two goats utilize the semi-arc, or *knocked off* symbol, to indicate this. Their advanced position and the superimposition of one of these goats behind one belonging to army *b* also indicate this initial penetration *behind* the lines of army *b*. Symbol *d* further illustrates that army *b* was initially pushed back—note the extra slant of the legs.

The quick success of army *a*, however, did not last long. They were *knocked back off* from the ground they had gained, indicated by the horn of goat *e*. (Throughout this panel the army to which each quadruped belongs is distinguished by facing them in the same direction as their respective front-line combatants.)

Army *b's* success in pushing back army *a* was due to the reckless bravery of their soldiers. This is indicated by the barefoot track (*exposing oneself to danger*) —symbol *g*. This track also has the point from one of the fallen bodies (*f*) incorporated into its heel to say that *many fell* because of their reckless bravery. Note the bodies (*f*) of both armies scattered over the battlefield.

The superimposition of quadrupeds and bodies indicates the trampling or mingling of bodies among the living as the battle raged on; it does not mean that these symbols were pecked at different times, as may be supposed. This is apparent

Turkey (pictograph)

from the position of these symbols, their places in the story, and the affinity all have to each other. These fallen bodies appear to resemble daggers or swords, and may represent the sword bearers which have fallen in battle. However, Indian pictography occasionally utilizes the same long necks and pointed bases to portray human figures.

The ultimate outcome of this battle is indicated by the many stag-like animals (*h*), the deer (*i*), and the one-of-a-kind quadruped (*j*) with its legs slanting much further to the front than the other quadrupeds of army *a*, indicating that this side *had been pushed way back*.

The horns of the stag-like animals (*h*) reveal that army *b* finally broke through and scattered the soldiers of army *a*, who then fled. The *V*-shaped horns of these stags mean an *opening up*, or *breaking through*. The lines radiating to each side of the *V* represent a simultaneous and broad movement in these two directions, hence a *bursting* or *scattering to each side* by army *b*.

In America, deer horns are often conveniently subsitituted for deer tracks. This appears to be the case in this account, in which symbol *i* shows army *a* fleeing like a frightened deer, with army *b* hot on its heels (*k*). Symbol *l* indicates that some of the wounded were carried on this retreat by those who still had strength left.

This bloody battle account contains many symbols already explained in Indian pictography — symbols which show absolute affinity and coherency in the reading of this panel. Not one of these symbols appears to vary even the slightest in meaning, uncanny as it may seem. Quadrupeds lined up in this type of battle line are, however, not common in America; Indians did not customarily fight their battles in this manner.

This panel is a classical example of the ingenious use of quadrupeds to facilitate depiction of lateral actions—actions which would be much more complicated to illustrate using any other pictorial method. It would be difficult to offer a rational explanation of this panel as a conflict between bulls (some armed with swords), stags, ibexes, and dogs!

This particular battle, which involved so much daring and personal sacrifice, ending in victory over a much larger force, was an event to be long remembered by the people of the era, and would surely have been passed down to their descendants — in oral or written form, or both. Perhaps traces of this battle still exist in stories and myths of this part of the world. But whether they do or not, the rocks still tell the story and, more than that, are evidence of a powerful motivation for undertaking the arduous task of inscribing it in stone. It obviously had much more significance than a mere hunting scene or other commonplace event would have had.

Chart 6.

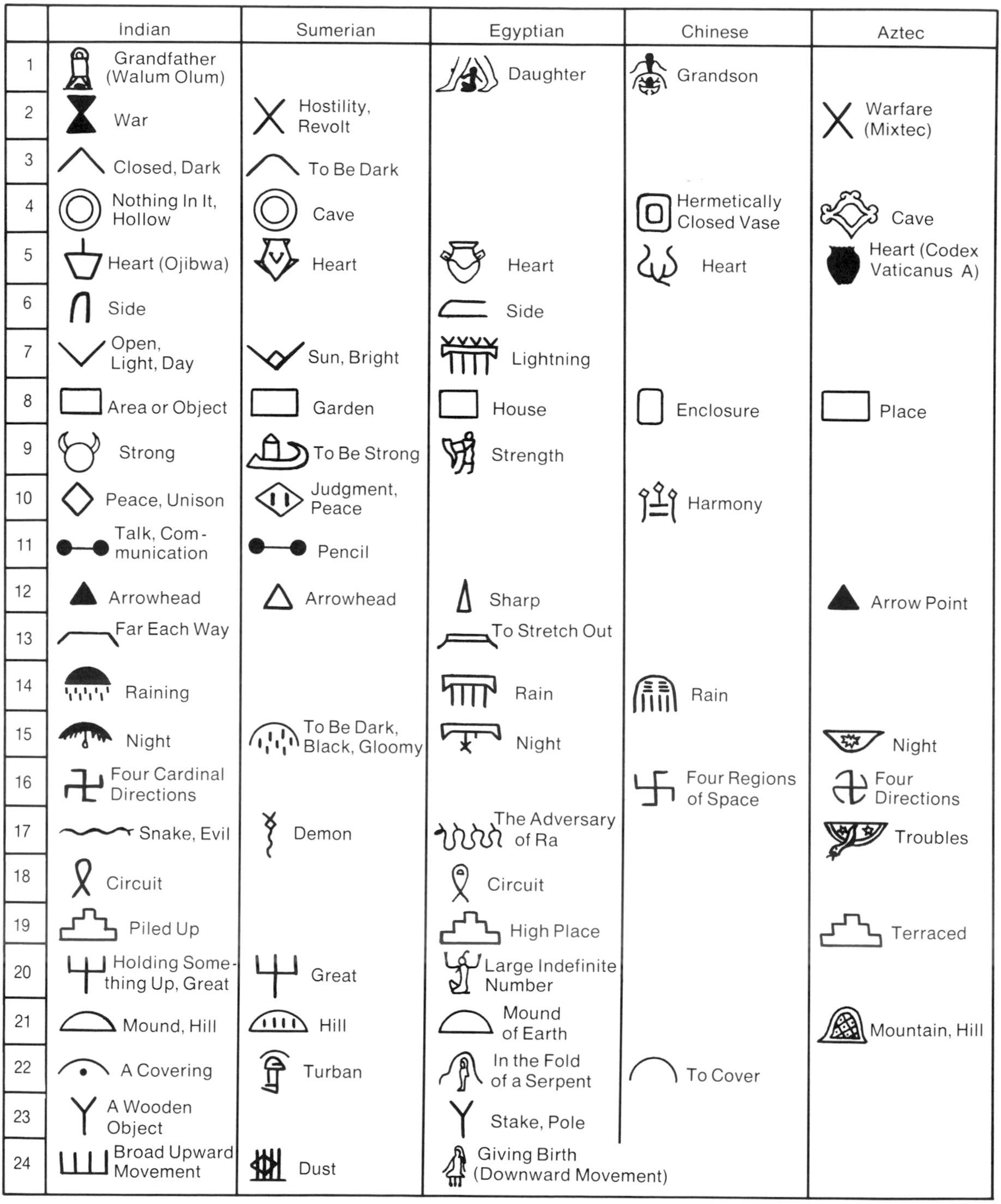

	Indian	Sumerian	Egyptian	Chinese	Aztec
1	Grandfather (Walum Olum)		Daughter	Grandson	
2	War	Hostility, Revolt			Warfare (Mixtec)
3	Closed, Dark	To Be Dark			
4	Nothing In It, Hollow	Cave		Hermetically Closed Vase	Cave
5	Heart (Ojibwa)	Heart	Heart	Heart	Heart (Codex Vaticanus A)
6	Side		Side		
7	Open, Light, Day	Sun, Bright	Lightning		
8	Area or Object	Garden	House	Enclosure	Place
9	Strong	To Be Strong	Strength		
10	Peace, Unison	Judgment, Peace		Harmony	
11	Talk, Communication	Pencil			
12	Arrowhead	Arrowhead	Sharp		Arrow Point
13	Far Each Way		To Stretch Out		
14	Raining		Rain	Rain	
15	Night	To Be Dark, Black, Gloomy	Night		Night
16	Four Cardinal Directions			Four Regions of Space	Four Directions
17	Snake, Evil	Demon	The Adversary of Ra		Troubles
18	Circuit		Circuit		
19	Piled Up		High Place		Terraced
20	Holding Something Up, Great	Great	Large Indefinite Number		
21	Mound, Hill	Hill	Mound of Earth		Mountain, Hill
22	A Covering	Turban	In the Fold of a Serpent	To Cover	
23	A Wooden Object		Stake, Pole		
24	Broad Upward Movement	Dust	Giving Birth (Downward Movement)		

152

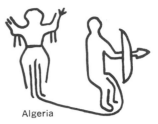

Algeria

In spite of similarities in the meanings of symbols in the foregoing panel to those of American rock writing, it is still much too early to conjecture too broadly about them. A few of these symbols may be due to coincidence; but this seems highly unlikely, especially in this panel.

There are some writing systems of the world (not basically rock writing) about which more is known; some interesting comparisons can be made with these — Egyptian hieroglyphics, Sumerian cuneiform, and Chinese are all based upon symbols from picture-writing systems.

Many Egyptian picture symbols are employed in both a pure picture-writing sense and as representing sounds derived from the world value of that symbol. For example, the word *owl* is *mulotch* in Coptic, an Egyptian dialect. Whenever this owl symbol (figure 81) was used strictly as a sound value, it took the alphabetic value of *m*, the initial letter of the word *mulotch* (Budge 1966). This symbol could therefore stand for the sound of the consonant *m*, or for the actual owl, depending on the use intended.

Because this symbol retained both its values down through the ages, we are able, once deciphered, to determine its pictographic applications. Many other symbols of Egyptian and of Sumerian utilized a similar principle, resulting in double use.

The interest of several scholarly writers, including Mallery, has been aroused by some of the similarities existing between the symbols of these systems and those of American Indian pictography; various allusions to these similarities have been made in several publications. In view of recent decipherments, however, some of which are presented in this work, a considerable amount of new knowledge concerning Indian pictography is now available from which world comparisons can be drawn with more confidence.

Chart 6 compares many symbols of Indian pictography with those of the Old World. Only those symbols bound to all cultures by a common usage are included.

Many things have been taken into consideration in preparing this chart and in presenting these comparisons. Most realistic depictions have been omitted for the simple reason that most of mankind is inclined to depict a horse to look like a horse, a cow like a cow, and so on. This is true also in the depiction of some flora and fauna, and other objects of nature.

Symbols for items known only to one culture are, of course, not comparable, and are therefore not included. For example, the Egyptians had symbols for items of Egyptian culture—baker, crown, papyrus, giraffe, helmet, chariot, silver, and many other things that did not exist in the pictography, nor in the spoken language, of American Indian tribes. Likewise, Indian cultures used words not found in Egyptian writing—warbonnet, tomato, tipi, scalp, moose, peace pipe. This greatly limits the number of symbols which can be compared.

Fig. 81.

In the case of Egyptian symbols, for example, Gardiner's symbol list was used—a list which contains a total of approximately 723 symbols. Out of these, a total of 265 were not applicable (not mutual to both cultures), and, of these, 67 are realistic depictions of animals or other naturalistic depictions. This leaves about 391 symbols which can be legitimately compared.

The Sumerian pictographic symbols were taken from Rene Labat's symbol list of these old forms, a total of approximately 267 symbols (minus duplications). Of these, 66 are not mutual to both cultures and are not comparable; 23 are realistic depictions; only 177 are in any way comparable.

It can therefore be seen that both Egyptian and Sumerian systems consist of an unusually high percentage of words peculiar to their civilized cultures. Pictographic values which would be of the most good in these comparisons are in many cases unknown in the Egyptian and Sumerian systems; the records from which this symbol list was compiled consisted of topics in which there was no occasion to use symbols comparable to those common to American Indian pictography. In fact, the writing systems of the Egyptians and Sumerians served completely different purposes than the writing system of the Indians. These civilized systems functioned basically as methods of keeping economic, administrative, magical, religious, legal, mythological and other restricted records, and as such used phrases and symbol combinations rarely found in Indian pictography.

Because of the nature of the subjects recorded, only an elite small percentage of the population understood and used these systems. Writing was the exclusive "secret treasure" or "mystery" of professional scribes. In fact, many a king or pharoah could not read the writing of his own country, and had to rely upon the scribes for interpretations. It is no wonder that Ashurbanipal (668-626 B.C.) greatly boasted of the fact that he was the first king who could read cuneiform (Driver 1944). Indian pictography, on the other hand, was available to all classes of the entire population, and recorded topics of a more general and personal nature closer to the bloodstream of life throughout the world.

Thus we find an impasse in drawing any conclusive comparison of Indian pictography to Egyptian and Sumerian, since too few comparable words are available to sway the balance of doubt. Out of the 391 comparable characters of Egyptian and the 177 of Sumerian, many characters are used in a manner or phrase so peculiar to their advanced cultures and restricted topics that their value in comparisons is greatly diminished. Compounding the problem is the lack of understanding of concepts behind many Egyptian and Sumerian symbols, a knowledge which is basic to the formation of any accurate conclusions.

Old Chinese Vase

Chart 6, even though it is highly condensed and is not complete, does present a substantial number of symbols identical to those of Indian pictography. The similarities involved cannot be ignored. The next question is automatically one of how these similarities came to exist.

Some can be accounted for simply by man's instinct to depict certain ideas in the most suggestive and the plainest manner possible; people from different parts of the world would naturally come up with identical, self-interpreting symbols. But many symbols on this chart cannot be explained away in this manner —*dark* (line 3), *hollow* (4), *heart represented by a vase* (5), *side* (6), *strong* (9), *writing* (11), and many others. This also applies to many of the symbols in the panel from Camonica Valley (figure 80)—*dangerous, fleeing*, lateral action, and *breaking through*—similarities for which the only logical explanation can be that either borrowing from one another occurred at some time during the time when these systems were widely used (somewhat difficult for Indians living on the remote American continent), or that these writing systems had a common origin.

It is a fact that most writing systems, even English, can be traced back to a time when they consisted of many or even entirely of picture-writing symbols. When any of the now known systems are traced back to this stage, we find that many of the characters are identical in meaning and shape to each other as well as to Indian pictography. This evidence definitely suggests, but does not conclusively prove, a common origin of these systems.

But when we reach the point in antiquity when such comparisons can be made, we find ourselves but one step removed from a relative ignorance and darkness in understanding and reading these and other ancient parent forms of pure pictographies that do not contain the use of sounds. Many such undeciphered Old World examples of what appear to be a pure pictography, and hence possibly the one common source of the world's writings, exist in the museums and archeological collections of the world and upon the rocks of various countries. However, in these examples we are again faced with the fact, as in America, that these pictographies cannot be fully understood. Until these oldest records are deciphered, a complete comparison of Old and New World pictographies cannot be made, nor can the theory of a common origin be conclusively proved.

Chinese is another excellent example of a system which is based upon picture-writing symbols. Today these old symbols are still used, but in an abbreviated form more conducive to speed in writing than the older, more recognizable picture forms. Sumerian cunieform likewise evolved from recognizable pictures to forms more readily adapted to their wedge-shaped writing tool.

Sound values have been added to Chinese characters, as they were to Egyptian and Sumerian. So today Chinese is no longer a pure pictography, although the

155

pictographic values of many Chinese symbols are known. Note how similar in meaning and shape Chinese symbols in chart 6 are to symbols of Indian pictography.

Whether Chinese had a common origin with these other systems, as this chart suggests, is still a matter to be proven—but the possibility does exist. Chinese is not nearly as old as either Egyptian or Sumerian. The systematization of Chinese writing is attributed to Huang-Ti, the founder of the Chinese empire in the twenty-fifth century B.C. (Wieger 1965), while Egyptian has been estimated to have taken its characteristic shape about 2900 B.C., and cunieform at about 3500 B.C. The reliability of these dates is not certain. For example, the date of the unification of Egypt under King Menes (when Egyptian script took shape) has been constantly revised, from Champolion's first estimate of 5867 B.C. closer to the present estimate of 2900 B.C. (Ceram 1954).

Scholars have already presented evidence that Egyptian is of Sumerian origin (Wadell 1930). Some have even attempted to prove that Chinese is of the same origin, but have not yet convincingly done this. However, proving that Old World writings originated with Sumerian picture writing is not the last step in such studies. Sumerian picture writing itself must still be studied in conjunction with older and still undeciphered picture-writing examples upon the rocks to determine whether all have a relationship, or are separate and distinct systems.

Regarding the question of the possible Old World origin of American Indian pictography, it has long been recognized by most scholars that the American Indian did, in fact, come from the Old World; he could well have acquired a picture-writing system in the place of his origin and perpetuated it on this continent. This could not have been a system derived from Egyptian, Sumerian, or Chinese in their stabilized and advanced forms. These were not only limited in symbols but relied basically upon sounds. Indian pictography would have had to stem from an older and purer pictography. The fact that there are many unexplained similarities among these systems may indicate that the older pictography in question was not only the parent of the Indian system but also of Egyptian, Sumerian, and Chinese.

To Call	A Baby (Sucking Finger)	Man (Right Index Held in Front of Body)	To Give
Friendship (Clasped Hands)	Eat	To Raise Up	Foreign (Distant)
Child (Showing the Child's Height)	Tired (Dropping the Arms)	Negation (Pushing Aside)	Aged (Walking with a Staff)

Chart 7.

156

Siberia

If this *is* the case, then Indian pictography is not only the oldest writing system in the world, it has also been in use longer than any other! If we are to predate it to Sumerian pictography, the life span of the Indian writing system would be close to 6000 years. Whether Indian pictography has remained unchanged for this lengthy period is yet a matter of research. It should not seem too remarkable — both Sumerian and Egyptian existed for 3000 years, and furthermore Egyptian underwent only a "slight modification of form" in all these years (Budge 1966).

If it is eventually proven that Indian pictography underwent little change from the day of its inception until the day of its death, it would most likely be due to its refusal to adopt sounds into its structure. It may also be due to the lack of change in the simple Indian cultures which have remained fairly well hidden and thus immune to the influence of Old World complexities in writing.

If Indian pictography stemmed from the same source as Sumerian, it does not necessarily mean that the ancestors of the American Indian came to this country at that time. Many rock-writing panels throughout the Old World contain symbols whose character and subject (such as iron weapons) can be dated as historic. It is therefore apparent that in the less civilized areas of the world, Old World pictographies persisted into historic times. It is also reasonable to theorize that it existed for some time in more advanced civilizations as the basic means of communication among the general population. It has already been shown that these people were not initiated into the "mysteries" of the more complicated forms.

If Indian pictography is eventually proven to be identical to the original Old World system, then it represents the survival of the actual parent system of almost all writing right up until the beginning of our modern era!

The theory of the common origin of all pictographies is harmonious with the idea that Indian pictography is based upon the sign language. If personal communication among the many Indian tribes, who spoke completely different languages, was accomplished by a universal sign language, then it is feasible that this universal sign language provided the same practical answer to the same language dilemma of the Old World.

Whether Indian and Old World sign languages also had a common origin is not known. That there are indeed similarities between the two systems extending far back into antiquity was recognized long ago by Mallery. He also recognized the fact that some Egyptian heiroglyphics were based upon hand signs; in fact, he delved rather deeply into this relationship.

Chart 7 shows a few of Mallery's comparisons, and some additional Egyptian symbols which were recently found to indicate that they were based upon hand signs. These hand signs are identical, both in manner of execution and meaning, to those of the American Indian, as explained in this chart.

157

Mallery elaborates upon this subject by comparing classical Greek and Italian signs to identical signs of the American Indians. He also conducted an interesting study comparing the Indian sign language with the Old World sign language of deaf mutes. On March 6, 1880, he personally took seven Utes to the National Deaf Mute College in Washington, D.C., to converse with deaf mutes in their respective sign languages, under test conditions. It was found that the deaf mutes and the Utes understood each other's stories; only a few signs were not comprehended. A detailed description of these tests may be found in Mallery's work upon the subject published in 1881.

In summarizing what we know of the world's rock-writing and writing systems in their pictographic stages, we find it a dark chapter in our enlightened age of knowledge. Why has it been ignored so long? Picture-writing systems of the world have either proven to be the hardest of all for modern men to crack, if we are to compare our accumulated knowledge of them with other deciphered systems, or else modern men have been embarrassed and reticent about prying into the educational capabilities of men they have previously termed primitive and have thus exploited.

The efficiency and speed of Indian pictography cannot of course be compared to modern alphabets (which indeed still have much room for improvement), but they nevertheless fulfilled the existing needs of the American Indian for a period of uncounted centuries. It enabled him to record his thoughts and to communicate them satisfactorily to his contemporaries. What more was needed? He should be credited for this intellectual achievement.

This long overdue recognition should be all the more forthcoming when we consider the illiteracy of the general population and even of the royalty of Egyptian and Sumerian civilizations. The literacy rate of the American Indian was much higher than these, if gauged by what is known of the reading and writing capabilities of the general public. In fact, during the dark ages of Europe when only the elite could read, the American red man was basically literate! The evidence is on the rocks for all to see — no-trespassing signs, simple histories, land claims, maps, absentee messages, and panels relating the consequences to be inflicted if certain warnings were not heeded.

It could even be argued that the simplicity and thoroughness of the American Indian system (which could easily be committed to memory), when compared to the "ambiguity," "restriction of expression," "complexity," and "excessive multiplication of characters" in the Egyptian and Sumerian writings (to use the words of scholars upon these subjects), would make it in fact the superior system!

But many undeciphered examples of pictography and rock writings exist in the Old World. There could well have been a time in these cultures when the general population understood a simple, universal pictography — one which eventually died out when man's ingenious or selfish and monopolizing spirit led him to introduce sounds and thus complicate writing to the point that it eventually became the exclusive right and mystery of a few individuals for many dark ages often erroneously termed "enlightened."

10.

Conclusions

THE MATERIAL PRESENTED has been carefully selected for this study from thousands of panels. Care has been taken to choose only those panels in which historical, geographic, and/or cultural evidence can be offered to the reader so that he need not rely upon cryptanalytical evidence alone. In so doing, we have omitted many interesting panels which can be read in a method based solely on symbol consistency and other cryptanalytical evidence. Likewise, panels of a more artistic or photogenic nature have been omitted.

The material used here is, however, conclusive and self-proving when applied to other panels, even *without* the aid of geographic, historical and other subordinate evidence. This test of consistency is the ultimate cryptanalytic proof of accurate decipherment. If a symbol can normally be read wherever it occurs, and if it shows coherency and proper affinity to other symbols in the panel, then it can be considered deciphered, even though refinements in meaning and concept might later be made.

Examples of this consistency have been rife throughout this work, and a master consistency table is presented here (chart 8) showing the number of times many of the more common symbols were used with consistent meaning. The table is, of course, based only on the panels presented. If all the readable panels on hand had been included, then the frequency of consistency for these symbols would have been greatly increased. But these additional panels are too numerous to present here for the reader to evaluate to his own satisfaction.

On the other hand, the consistencies in this chart alone are more than sufficient to show that these symbols are similar in concept throughout many areas of the country, and that Indian rock writing is a definite system of communication. It is this very consistency which makes this writing a method of communication; it obviously could not exist unless the parties using these symbols had a mutual understanding of their meanings — the basis for all writing by which men are able

159

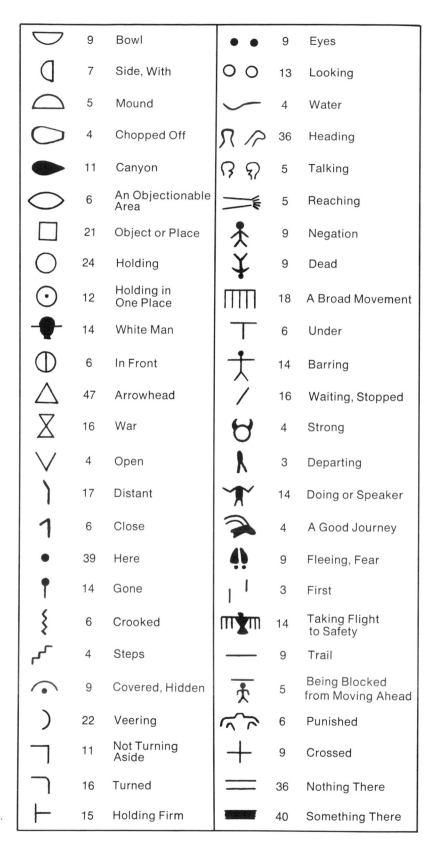

⌣	9	Bowl
⟩	7	Side, With
⌒⌒	5	Mound
⬯	4	Chopped Off
⬤	11	Canyon
⬭	6	An Objectionable Area
▢	21	Object or Place
○	24	Holding
⊙	12	Holding in One Place
⬤	14	White Man
⊘	6	In Front
△	47	Arrowhead
⧖	16	War
∨	4	Open
\	17	Distant
↑	6	Close
•	39	Here
⬤	14	Gone
⌇	6	Crooked
⌐	4	Steps
⌒•	9	Covered, Hidden
)	22	Veering
⌐	11	Not Turning Aside
⌐	16	Turned
⊢	15	Holding Firm

• •	9	Eyes
○ ○	13	Looking
⌣	4	Water
Ω ⌢	36	Heading
⌢ ⌢	5	Talking
⟶	5	Reaching
⚹	9	Negation
⚹	9	Dead
⊓⊓⊓	18	A Broad Movement
⊤	6	Under
⚹	14	Barring
/	16	Waiting, Stopped
⚹	4	Strong
⚹	3	Departing
⚹	14	Doing or Speaker
⚹	4	A Good Journey
⚹	9	Fleeing, Fear
⎸ ⎸	3	First
⚹	14	Taking Flight to Safety
—	9	Trail
⚹	5	Being Blocked from Moving Ahead
⌢	6	Punished
+	9	Crossed
=	36	Nothing There
▬	40	Something There

Chart 8.

160

Wayne Co., Utah

to communicate. Since Indian pictography fulfills this requirement, it must be classed as a writing system!

Indian pictography is also complete in its ability to communicate anything (other than sounds) that an Indian could say in his spoken language. The wide range of topics and expressions attest to this. This pictography is not a mnemonic (memory-aiding) system, although it was often employed as such on calendars and in other records where there was not sufficient space to record each event in full. Indian pictography may therefore be classed as a *complete* pictography and an adequate substitute for the spoken language of the American Indian.

The answers to questions of the degree to which this system was used throughout North America, and how many symbols each tribe understood hinges upon the complete decipherment of all symbols in this country. Any definite conclusions concerning this will have to be delayed until this is accomplished.

There are certain indications in Mallery's and Schoolcraft's works that a few minor differences in the meanings of some symbols do exist (e.g., Schoolcraft's interpretation of war symbols as headless bodies). It is apparent that some of these differences exist because of the personal interpretations put upon the more obscure symbols by these men themselves. Not to be overlooked as a possible reason for these differences is the proclivity of the Indian to mislead or deceive any gullible interrogator. This trait will be vouched for by many modern anthropologists. The application of cryptanalytic principles to many of the symbols contained in the works of these scholars (particularly Schoolcraft's headless bodies) indicates this may have been the case. In spite of these discrepancies, the works of these early scholars remain the foundation and the sounding key to much of our knowledge of Indian pictography today.

Whether there are other differences throughout North America is not yet known. The various methods used in saying the same thing (such as the wavy water line used by the Kiowa versus the cupped-hand water symbol) cannot be readily classified as peculiar to the tribes using them, at least until numerous similar examples are translated from the same tribes. Aside from these minor differences, the accumulated evidence reveals that one basic system of pictography was used by most, if not by all, of the tribes which practiced picture writing to any extent. It does not necessarily mean that every Indian used exactly the same symbol, fixed combination or incorporation, or the same arrangement in constructing any given sentence. Indian pictography is so versatile and so abundant in symbols that one sentence composed in a variety of ways could still be understood.

Caution must be exercised in reaching conclusions pertaining to the development of Indian pictography until the complete system is deciphered. We can say with certainty, however, that many symbols of Indian pictography are based upon the sign language, and it therefore must be the older of the two systems. It seems

161

only logical that ancient man would have a more urgent need to converse directly with his neighbors of a different language than he would have need to write to them, or record important events for his own descendants.

The nature of the sign language is in and of itself universal; it seeks to employ the simplest of signs so that all men of any languages can understand. Since Indian pictography is based upon the sign language to a great extent, it may also be classed as a universal system.

Both Indian sign language and pictography have recently adopted signs and symbols to fit the changing times and to portray items foreign to their ancient culture, such as the trains and horses of pictography, and such other modern innovations as *jail, gas, driver's license, wine,* and many others adapted to the sign language. It is probable that this ability to change and adapt dates back to their origins, and that both the sign language and the pictographic system developed in a gradual, natural manner which fulfilled existing needs as they arose, until both systems reached their total capabilities.

Conclusions as to the place of origin of the sign language and of Indian pictography must be postponed until extensive research into Old World writing can be accomplished. Many similarities exist among American Indian pictography and the rock-writing and writing systems of the Old World. Many of these similarities are probably coincidences resulting from man's natural instinct to use similar signs to denote the same thing. Other symbols, however, differ too much from any natural portrayal to have originated independently of one another, and thus cannot be accounted for in this manner.

Thus we are faced with the intriguing possibility that American Indian pictography had a common origin with some Old World pictographies at some place on the other side of the globe, or that it was at some time highly influenced by them.

If these writing systems *do* have a common origin, then the pictography of the American Indian is not only the *oldest* writing system in the world, it is the one in *longest continuous use,* having been practiced from its inception in the remote past right up to the beginning of our modern era. It may even be proven to be the perpetuated ancestor of our modern writing systems.

The degree to which Indian pictography has remained unchanged down through the ages cannot be determined until such time when all the ancient and more recent examples of rock writing have been deciphered and some comparative dating methods established. Rock patination is our only method for even a relative dating of ancient panels. The age differences of certain panels, determined by the degree of rock patination, definitely indicate considerable stability in form down through countless centuries of use. Figures 35 and 65, and most of the early locators are panels of considerable age. We know this to be true since they are covered with a high degree of patination. In comparing these panels with very recent panels (evidenced by the *lack* of patination), we find symbols identical in both form and meaning.

When the decipherment of Indian pictography is complete, and when all

Algeria

resultant translations can be readily accomplished, a new and highly valuable tool in the study of ancient men will be available, for written upon the rocks lie many of the answers to the riddles that have long puzzled archeologists and students of the American Indian. We can then hope to unravel some of the mysteries surrounding the origins of many Indian tribes, their divisions and long migrations. We can then sift from the traditions and myths that material which is actually based on fact. (An example of this is the verification of the claim of the Hopi Snake Clan that they once lived in Utah. The translation of the panel relating the origin of the Hopi Snake Dance proved this claim to be a valid one.)

The acquisition of this information will take many years of work by many scholars working together in fitting the numerous small pieces of history into some semblance of order and chronology. Even with the little that has already been deciphered of Indian pictography, many of these missing links of history are beginning to fall into place.

A point that cannot be justifiably overlooked in this evaluation is the present lack of knowledge and ability in reading Indian pictography. Aside from cultural conflicts existing, a great factor contributing to the meagerness of knowledge is the lack of appropriate university courses which might prepare a student to undertake such a study. Educational pursuits are so specialized today that it is almost impossible for a graduate to come out of college with the three educational prerequisites to approaching the subject: (1) an understanding of the sign language, (2) a working knowledge of Indian languages and cultures, and (3) a basic understanding of cryptanalysis. None of these requirements can be overlooked in a thorough and scientific study of a pictography.

Cryptanalysis is not generally taught in our colleges and is consistently overlooked in the field of anthropology, even though it played a paramount role in deciphering some of the forgotten writing systems of the past. Also overlooked is the fact that a great deal of pertinent cultural information which can be obtained only from the Indians themselves is yet unrecorded. We have already lost much by this neglect.

All of this means that there are very few who are qualified to pick up the study of Indian pictography where earlier scholars left off. Consequently, no significant work has been done upon the subject in this century, although many books have been published upon the subject. Only one man in this century having one of the three prerequisites — knowledge of the sign language — approached this work on the premise that pictography was based on the sign language. Richard P. Irwin's *Indian Rock Writing in Idaho,* which presented many translations, was published in the *Twelfth Annual Report of the Idaho Historical Society* in 1930. Although this book approaches rock writings from a correct standpoint, the author overlooks

163

the method of cryptanalysis to prove his interpretations and thus fails to show consistency in symbol meaning.

In summarizing our study so far we might appropriately borrow from Mallery (1881) who states, "The result of the studies so far as prosecuted is that what is called *the* sign language of Indians is not, properly speaking, one language, but that it and the gesture systems of deaf mutes and of all peoples constitute together one language—the gesture speech of mankind—of which each system is a dialect."

Perhaps this statement — applied to the pictographies of the world — will suffice, at least for the moment, until more information is obtained in the long years of research that lie ahead in this untended field of fascinating research.

The Rocks Begin to Speak

Part II

1.

The Red Man's
Trampled Pencil

WE KNOW THAT INDIAN PICTOGRAPHY existed right up into the dawn of our modern era. The recent use of symbols identical in meaning to those used thousands of years ago prove that Indian pictography did not perish ages ago as theorized by some. Instead, it breathed its last right under our very noses!

Why did Indian pictography die?

The answer to this question is quite obvious to the student of American history, and we need not delve very deeply into the subject to obtain our answer. Factors in the cause of its death were the constant warfare, distrust, animosity, and neglect that characterized the relationship of Indian and white man from the day of the Pilgrim to the last official Indian war with the Southern Paiutes in 1915.

It is no wonder that there was dissension and bloodshed. Vast differences existed between the cultures and religions of the two races. The taking of Indian lands to satisfy the early colonizers' insatiable quest for land was often rationalized with the excuse that the Indians were uncivilized savages, and therefore had no right to the land.

This attitude was exemplified at a town meeting in Milford, Connecticut, in 1640, where it was "Voted: that the earth is the Lord's and the fullness thereof. Voted: that the earth is given to the saints. Voted: that we are the saints" (Willison 1945). This attitude was hardly conducive to recognizing the merits of a people being conquered; indeed, as an excuse for conquest their merits were often purposely ignored. It has often been a practice of civilized nations to measure the intelligence of another race by whether or not it had a writing system. It thus became convenient to ignore Indian pictography, or to classify it as crude caveman scribbling which only the writer himself could understand.

In the conquest of Mexico it was not so easy to ignore the huge libraries of the Mayan Indians and thus tag their advanced civilization as savage. Zumarraga, Bishop of Mexico, and Landa, Bishop of Yucatan, neatly surmounted this obstacle by building huge bonfires with the Mayan writings — declaring them "works of the devil." Their destruction was so thorough that only a handful of manuscripts survive today.

Warfare and conquest cannot alone take the blame for the recent destruction and abandonment of Indian pictography. The well intentioned and seemingly harmless efforts to civilize and Christianize the Indians were often just as devastating. Some of the most ardent workers dedicated to this project were the early missionaries and priests who were in many cases the first to set foot on unexplored Indian territory. Perhaps no one had a better opportunity than they to witness and record Indian culture and pictography while yet in a stage completely untouched by the smothering hand of progress. But the primary purpose of these missionaries was to *civilize* and *convert* the Indians, not to study and observe them, and as a result the recording of then-flourishing cultures was often neglected.

Glimmers of valuable information pertaining to Indian picture writing may, however, be obtained from some of the notes of these Christian adventurers. For

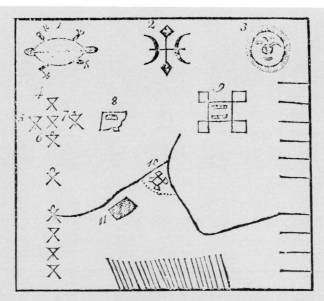

XXII. *Observations on the* Indian *method of Picture-Writing by* William Bray, *Esq. In a Letter to the Secretary.*

Read March 1, 1781.

SIR,

IN a memoir lately communicated to the Society by governor Pownall on the origin and nature of picture and elementary writing he observes that he has heard of painting on trees by the Indians in North America, but that he never saw any of them.

From "Observations on the Indian Method of Picture Writing by William Bray, Esq.," 1781

Missouri

example, one early missionary in the Rocky Mountains — Father Nicholas Point — did not ignore the practical value of using Indian "hieroglyphic forms" to teach the Indians "what is necessary to believe to be saved" (Donnelly 1967). This recorded note speaks loudly for the completeness of Indian pictography and hence is of value to us today.

By the time the geographic confines of civilization reached the habitat of many Indian tribes, they were often well on their way down the white man's road. This work of civilizing the Indian was greatly augmented by the attraction of many mechanical oddities and the never-ending pressures upon the Indians to abandon their cultures.

Soon the Indian was wearing the white man's clothes, riding in his wagon, living in his house, speaking and writing his language, drinking his whiskey, and depending upon him for a livelihood. There was no longer any need for the "old ways." This of course included pictography. The sign language suffered the same lingering death in certain parts of the country. With the advent of the English language in the East, Spanish in the Southwest, and the Chinook jargon in the Northwest, a practical need for the sign language no longer existed, and the first tribes to learn these new languages were the first to abandon it. Having once served as a means of communication among the numerous tribes of America who spoke completely different languages, it remains in use today only among the Plains tribes, Utes, and a few others whose elderly people never quite mastered English.

It was only during the final gasping breaths of the Indian way of life, perishing before the steady western onslaught of civilization, that a handful of men came upon the scene to salvage what they could. Were it not for their efforts we would know nothing of Indian pictography in the light of what the practitioners remaining at that time could tell. Their task was not an easy one. The distrust which had grown between white man and Indian was sometimes insurmountable. Many an Indian would rather take to the grave the things he held sacred than to reveal them to the white man. He succeeded to a great extent in doing just that. To those he knew he could not trust or those he felt were out to exploit him, the Indian would often play defensively dumb or make up stories rather than tell what he knew. This is a practice persisting among the Indians to this day, frustrating scholars and impeding their research.

But there were a few men who won the confidence and trust of the Indian in one manner or another, and it is due to their efforts in researching and writing that the world was not left in total ignorance of the literary efforts of the American Indian.

One of the earliest accounts pertaining to Indian pictography was published under the title, "Observations on the Indian Method of Picture Writing by William Bray, Esq., in a Letter to the Secretary Read March 1, 1781." In this letter William

169

THE number of scalps or prisoners taken in each expedition are set opposite to it, viz. The first time he went to war he was unsuccessful, taking none; the second time he took one man's scalp; the third time he took a woman's scalp, a man's scalp, and a woman prisoner.

THE figure under the turtle, N° 8. is intended for a fort which he was at the taking of; he believes it was one of the small forts on lake Erie which was surprised by the Indians about 1762.

THE fort N° 9. is intended for Fort Detroit, which was besieged by the Indians in 1762 under the command of the famous Pontiack, but bravely defended by major Gladwin. The other, N° 10. is Fort Pitt, with the town, N° 11. and the Moningalialy and Alligany rivers; which was besieged by the Indians about the same time.

THE space between the sixth and seventh horizontal strokes, shews that he did not go to war for some time.

THE twenty-three strokes at bottom shew the number of warriors he had with him at the time he made the war-marks; their inclining to the left, with their backs to the sun, shews that they were going to the northward.

HE says that the marks they make on their return are generally done with vermillion, which is a peaceable color, and shews that their anger is no more. At those times they put the scalps and prisoners in the rear of their men, in this manner $\backslash\backslash\backslash\backslash\ \bar{x}\ \bar{\tilde{x}}$, and if they had been out two moons and an half they would put two round black or red spots on the right of the prisoners, and a semicircular one for half a moon. Their loss they would express by making horizontal strokes between the prisoners and the moons in this manner $\backslash\ \backslash\backslash\backslash\ \bar{x}\ \bar{\tilde{x}}\ \equiv\ \Theta\Theta\complement$

THE Delawares are divided into three tribes, the turtle, the wolf and the eagle tribes. Each makes use of their respective

VOL. VI.   Y   badge,

From "Observations on the Indian Method of Picture Writing by William Bray, Esq.," 1781

Walum Olum

Bray explains the meaning of the symbols used in a war account of a Delaware Indian painted upon a peeled section of a tree. The original interpretation was given by Captain White Eyes, a Delaware chief. In this brief letter he explains that every Indian nation practiced the art of recording by writing their war achievements, but differed somewhat in methods used.

The meaning of more Indian symbols came to light in Tanner's narrative first published in 1830. John Tanner was captured by the Indians at the age of nine, and spent thirty years of his life as a captive among them. In his narrative he relates the events of his life among the Indians, and includes symbols and translations of several medicine, war, hunting, and love songs.

Another, and perhaps the most valuable, translation of Indian symbols appeared in 1836 in a document known as the *Walum Olum* or "Red Score" of the Delaware Indians. This was a painted record or tally (hence the name "Red Score") of the most notable events in the history of the Delaware people from the time the world was created until the arrival of the white man upon the eastern shores of this continent.

This record consists of 184 units of many combined symbols painted upon sticks (figure 82). A translating song accompanied each set of symbols. These included the creation of the earth, the flood (known to almost all native races), their long migration to this land, tribal divisions, battles, and the names of many of their chieftains. Its last entry ends with the arrival of the white man: "They are peaceful; they have great things; who are they?" (Brinton 1885).

A similar practice of recounting ancient events or myths through a succession of short songs also exists among the Cahuilla, Mojave, and Southern Paiute. They are still sung at their funerals — the reason these stories are alive today.

The preservation of the *Walum Olum* and its first published account is due to the efforts of Constantine Samuel Rafinesque. At one time he was professor of historical and natural sciences in Transylvania University in Kentucky. His other interests and studies included botany and zoology. He began writing at the age of nineteen, and wrote fluently in English, French, Latin, and Italian.

The painted records of the *Walum Olum* were actually acquired from the Indians in Kentucky in 1822 as a reward for a medical cure accomplished by Dr. Ward, a friend of Rafinesque's. Rafinesque acquired this information from Dr. Ward but could not translate the Delaware songs. He therefore studied Delaware, with the help of the grammars of the missionaries Zeisberger and Heckewelder, and published his subsequent translation in 1836 (Brinton 1885). Since Rafinesque's translation, other authoritative works and revised translations of the Delaware songs have appeared. All of these critical studies stamp the *Walum Olum* an authentic native record.

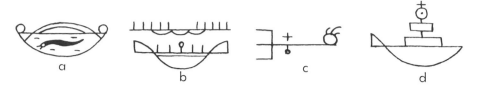

Fig. 82. Sample units from the *Walum Olum:* (a) flood created by a serpent, (b) ten thousand crossing a frozen sea at night, (c) moving east because of a drought, and (d) arrival of the white man off the East Coast.

In these lines Rafinesque makes an important statement, which has been amply verified by the investigations of Col. Garrick Mallery, Dr. W. J. Hoffman and Capt. W. P. Clark, within the last decade, and that is, that the Indian pictographic system was based on their gesture speech.

So far as I remember, he was the first to perceive this suggestive fact ; and he had announced it some time before 1840. Already, in "The American Nations" (1836), he wrote, "the Graphic Signs correspond to these Manual Signs." [1]

Here he anticipates a leading result of the latest archæological research ; and I give his words the greater prominence, because they seem to have been overlooked by all the recent writers on Indian Gesture-speech and Sign-language.

The *Neobagun,* the Chipeway medicine song to which he alludes, is likewise spoken of in "The American Nations," where he says : "The Ninniwas or Chipiwas * * have such painted tales or annals, called Neobagun (male tool) by the former." [2] I suspect he derived his knowledge of this from the Shawnee "Song for Medicine Hunting," called " Nah-o-bah-e-gun-num," or, The Four Sticks, the words and figures of which were appended by Dr. James to Tanner's *Narrative,* published in 1830. [3]

tem," by which all interested could soon become large capitalists. He published a book on it (of course), which might be worth the attention of a financial economist. The solid men of Philadelphia, however, like its scholars, turned a deaf ear to the words of the eccentric foreigner.

[1] *The American Nations,* etc., p. 78.

[2] Ibid, p. 123.

[3] Tanner's *Narrative,* p. 359.

From *The Lenape and Their Legends,* by Daniel G. Brinton, M.D., 1885

Washington Co., Utah

One of these studies was made by Daniel G. Brinton, M.D., and appeared in his 1885 publication, *The Lenape and Their Legends*. The Indiana Historical Society conducted a more recent study with the help of professional scholars, and published its findings in 1954 under the title, *Walum Olum*.

Brinton credits Rafinesque with having been the first to recognize that Indian pictography was based upon the sign language. In this regard Brinton quotes Rafinesque: "Of those I have now, 60 used by the Southern or Floridian tribes of Louisiana to Florida, based upon their language of signs—40 used by the Osages and Arkansas, based on the same—74 used by the Lenapian (Delaware and Akin) tribes in their Wallamolum or Records—besides 30 simple signs that can be traced out of the Neobagun or delineation of the Chipewas or Ninniwas, a branch of the last."

Brinton (1885) comments on this: "In these lines Rafinesque makes an important statement, which has been amply verified by the investigation of Col. Garrick Mallery, Dr. W. J. Hoffman and Capt. W. P. Clark, within the last decade, and that is, that the Indian pictographic system was based on their gesture speech."

Following Rafinesque's work came the writings of George Copway, a Chippewa chief who gave the meanings of some Ojibwa symbols in his 1850 publication. This was followed in 1851-57 by the works of Henry R. Schoolcraft, who was married to an Ojibwa woman and was thus in an excellent position to gain information. His well known work was collected and prepared under the direction of the Bureau of Indian Affairs.

Schoolcraft's chief interest was in the symbols of the medas or priests of the Ojibwa tribe, the meanings of which were known only to the priests themselves and not to the rest of the members of the tribe. He says that the Ojibwa called these symbols of the priest "Kekeenowin." These were used in ceremonies, hunting and war songs; and Indian initiates " . . . always pay high to the native professors for this knowledge."

Schoolcraft's numerous symbols obtained from the meda priest are therefore not always applicable for comparison with the more general type of picture writing covered in this work. He does, however, give many symbols used by the body of the Ojibwa tribe and also some from neighboring tribes. He states that the Ojibwa call the type of picture writing generally understood by everyone by the name *Kekeewin*. It was used to leave information by hunting and traveling parties, on grave boards, and on *rock writings*.

birch-bark, is deposited in the miscellaneous cabinet of the New York Historical Society.

It is remarkable that the system of pictography of the North American Indians becomes universal to the cognate tribes, at the moment that its symbols are committed to record. Bark, skin, tabular pieces of wood, or smooth faces, or angles of standing rock, or boulders, may constitute the material chosen for inscription. This is a matter of pure caprice, choice, or convenience. Its interpretation is not a question of distinctive symbol language. The system is one of recording — not words, but concrete ideas, and this is done by the power of association. The picture of a bear recalls the ideas, not simply of a particular kind of quadruped, but of a strong, black, clumsy, cunning animal, with powerful claws, whose flesh is deeply coated with a tender kind of white fat; whose skin is suitable for particular purposes. These are but parts of the ideas recalled by the symbol. The animal is fond of sweet fruits and berries, loves certain precincts, and is to be hunted in a certain way. To capture him, and to foil his natural sagacity, is a prime achievement.

To ensure success in this, the Indian seeks necromantic knowledge. He draws the figure of the animal, depicting its heart, with a line leading to it from the mouth. See Figs. 4, 8, 13, 37, 47, Plate 57. By uttering a certain incantation of charmed words, he conceives himself to get a necromantic power over this heart. He believes he can control its motions and desires. He believes this firmly. He raises his song in confidence. Already he sees his victim in his power. He draws him from his lair. He leads him into his own path in the forest. He exults in an imaginary triumph.

With such views this scroll is inscribed. It is a Sioux, (Dacota.) It resembles in some respects Plate 54, 1st Part. The chief figure, No. 1, is a man named Catfish. He is represented as completely armed. He begins to recite his arts and exploits. The leading ideas of the song, dismissing charms, and some verbiage, may be concentrated thus:

      1. Hear my power (alluding to voice, or drum.)
      2. My swiftness and vengeance are the eagle's.

From Schoolcraft, 1853, Vol. 1

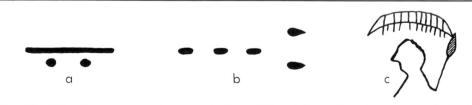

Fig. 83. Mallery's examples demonstrate the ability of the Indian to express abstract ideas in picture writing: (a) fear—eyes hiding beneath a base line, (b) comes in sight—footprints leading up to a pair of eyes, and (c) froze to death—a frozen pond upside down over a man with an arrow in his back.

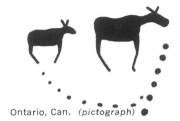

Ontario, Can. *(pictograph)*

In his study of this picture writing, Schoolcraft makes the following pertinent observation: "It is remarkable that the system of pictography of the North American Indian becomes universal to the cognate tribes, at the moment that its symbols are committed to record" (Schoolcraft 1853, Vol. 2, p. 227). He further states in referring to the Ojibwa picture writing, ". . . this system of picture writing was as familiar to the Dakota as we had found it among the Algonquin race" (Schoolcraft 1853, Vol. 1, p. 338). The Dakota and Algonquin languages are not related.

To Colonel Garrick Mallery goes the honor of having done the most extensive and authoritative work in the field of Indian pictography. His copious works are to be found in the *First, Fourth,* and the *Tenth Annual Report of the Bureau of American Ethnology.* He was also a fervent student of the sign language, and makes many comparisons between it and Indian pictography, showing them to be related.

He also delves into the matter of minor differences in the sign language throughout the tribes of North America, including Alaska, and says (1881): ". . . at the time of the discovery of North America all its inhabitants practiced sign language, though with different degrees of expertness . . ."

Mallery also explores the peculiarities of Indian pictography and gives many translations of writings obtained from several Indian tribes. He presents evidence that refutes many of the false theories prevalent in his day, one of which was that the Indian could not represent abstract ideas in picture form. He clearly demonstrates that they could (figure 83).

His works also include a study of the rock writings of America and of the world, and his comments are very pertinent to our present study. He assigns meanings to them similar in character to Indian pictography on other material such as trees, hides, and barks, and makes no distinction between writing applied to rocks and that applied to other materials.

Some of the topics Mallery assigns to rock writings are battle accounts, famine, abundance, sign posts to show the direction of springs, the line of established trails, or the paths that would shorten distance in travel, rites, ceremonies, and other topics.

Mallery further makes this important statement concerning rock writings (1893, emphasis added): "With certain exceptions they were intended to be understood by *all observers* either as rude objective representation or as ideograms. . . ."

The Reverend John Heckewelder, a fervent missionary to the Delaware and a man who understood their ways and language well, makes a similar observation (1819): ". . . yet they have certain hieroglyphics, by which they describe facts in so plain a manner, that those who are conversant with those marks can understand them with the greatest ease, as easily, indeed, as we can understand a piece of

The studies thus far pursued lead to the conclusion that at the time of the discovery of North America all its inhabitants practiced sign language, though with different degrees of expertness, and that while under changed circumstances it was disused by some, others, in especial those who after the acquisition of horses became nomads of the Great Plains, retained and cultivated it to the high development now attained, from which it will surely and speedily decay.

MISTAKEN DENIAL THAT SIGN LANGUAGE EXISTS.

The most useful suggestion to persons interested in the collection of signs is that they shall not too readily abandon the attempt to discover recollections of them even among tribes long exposed to European influence and officially segregated from others. The instances where their existence, at first denied, has been ascertained are important with reference to the theories advanced.

Rev. J. Owen Dorsey has furnished a considerable vocabulary of signs finally procured from the Poncas, although, after residing among them for years, with thorough familiarity with their language, and after special and intelligent exertion to obtain some of their disused gesture language, he had before reported it to be entirely forgotten. A similar report was made by two missionaries among the Ojibwas, though other trustworthy authorities have furnished a copious list of signs obtained from that tribe. This is no imputation against the missionaries, as in October, 1880, five intelligent Ojibwas from Petoskey, Mich., told the writer that they had never heard of gesture language. An interesting letter from Mr. B. O. Williams, sr., of Owasso, Mich., explains the gradual decadence of signs used by the Ojibwas in his recollection, embracing sixty years, as chiefly arising from general acquaintance with the English language. Further discouragement came from an Indian agent giving the decided statement, after four years of intercourse with the Pai-Utes, that no such thing as a communication by signs was known or even remembered by them, which, however, was less difficult to bear because on the day of the receipt of that well-intentioned missive some officers of the Bureau of Ethnology were actually talking in signs with a delegation of that very tribe of Indians then in Washington, from one of whom, Nátci, a narrative printed in this paper (page 500), was received.

The report from missionaries, army officers, and travelers in Alaska was unanimous against the existence of a sign language there until Mr. Ivan Petroff, whose explorations had been more extensive, gave the excellent exposition and dialogue now produced (see page 492). Collections were also obtained from the Apaches and Zuñi, Pimas, Papagos,

From "Sign Language Among the North American Indians," by Mallery, 1881

Lincoln Co., Nev.

writing. . . . all Indian nations can do this, although they have not all the same marks; yet I have seen the Delawares read with ease the drawings of the Chippeways, Mingoes, Shawanos, and Wyandots, on similar subjects."

In addition to this, Edwin T. Denig, in the *Forty-Sixth Annual Report of the Bureau of American Ethnology* (1930), comments on the picture writings and maps of some of the tribes of the upper Missouri. He states that while warriors are off on the warpath, the main camp will move and, due to rain or snow, their trail may become obliterated. In such instances the Indians ". . . leave intelligence in pictorial devices in some of their encampments as guides to the returning absentees . . . . There is, however, this danger in these records, that if they are stumbled upon by their enemies in their war excursions they are as certain a guide to them as to their own people, and this is one of the reasons why it is seldom done. . . . All warriors read and understand the devices of their enemies. . . ."

Nelson Lee, a Texas Ranger and former Comanche captive, states (1859): ". . . they have certain hieroglyphics by which they contrive to communicate intelligence with as much accuracy as if they understood the epistolary art."

Another former Comanche captive says: "The Comanche didn't go in for signs much, just as signs. They usually tried to paint the things they were thinking about in full" (Shuffler 1934).

The writing ability of the American Indian is further substantiated by a statement made by the Abbe' J. A. Maurault (1866), concerning the Tetes-de-Boule (a band of the Ojibwa): "We often saw during our instructions or explanations of the catechism that the Indians traced on pieces of bark, or other objects very singular hieroglyphs. These Indians afterward passed the larger part of the following night in studying what they had so written, and in teaching it to their children or their brothers. The rapidity with which they by this manner learnt their prayers was very astonishing."

In studying the observations and statements of these early observers gleaned from dusty history books, we conclude that they were unanimous in thinking that Indian pictography served the purpose of conveying information, and several present evidence that the general Indian population was able to read these messages without the aid of the authors. This included tribes who could not speak the language of the person leaving the message.

Those scholars acquainted with the sign language are unanimous in stating that Indian pictography was based upon the hand signs of the sign language, which Mallery (1881) claims was once practiced universally throughout America.

And finally, two of the foremost scholars conclude that rock writings consisted of the same symbols and pictography used upon materials such as bark, trees and hides.

The conclusions which may be drawn from these findings are identical to those established by cryptanalysis. If Indian pictography was based upon the sign language, which was mutually understood by all tribes, then pictography would have been equally intelligible to them all. In other words, Indian pictography was understood by most if not all tribes, but with perhaps the same minor differences from area to area as those found in the sign language.

Another important collection of information obtained from the works of these early scholars concerns the broad range of topics in which the Indians could communicate: war, medicine, hunting and love songs, traditions, myths, histories, migrations, biographies, maps, battles, declarations of war, treaties, expeditions, hunting, religious ceremonies, tribal rosters, census lists, calendar histories, accounting, grave-post records, dreams, departure and directional notices, absentee messages, appeals to the United States Government, and tribal, clan and personal names. This wide range of topics can stand alone in behalf of the Indian's ability to express almost anything he desired to express.

Although these scholars left us with many valuable observations, the total of all known symbols collected by them does not amount to very much. The majority of the pictographic examples were personal and tribal names, highly abbreviated memory aids to songs, and calendar histories. Those examples which might have aided greatly in our study are sadly lacking, and we are left with only a smattering of what is needed to effectively read the bulk of Indian pictographic symbols.

Indian pictography may not have suffered its sad fate if the meeting ground of white man and Indian had not been so bloody and the differences in their cultures had not been so broad. Instead, the paintbrushes and stone chisels of the Indian pictographers have been trampled into the dust, along with much of the pride of the red man himself.

2.

Cryptanalysis— The Forgotten Tool

THE DECIPHERING OF INDIAN ROCK WRITING is an ideal problem for the science of cryptanalysis. And it is the *only* appropriate science with which to decipher them. The basic requirement for such a study is an abundance of raw material, and America's supply of rock writings, with its hundreds of thousands of panels scattered throughout the country, amply fills the need.

Before any unknown communication system can be deciphered, however, it must have consistency in the meaning of its symbols, characters, or letters, and in its structure. **If it is consistent it can be deciphered, no matter how crude the system may be.** This principle of consistency is the foundation of all languages. Without it, no language could be understood! Without it, cryptanalysis would not exist!

The science of cryptanalysis, supplemented with considerable experience on the part of the researcher (for the pencil is no more accurate than the man who wields it), is the tool with which consistency can be established and an unknown communication system eventually deciphered. Since cryptanalysis works hand in hand with the consistent and established features of communications, its methods are therefore "those of the physical sciences" (Kahn 1967).

If Indian rock writings were meant to convey any information at all which might have been read and understood by other Indians of the same time and area, the symbols would have had to contain a distinguishable consistency. The science of cryptanalysis, after being applied to these writings, has ferreted out these consistencies, thus establishing it as a system of communication!

Most writing systems were not intended to baffle the reader. This of course is not true of codes and ciphers purposely designed to disguise consistency in order to elude or delay deciphering. Consistency, although disguised, cannot be completely abandoned; that is why some of the most ingenious codes and ciphers created have eventually been cracked. It is only by constantly changing codes and ciphers, thereby not giving one's opponent enough time or material to work with, that such systems are still used with effectiveness today.

Fundamental tools in deciphering some of the more simple ciphers are frequency lists, based upon the principle that, in any writing system, some sounds or letters occur more frequently than others. For example, the letter occuring most frequently in the English language is *E*. The next eight letters, in the order of frequency, are *T*, *A*, *O*, *N*, *R*, *I*, *S*, and *H*. Therefore; in any cipher wherein symbols or letters are substituted for those of the English alphabet, it would follow that the most frequently occurring unknown symbol or letter would equal the value of *E*. Going on down the line, one may match the frequency of unknown letters with known frequencies until many are determined. Words are soon recognized, and a message is read. (This is of course an over-simplification. There are numerous other type of frequencies and many other cryptanalytic principles which enter into the problem.)

Frequency lists are based upon the consistent spelling rules necessary in modern language. They cannot be applied to Indian pictography since it contains no sounds and therefore has no alphabet or spelling. However, frequency lists for a pictography can be established based upon the most frequently used symbols in the system itself. Any pictography efficient enough to be understood by other Indians would automatically follow the spoken pattern of some words or phrases occurring more frequently than others. This is true, also, of the sign language, wherein many signs occur much more frequently than others, depending upon the topic.

In deciphering Indian rock writing through controlled experimentation this symbol frequency can be very helpful in associating the most frequent symbols with the most frequent words. However, to do this one must have a definite understanding of more than one Indian language, since Indian expression varies from tribe to tribe. One would not expect to find common Hopi words—*kiva, prayer stick, clan, kachina*—used by a nomadic tribe whose culture would have no use for these words. Moreover, many tribes do not distinguish, in words, the difference between blue and green, or orange and red. Some tribes also express the ideas for *wants* and *needs* with the word for *likes*.

Similarly, some Indian words bear no relationship to English expressions. For example, one does not find the exact English equivalents for *faith* and *hope* in many Indian languages. These concepts are often expressed by Indian words for *believe, holding on to, know,* which to an Indian express similar concepts.

Word-frequency lists taking all these and many other things into consideration can thus be very helpful in deciphering Indian pictography; conversely, if such points are not taken into consideration, they can be disastrous. Frequency lists are designed basically to reduce the amount of guesswork necessary in deciphering unknown symbols. But—since frequency lists will not include all symbols, especially those symbols having neither a high nor a low frequency rate — they have a very limited use in pictography.

The burden of the task of deciphering falls, then, upon other principles of cryptanalysis—topic elimination, grammatical elimination, controlled experimentation, affinity checks and tests, deduction and induction. Most of these tests are

Phoenix, Ariz.

designed to reduce the amount of guesswork necessary, and then to test the accuracy of any remaining guesses through consistency tests. A consistency test, however, cannot be made without a few educated guesses to work with, arrived at with the help of imagination, intuition, symbol suggestiveness, research and other sources, after all possible elimination has been accomplished. All such guesswork must be checked thoroughly for consistency; otherwise it becomes no more than one man's opinion. Many sincere attempts at translation have failed because the translator failed to apply tests of consistency to guesswork. The author of an unknown writing system does not need to be on hand in order to establish a conclusive and accurate translation. **All communication systems, due to their built-in consistency, are self proving.**

The odds against a person's accurately guessing the meaning of just one symbol without the aid of any cryptanalytic or other help is several thousand to one. Without clues, one has the complete language to choose from—quite a task! But if he can eliminate all but a few of these words for each symbol, he is well on his way to a successful translation.

In order to reduce the boundaries of this almost infinite field of guesswork, one must first establish a tentative topic, automatically eliminating words foreign to that topic. For example, battle accounts, migrations, and religious ceremonies all have words peculiar to each. One would not commonly find rain-making ceremonies described in a battle account. (All topics, however, do contain words common to all, the incidence of which is in itself a useful tool.) Therefore, the key to isolating the topic of a panel is to first know the meaning of at least one or two symbols it contains which are not common to all topics. Thus the topic of the panel must bear a relationship to such known symbols.

The content of phrases and sentences may also be determined, further reducing the guesswork necessary. For example, it is common to find such words as *high*, *rugged*, and *snowy* occurring together with the word *mountain*. There is a definite relationship or affinity here; or, grammatically speaking, these words are appropriate adjectives used to describe the noun *mountain*. Conversely, the word *mountain* is seldom, if ever, found used next to words such as *later, ready, today,* and *now*. Such words have no kinship, or affinity, and their use would be grammatically unsound. This knowledge aids in simplifying the processes of translation.

In some examples wherein only two symbols are being studied, each of which is equivalent to only one word, deciphering is aided by simple grammatical elimination. However, in the more common cases wherein one symbol is equivalent in meaning to several words in English or a short phrase, it then becomes only a matter of completing that phrase. There are not many words or phrases in a language which can be properly used with the meaning of one known symbol. This type of cryptanalytic principle or affinity elimination process is thus very valuable

Chart 9.

182

Lincoln Co., Nev.

in enormously reducing the guesswork necessary. The value and necessity of having a few known symbols with which to work becomes obvious.

An example of how elimination by affinity can serve in an almost wholesale elimination process is found in chart 9. This multiple-use chart is only a condensed version of the numerous, lengthy charts, tediously compiled from each cultural locality, actually used in cracking Indian pictographic symbols. Column *A* represents basic symbols which cannot be broken down further without changing their meaning. Each of these symbols represents an assigned phrase, word, or idea suggested by its shape. The symbols in column *B* represent a few of the numerous variations, combinations, incorporations, and attitudes in which the symbols in column *A* have been found upon the rocks — each contains its respective base symbol in column *A* as part of its makeup. This chart therefore categorizes and distinguishes combinations, incorporations, and basic symbols.

For example, the symbol in line 3 in column *A* indicates *veering* or *curved*. It must retain this meaning in all its variations, combinations, and incorporations in column *B,* while at the same time soundly formulating in these embodiments additional linguistic meaning. A considerable amount of guesswork is thus eliminated, since not many meanings exist which can appropriately combine with this one known symbol.

Symbols must also retain their basic meanings throughout all the various attitudes presented in column *B*. By virtue of these attitudes and variations these symbols suggest their own meanings. For example, in line 5, symbol *a* is known to mean *close* or *near*. Thus symbol *b*, pointing downward, suggests *close down*; symbol *c,* pointing upward, suggests *close up, or a short way up;* symbol *d* suggests *bunched,* or *close together.* If these suggested meanings are indeed correct, then these translations must prove applicable and correct at all times in conjunction with other symbols in actually reading panels.

This chart, in addition to its use as an elimination process, serves equally well as an effective consistency test, once a few symbols are known. For instance, the two symbols *curved* and *near* must be consistent in each of their embodiments in column *B* — if they have been correctly deciphered, if there are no symbols wrongly placed in this chart, and if no tribal variations in meaning exist. Such symbols, because they do not meet the criteria of consistency, are thus identified and eliminated.

Another method of using this chart as a consistency test in checking the validity of guesswork is illustrated as follows: Lines 6 through 10 show five basic symbols, all of which have identical appendages attached to them in column *B*. Whenever any guess is applied to the meaning of any of these appendages, it must retain that meaning in use with all of the other basic symbols in order to prove its accuracy. This of course ultimately requires a knowledge of the meanings of all the basic

183

Chart 10.

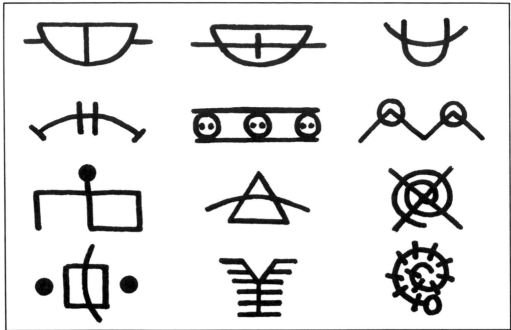

symbols. However, by initially knowing the meaning of only one or two of these basic symbols, a certain degree of accuracy can be assigned to appended symbols that pass this test. If any guesswork fails to stand up, then it must be reevaluated. The efficiency of this test increases with the increase in numbers of known symbols.

The symbols presented in chart 9 present an excellent example of how cryptanalysis works. Space does not permit the chart to be shown in its entirety; nevertheless, it gives a relative demonstration that linguistic principles exist in Indian pictography. Charts of this type compiled early in this study were necessarily crude and often contained misplaced symbols, but their makeup improved with experience and increased knowledge of symbol meanings.

The existence of linguistic principles in Indian pictography is enhanced by the hypothetical symbols presented in chart 10. These imaginary artistic combinations and incorporations of many of the basic symbols from chart 9 do not exist; such arrangements lack grammatical soundness and affinity. It demonstrates that Indian pictography has a noticeably limited number of symbols and methods in its makeup with which communication can be accomplished. This is true of all writing systems, but is more pronounced in some than in others. For example, in English two *x's* (*xx*) or two *q's* (*qq*) are never found together in the correct spelling of written words. Words consisting entirely of several consonants or vowels are also normally lacking. Chart 10 demonstrates a similar principle as it exists in Indian pictography. The possibilities in creating such hypothetical artistic combinations as those in this chart are unlimited. However, it may even be possible that some of these combinations actually do exist! After all, much is still to be learned about Indian pictography, and there are countless panels yet to be studied.

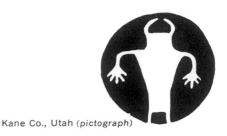

Kane Co., Utah (pictograph)

If linguistic limitations did not exist, then this system might realistically be classed as art, doodling, or magic—not limited by such restrictions. Such limitations are, however, necessary in any pictography, and the limits to which each basic symbol can be used is indicative of how extensive and effective a pictography is. From the many charts compiled, it must be concluded that Indian pictography is equal in communicative ability to Indian languages.

Limitations, affinities, and other linguistic principles are fairly consistent over much of the country, thus ruling out the theory that rock writing contains only individual or local meaning. If each cultural or tribal area contained a different method of pictography, then the foregoing tests should show a noticeable variation from area to area in the affinities and limitations shown. No pronounced variations, however, have been encountered so far in this study.

This brief review of some cryptanalytic principles reveals their value and indispensibility in deciphering Indian pictography. The fact that these principles are especially well suited to this type of study demonstrates the versatility of the science of cryptanalysis.

Appropriate cryptanalytic principles are not readily found in textbook form. Because of this, and because of the fact that almost nothing is known of some forgotten writing systems, it often takes a considerable amount of time to establish workable cryptanalytic devices. This difficulty in establishing suitable methods causes the deciphering of unknown writing systems to take much longer than the cracking of codes and ciphers.

In the deciphering of the unknown writing systems of the world—Egyptian, cuneiform, Linear B, Hittite, and parts of Mayan—this science has played the basic role. The men involved were not always trained cryptanalysts, but they nevertheless had a deep insight into its principles and thus eastablished precedents to be used in this type of deciphering. Most of these men were non-professionals in the field of anthropology. They often came with titles quite unrelated—teacher, army officer, architect, engineer. But most were also avid students of history, fluent in other languages, and possessed with a *positive* attitude that the unknown writing system they were studying could be deciphered. Without this approach, many of these systems and their forgotten histories would still be unknown. The idea that an unknown writing system cannot be deciphered without the aid of the authors is old-fashioned and is based upon a complete ignorance of the science of cryptanalysis.

Chart 11.

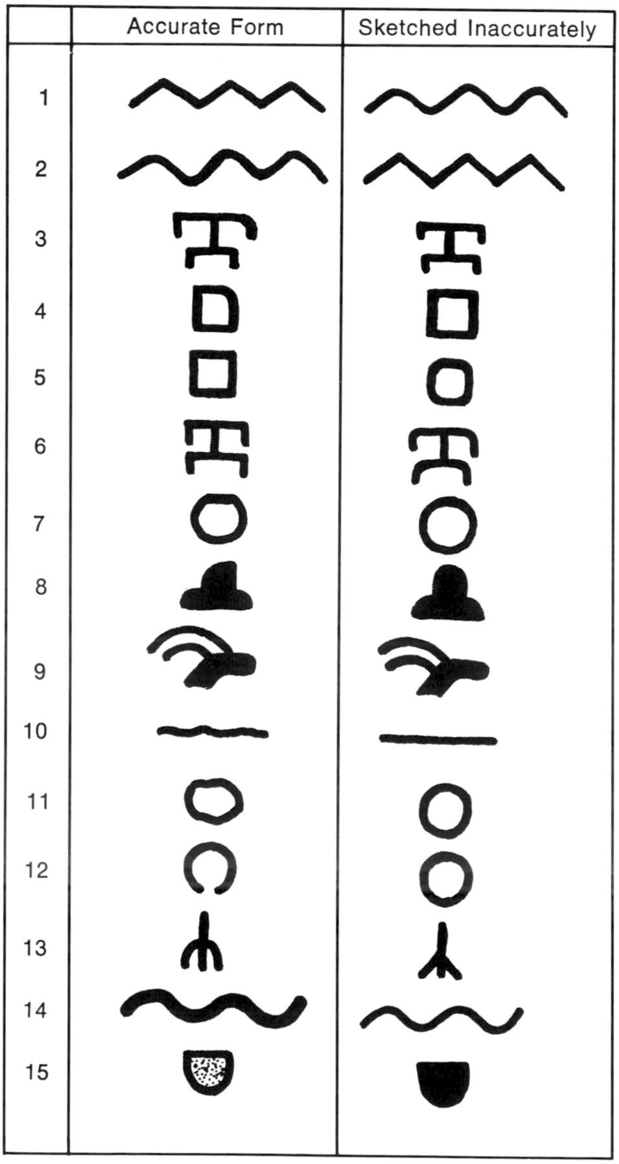

	Accurate Form	Sketched Inaccurately
1		
2		
3		
4		
5		
6		
7		
8		
9		
10		
11		
12		
13		
14		
15		

3.

Recording Technicalities

It is not a simple task to convince an artist that his sketches of Indian rock writings are inaccurate! It is often just as difficult to impress him with the importance of accuracy, especially when he considers it "rock art" and not a writing system. However, in the deciphering and reading of rock writing, everything depends upon proper and accurate recording methods. This lesson was not fully appreciated nor my own inaccuracies noticed until many years of painstaking sketching had passed in which close to a thousand panels had been drawn.

The pride and confidence I felt regarding the accuracy of those early sketches was further lessened when I recognized the principles of symbol and rock incorporation. It then became necessary to revisit sites and compare my sketches with the actual panels. So many mistakes came to light that sketching was almost entirely abandoned, with the exception of small panels, and photography substituted.

Chart 11 shows some of the more common symbols which are often sketched wrong. Column *A* shows symbols in their accurate form; column *B* shows them as they are often erroneously sketched. One of the most common errors is the rounding-off of squared corners, or vice versa (lines 1 through 6). Another common offense is the rounding out of symbols which were intended to have flat sides (lines 7 and 8). Proper positioning of some horns is also overlooked. For example, in line 9 the horns originate on the upper face, but are sketched as originating from the top of the head where the sketcher thought they *should* have been. In other words, a sketcher, in his attempts to make his sketch more realistic, may unconsciously rob it of its intended meaning.

Some symbols seemingly poorly sketched or crooked were intentionally drawn that way in order to incorporate certain meanings. These should not be improved upon or perfected in recording (lines 10 and 11). Likewise, perfectly drawn symbols should always be matched in perfection, since this may be intended to imply added meaning. Sloppy, overzealous, and inaccurate sketching thus actually changes, distorts, or omits intended meanings, resulting in the hindering of accurate decipherment. The more common errors shown in chart 11 should be carefully studied if one plans to do any reliable sketching.

Those who have practiced the art of sketching panels will undoubtedly find some of these mistakes existing in their own work. The difficulty of sketching accurately might be compared to a child learning to print. He will make many mistakes until he becomes thoroughly familiar with the letters and what they stand for. After he obtains facility in writing, he becomes justly confident—perhaps even sloppy—without sacrificing readability. Rock writings, too, can be accurately sketched once *all* principles and symbols are clearly understood.

In my early work, sketching mistakes had of course a drastic effect in deciphering. Some panels based on sketches thought to be deciphered were found, instead, to have been wrongly sketched, and could under no circumstances be considered solved. I was not alone, however; similar mistakes were found to exist abundantly in the works of some modern professional artists far superior to me in their artistic abilities. Mallery was well aware of this trend and said: ". . . sketches, even by artists of ability, are not of high value in accuracy, as shown by the discrepant copies of some of the most carefully studied pictographs, which discrepancies sometimes leave in uncertainty the points most needed for interpretation" (1893).

Almost every available modern published work containing sketches was obtained for reference, but upon the discovery of my own copious sketching mistakes, these were found to be equally misleading and of no use in deciphering projects, *unless* they contained photographs. Many of these sincere efforts contain inaccurate sketches of panels lost forever to us—destroyed by highway construction and dams. It is deplorable that photographs were not taken before their obliteration; full and accurate decipherment of such panels may now never be obtained.

Another deficiency existing in sketching panels is the difficulty in recording all the rock features, some of which—unknown to the artist—might be serving as rock incorporation. Whenever sketches are made, *all* rock features—including the rock outline, proximity of symbols to the rock's edge, humps, dips, holes, cracks, and rock angle (whether the panel face is flat, vertical, or tilted)—should be recorded. The direction in which the viewer is facing while looking at the panel should also be noted, since many panels are purposely oriented as to direction.

Photography automatically includes most rock features, and picks up many faint symbols the sketcher often overlooks. It is, then, the most effective method of accurate recording. Even photography is not foolproof; it must be practiced with caution and experience. Certain universities and individuals have attempted to photograph panels soon to be covered by dam waters, but in some of these photos many symbols could not be discerned, and are now forever lost. Reasons for poor photography may have been the inexperience of the photographer, using the wrong kind of camera, poor angles, being too far away from the panel when the picture was snapped, and either lack of time or fear in chalking very faint panels. All of

Graham Co.,
Ariz. (pictograph)

these points must be taken into consideration when photographing, *especially* if it is to record panels marked for oblivion.

It is always wise to have two cameras along—one for black and white, and one for color—since it cannot always be determined, without considerable experience, which type of film will produce the most distinct shot. Panels which are so large or long as to require a distance shot in order to get all the symbols into one picture should be photographed close up and in overlapping sections, thus allowing the panel to be pieced together when the pictures are developed. A distant over-all shot, when used in conjunction with closeups, is also helpful. Wide-angle lens cameras are useful, but often distort symbol shapes. A telescopic lens is sometimes required for panels high up on cliffs and out of reach.

A camera should be chosen which allows the photographer to get as close to a panel as possible and still get the entire panel in the picture. Greater detail can be picked up by remaining as close as practical to a panel, unless one has the proper lens for distance shots.

A photograph should always be taken from directly in front of a panel—not from an angle, which may cause distortion of the shape of symbols. Exceptions occur where this cannot be done because of the position of the panel; these exceptions should be supplemented with sketches for comparison with the photos, thus identifying possible distortion.

Rock glare will show up in a picture as a very white area, and may hide many inscriptions lacking much contrast. This glare may be avoided by changing the angle of the shot a little so that the glare will move away from the subject, or by waiting for different lighting.

Excellent pictures may often be obtained of panels containing deep grooves by photographing them in the early morning or late evening when the sun produces distinct shadows in the grooves. At such times a flash shot should definitely be avoided. However, if one is using an inexpensive camera, flash shots are often useful during certain parts of the day when part of a panel is shaded. A flash will equalize and lighten these shaded areas. On some rocks flash shots are more successful with colored film. With black-and-white film, or if one is too close to the rock, the flash occasionally overexposes and therefore obliterates the symbols. Painted panels should always be photographed in color.

Water should not be thrown on every painted panel, as some careless people will do in the hope of making them more distinct. This tends to wash the paint itself from the panel and hasten its destruction, especially if the panel has not normally been exposed to water or if it was painted with charcoal. On certain rocks the application of water actually makes the panel *less* distinct, and postpones the opportunity for a good picture until the panel has dried. Under no circumstances

Fig. 84. This panel near the Santa Clara River in Utah contains two distinct inscriptions made at widely separated times. The brightest symbols may be as recent as 100 years ago. They are superimposed on similar symbols inscribed hundreds, perhaps even thousands, of years earlier.

should oil or kerosene be applied to paintings! This does much damage to the paint and remains on the rock a long time.

Paintings should never be chalked; the chalk will remain almost indefinitely, since most paintings are in caves or under overhangs where the rain seldom reaches to wash the chalk away. This is, in fact, the reason such places were chosen in the first place—so that the rain would not wash away the fresh paint. Under no circumstances should crayons be applied to a painted panel.

Some photographers have experimented, with varying success, with infrared film to bring out the dim areas of a faded painted panel. The drawback is that it may cause a distortion of colors; but if this is properly noted, this method may still be useful.

Many petroglyphs will be found in which the symbols are so covered with patina that they can barely be discerned; even the best photography cannot bring out the necessary details. In such cases, a photograph of even a poorly chalked panel is better than one in which little can be seen.

Chalking a pecked rock does not damage it unless it is of very soft material. Most rocks are of course much harder than chalk, and besides it will soon be washed away by rain if properly exposed. However, it is always desirable to wash the chalk off after a photograph has been taken, so as not to attract vandals. It is also polite, for there is a chance that if it has been chalked inaccurately it will irritate following photographers.

190

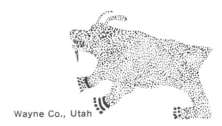

Wayne Co., Utah

Accurate chalking is a very touchy and exacting art. It often requires several colors of chalk, a knowledge of pecking techniques and their meanings, and considerable experience. The basic thing to remember is that a panel should not be chalked too heavily; it should be done lightly so that the pecking can actually be seen through the chalk itself. Then, if it is chalked erroneously, mistakes can sometimes be discerned through the chalk.

Many panels do not need to be chalked entirely. Leave the distinct, visible symbols alone. Chalk only those which are the dimmest (figure 38). This applies especially to panels which are to be photographed for purposes of deciphering — the *only* legitimate excuse for chalking! Chalking for the purpose of improving the aesthetic value of a pictograph in actuality only obscures its inherent beauty and age and should therefore be avoided.

Panels revealing different ages, or contrasting in symbol brightness, should be chalked in two different colors, if indeed the entire panel must be chalked. Normally, it is the older symbols only which require chalking. Age may be ascertained by the varying degrees of darkness in the coatings of patina on the symbols. The darkest patina—covered symbols are the oldest, and the lightest are the newest (figure 84). The difference in ages of symbols on the same rock is accounted for by the fact that Indians inscribed messages over panels hundreds of years old which had already acquired a patina corresponding in age. This was often done in preference to using another rock; consequently the same rock may contain two different messages from two different ages! This type of relative dating is very important for study purposes. Chalking of such superimposed panels should be completely avoided if at all possible!

Another point to remember in this respect is that Indians, during their own time, would often repeck some aged and dim symbols in order to make them more visible. Close examination will distinguish these, since some of the older patina-covered pecking can be seen beneath. This type of repecking should be properly noted and should not be confused with superimposition of different messages.

Caution should be taken in noting different degrees of darkness of some symbols. Water running down over only a portion of a panel will often darken only that section. This discoloration should not be assigned an age different from the remainder of the panel. Close examination of the rock and the other symbols will reveal whether the entire panel is of the same age.

Various techniques of inscribing rocks—solid pecking, light and scattered pecking, scratching, pits, deep grooves, and abraded or rubbed areas—should also be distinguished, if chalking is necessary, since each technique relates a pertinent meaning of its own.

In distinguishing a rubbed or abraded area from a solidly pecked symbol,

191

Fig. 85. This "rubbing" or "lifting" of a panel from Washington County, Utah, is an accurate, life-sized reproduction of the inscriptions from the rock itself. The five dots (arrow), however, are not pecked symbols; they are depressions made by erosion. This was not determined from the rubbing, but was noted while at the rock. This type of notation is a necessity if such rubbings are to be used for purposes of deciphering.

chalking on the rubbed area should be very lightly smeared, or two different colors of chalk should be used. In cases of scattered or sloppy pecking, each minute dot should be chalked individually or in a scattered manner which duplicates this technique. Care should be taken not to overchalk these different techniques. Figure 18 (although unchalked) is a good example of the necessity and the importance of this type of chalking.

All lines should be followed exactly in chalking, and differences between square- and round-cornered symbols carefully noted. Any symbol or part of a symbol which cannot be accurately discerned should be left unchalked. A photograph will sometimes bring out certain details that may later help in distinguishing this symbol. Guesswork in chalking these indistinct symbols negate the possibility of accurately recognizing them later in the photograph.

Remember that chalking is as highly subject to error as sketching, and that the symbols which are commonly sketched inaccurately (chart 11) should be understood clearly and these mistakes avoided in chalking. An inexperienced recorder will only transfer the mistakes he would have made in sketching to his chalking, if he is not extremely careful.

The ideal method of dealing with panels which must be chalked is to take two photographs of the same panel—one before chalking and one after. In using this

192

Grape Vine Springs, Nev.

method chalking mistakes can often be detected when the photos are compared.

Both color and black-and-white film will pick up most chalk colors if distinct colors have been chosen—white, yellow, or light blue.

A scaled arrow denoting direction and size should be placed near a panel so that it appears in the photograph. If a rock is flat, something should be placed on the arrow, or some method or note employed that will distinguish this flatness or slight angle in the photograph.

Other methods which are definite improvements over chalking can be used, provided the symbols have a little depth. One method is the application with a brush of a thin mixture of water and aluminum powder (Swartz 1963), or a mixture of water and "gouache" (Anati 1961). These thin, diluted mixtures concentrate in the depressions made by pecking. The rock is then rubbed over with a cloth to remove the excess dilution, but some will remain in the grooves of the symbols, which can then be photographed.

Caution should be taken to brush out dried dilutions from all extraneous cracks and holes. These will pick up the applications and consequently appear indistinguishable from symbols in the photograph. All rocks should be washed or brushed clean after the photographs are taken. This solution should *not* be applied to the softer sandstone or tuff, which tends to absorb the solution and smear the rock.

Another very useful method of recording petroglyphs is known as the "rubbing" or "lifting" method. This, again, can be done only on panels wherein the symbols have some depth. The first step in this rubbing technique is to stretch a piece of lightly colored or white cloth, such as an old sheet, across the face of a rock and then tape it tightly down with masking tape. Oil paint or printer's ink is then placed in a flat tray and a rubber roller rolled back and forth in this paint until its surface is lightly, but completely, covered with paint. The roller is then applied to the surface of the cloth. Paint is transferred to the cloth only where it comes in contact with the rock. The symbols, which are recessed, will show upon the cloth as unpainted areas. An example of this technique may be seen in figure 85.

This method does not damage the rock, since paint is applied only to the cloth and *not to the rock*. Caution should be taken not to so saturate the cloth that paint will seep through to the rock. Many thin coats are much better than one thick one. All material should be picked up, and hands wet with paint should be kept off the rocks.

The rubbing technique is valuable in that it will pick up minute details not apparent to the naked eye; however, it at the same time picks up cracks and holes which may appear as symbols on the finished print. It is therefore necessary to distinguish with notes, *while at the rock*, those lines which are only rock features.

193

This method will also pick up intended rock incorporation, but some features may not show up—shallow depressions and smooth humps, for instance. Rubbings also fail to show contrast in patination. It is best, then, to always supplement these rubbings with photographs and/or notes.

Tracing methods, in which large, thin, transparent paper is taped in place over a panel and the symbols actually traced on the paper itself, are useful in that they can be used on both petroglyphs and pictographs, and are exact in scale. Nevertheless, they are no better or accurate than the person doing the tracing. Mistakes common to sketching and chalking are also made in such tracings.

Color photography is essentially the most accurate and best method of recording; nevertheless it should be occasionally assisted with other methods since in a photograph it is sometimes difficult to distinguish rock discoloration and deterioration from the symbols themselves.

No substitute exists for the rock itself, and if possible each rock should be revisited many times. It was only after numerous visits to the same panel that I was able to decipher some of them. Such repeated visits still produce new and enlightening results.

It is a federal offense punishable by law to damage, destroy, or remove rock writings upon public lands. One of the practices most damaging to the successful reading of Indian rock writing is the removal of rocks from their original positions. Rocks should never be removed and used to beautify landscapes, gardens, floors, fireplaces, or to accent a collection of Indian artifacts. The writings on most panels are purposely oriented to surrounding geography, and often to other panels near by. Removal of a rock, therefore, may snatch a sentence or paragraph from its original context, thus losing the message in its entirety. When impending destruction does dictate the removal of rock writings, thorough notes and photographs should be taken in order to record permanently their original relative positions.

It might be said, in summary, that there is no single duplicating method which can be relied upon for accuracy in all instances. The only really foolproof method of recording is to be able to read the writings on the spot in their entirety, as they were intended by their Indian authors to be read. If one understands this pictographic system and all its peculiarities perfectly, he can accurately identify many hard-to-distinguish symbols, just as an experienced reader can read poor or faint handwriting as long as it is still barely visible. Other methods must suffice, however, to record rock writing for the time when this can be accomplished.

Glossary

AFFINITY.   The relationship or kinship in meaning one symbol has to associated symbols.

AGGLUTINATIVE.   A term used in the study of spoken languages wherein several words are combined into one word, and undergo no basic change in makeup, i.e. *newspaperman.*

ANIMATION.   An action or state of being portrayed in a nonrepresentational quadruped or human hymbol.

CLUSTER.   A group of symbols pertaining to a particular theme in a panel purposely concentrated in one particular area of the panel in a manner most conducive to clarity.

CRYPTANALYSIS.   The science by which an unknown system of communication is deciphered from nothing more than the symbols, characters, or letters of the communication itself.

DEDUCTION.   Conclusions obtained from the scientific compilation, analysis, and elimination of bulk material.

DETERMINATIVE.   An additional symbol or symbols used to clarify or classify the meaning of other symbols.

GOAT.   An animal-like symbol not intended to represent any particular animal, but which is used to depict lateral action and other meanings. Distinguished by its horn-like appendages. Also termed *horned quadrupeds.*

IDEOGRAM.   A symbol that expresses an idea or concept understandable to all people, regardless of differences in language. An idea expressed in a symbol containing no phonetic elements.

INDUCTION.   A conclusion arrived at by reasoning from a part to a whole or from particulars to generalities.

PANEL.   A symbol or group of symbols conveying a message either complete in itself or related to other panels nearby.

PATINATION (PATINA).   A natural process by which the surface of a rock becomes darker over a period of many years.

PETROGLYPH.   Symbols made upon a rock by pecking, incising, abrading or scratching.

PICTOGRAPH. Picture writing in a painted form upon any material. Also, a picture representing and expressing an idea.

PICTOGRAPHY. A method of communication in which pictures and ideograms are used upon any material, including rocks. A picture writing.

POLYSYNTHETIC. The fusion of several parts of a sentence into a single word in which the component parts are reduced to the simplest elements.

QUADRUPED. An animal-like symbol on which no horn symbol occurs. Used to depict lateral action and express other meanings. It may have any number of legs or none at all.

ROCK INCORPORATION. A symbol purposely placed in, on, or near any natural rock feature so as to incorporate such rock feature into the meaning of the message.

SIGN. Any method of communication as used in the sign language.

SYMBOL. Any depiction or drawing used in pictography to convey any type of meaning. One of the characters, combinations, incorporations, or units of pictography.

SYMBOLS (BASIC). A symbol in its simplest form or concept that is not intended to be broken down into component parts.

SYMBOL EXTENSION. Additional and related meanings naturally derived from or suggested by the basic concept of a symbol.

SYMBOL INCORPORATION. Two or more basic symbols embodied in one symbol in such a way that features of both share common sections of the same symbol.

SYMBOL SUGGESTIVENESS. The resemblance of symbol shape to its meaning.

UNIT. A distinct symbol constituted in its makeup of both symbol combination and incorporation. A combination or incorporation composed of many symbols.

Bibliography

Anati, Emmanuel. *Camonica Valley.* Translated from the French by Linda Asher. New York: Alfred A. Knopf, 1961.

Auerbach, Herbert S. "Father Escalante's Journal, 1976-77." *Utah Historical Quarterly,* Vol. II (1943).

Beckwith, Frank. *Trips to Points of Interest in Millard and Nearby.* Springville, Utah: Art City Publishing Co., 1947.

Bender, Henry E. *Uintah Railway, the Gilsonite Route.* Berkeley: Howell-North Books, 1970.

Brinton, Daniel G. *The Lenape and Their Legends.* No. V. Brinton's Library of Aboriginal American Literature. Philadelphia: D. G. Brinton, 1885.

Budge, E. A. Wallis. *Egyptian Language.* 8th ed. London: Routledge & Kegan Paul, 1966.

Clark, W. P. *The Indian Sign Language.* Philadelphia: L. R. Hamersly & Co., 1885. (Lithographed and bound in the USA by the Rosecrucian Press, San Jose.)

Clodd, Edward. *The Story of the Alphabet.* New York: D. Appleton & Co., 1902.

Colton, Harold S. *Hopi Kachina Dolls.* Rev. ed. Albuquerque: University of New Mexico Press, 1959.

Copway, George. *The Traditional History and Characteristic Sketches of the Ojibway Nation.* London: C. Gilpin, 1850.

Cox, J. Halley, with Stasack, Edward. *Hawaiian Petroglyphs.* Honolulu: Bishop Museum Press, 1970.

Denig, Edwin T. "Tribes of the Upper Missouri." *Forty-Sixth Annual Report of the Bureau of American Ethnology, 1928-29.* Washington, D.C., 1930.

Dibble, Charles E. *The Ancient Mexican Writing System.* Utah Anthropological Papers, No. 2, Vol. 2. Salt Lake City: University of Utah Press, 1940.

Donnelly, Joseph P. *Wilderness Kingdom, Indian Life in the Rocky Mountains: 1840-1847.* New York: Holt, Rinehart & Winston, 1967.

Driver, G. R. *Semitic Writing.* Rev. ed. The Schevlich Lectures of the British Academy. London: Oxford University Press, 1944.

Emmitt, Robert P. *The Last War Trail.* Norman: University of Oklahoma Press, 1954.

Franch, Jose Alcina. *Las Pintaderas Mejicanas y sus Relaciones.* Consejo Superior de Investigaciones Cientificas. Madrid: Instituto Gonzalo Fernandez De Oviedo, 1958.

Frobenius, L., and Obermaier, H. *Hadschra Maktouba, Urzeitliche Felsbilder Kleinafrikas* (Rock Writings of Northern Africa). Munich: Forschungs-instituts fur Kulturmorphologie, 1925.

Gardiner, Alan. *Egyptian Grammar.* 3rd ed. London: Oxford University Press, 1957.

Gunnison, J. W. *The Mormons, or Latter-Day Saints in the Valley of the Great Salt Lake.* Philadelphia: Lippincott, Grambo & Co., 1852.

Heckewelder, John. *An Account of the History, Manners and Customs of the Indian Nations Who Once Inhabited Pennsylvania and the Neighboring States.* Rev. Philadelphia: Abraham Small, 1819.

Hoffman, W. J. "The Mide-wiwin or 'Grand Medicine Society' of the Ojibwa." *Seventh Annual Report of the Bureau of American Ethnology, 1885-86.* Washington, D.C.: 1891.

Kahn, David. *The Codebreakers, The Story of Secret Writing.* New York: Macmillan Co., 1967.

Labat, Rene. *Manuel D'Epigraphie Akkadienne.* Paris: Imprimerie Nationale, 1948.

Laffin, John. *Codes and Cipers.* New York: Abelard-Schuman, 1964.

Lee, Nelson. *Three Years Among the Comanches.* Norman: University of Oklahoma Press, 1957.

Mallery, Garrick. "Sign Language Among the North American Indians." *First Annual Report of the Bureau of American Ethnology, 1879-80.* Washington, D.C., 1881.

Mallery, Garrick. "Pictographs of the North American Indians." *Fourth Annual Report of the Bureau of American Ethnology, 1881-82.* Washington, D.C., 1886.

Mallery, Garrick. "Picture Writing of the American Indians." *Tenth Annual Report of the Bureau of American Ethnology, 1888-89.* Washington, D.C., 1893. Reprinted New York: Dover Publications.

Maurault, Abbe J. A. Histoire des Abenaquis depuis 1605 jusqua' a nos jours. *Gazette de Sorel.* Quebec, 1866.

McCarthy, Frederick D. *Australian Aboriginal Rock Art.* 3rd ed. Sydney: Australian Museum, 1967.

McClintock, Walter. "Painted Tipis and Picture-Writing of the Blackfoot Indians." Southwest Museum Leaflet No. 6. Los Angeles: Southwest Museum.

Mooney, James. "Calendar History of the Kiowa Indians." *Seventeenth Annual Report of the Bureau of American Ethnology, Part 1.* Washington, D.C., 1898.

Newcomb, W. W., Jr. *The Rock Art of Texas Indians.* Austin: University of Texas Press, 1967.

O'Neil, Floyd A. "An Anguished Odyssey: The Flight of the Utes, 1906-08," *Utah Historical Quarterly* 36 (1968).

Powell, John Wesley. *The Exploration of the Colorado River.* Chicago: University of Chicago Press, 1957. (Abridged from the first edition of 1875.)

Schoolcraft, H. R. *Historical and Statistical Information Respecting the History, Condition, and Prospects of the Indian Tribes of the United States.* Philadelphia: Lippincott, Grambo & Co., 1853.

Seaman, N. G. *Indian Relics of the Pacific Northwest.* 2nd ed. Portland, Oregon: Binfords & Mort, 1967.

Seler, Eduard. "The Mexican Chronology." Bulletin 28, Bureau of American Ethnology. Washington, D.C., 1904.

Shuffler, R. Henderson. "Blue Mountain Caves in Indian Days Described by Captain Cook." *Odessa News-Times,* December 7, 1934.

Swartz, B. K., Jr. "Aluminum Powder: A Technique for Photographically Recording Petroglyphs." *American Antiquity,* Vol. 28, No. 3, January, 1963.

Tanner, John. *A Narrative of the Captivity and Adventures of John Tanner.* Edited by Edwin James, M.D. New York: G. & C. H. Carvill, 1830. (Minneapolis: Ross & Haines, 1956.)

Tomkins, William. *Universal Indian Sign Language.* San Diego: Neyenesch Printers, 1948.

Voegelin, C. F. *Walum Olum.* Indiana Historical Society, Indianapolis. Chicago: Lakeside Press, R. R. Donnelley & Sons, 1954.

Wadell, L. A. *Egyptian Civilization, Its Sumerian Origin and Real Chronology.* London: Luzac & Co., 1930.

Waters, Frank. *Book of the Hopi.* New York: Viking Press, 1963.

Wellmann, Klaus F. "Kokopelli of Indian Paleology." *Journal of American Medical Association,* Vol. 212, June 8, 1970.

Wieger, L. *Chinese Characters.* 2nd ed. New York: Paragon Book Reprint Corporation and Dover Publications, 1965.

Willison, George F. *Saints and Strangers.* New York: Reynal and Hitchcock, 1945.

Acknowledgments

Many years of research have gone into this study since its inception in 1956, but the material and findings presented here would not have been available for publication at this time were it not for many kinds of help given by many individuals.

Invaluable support in alleviating financial pressures during the critical times of this research was given by Deere and Edurine Kanosh, Florence Kanosh, Richfield, Utah; Carl and Minnie Jake, Cedar City, Utah; Morris Jake, Moccasin, Arizona; the George McFee family, Shivwits Reservation, Utah—all members of the Southern Paiute Tribe; Ernest and Delia Victor, Ray Kidde, and William Brown—members of the San Carlos Apache Tribe; Rhoda Poowegup and family, Gary and Betty Poowegup—members of the Ute Tribe.

Transportation on lengthy field trips was provided by Gaylord Staveley, Flagstaff, Arizona; Paul Lamoreaux and Clair Paxman, St. George, Utah; Vince Dull, Whittier, California; and D. L. Laidlaw, International Falls, Minnesota.

Site information and many photographs, rubbings, and books were supplied by Elfriede Tingleaf of Tonasket, Washington, and Janis Tower of Las Vegas, Nevada.

The people of the Glenbow Foundation, Calgary, Canada, made available to me much information concerning sites and recorded panels.

Many Indian friends furnished unpublished information that has been of inestimable worth: Jimmy Timmican, Florence Kanosh, Carl Jake, Woots Parashont, Isaac Hunkup, Morris Jake, Bessy Tillahash, Johnny Domingo (Southern Paiute); Harriet Taveapont, Ouray McCook, Russell Root (Ute); David Monongye, John Lanza (Hopi); Matthew Hoffman (Apache); and many others. Special guidance was given by Moounum.

Without the steadfast confidence and support of K. C. DenDooven over many years this work would not have been available to the general public. I am indebted to K.C. for his valuable suggestions concerning this manuscript.

My wife, Doris Kanosh (now deceased), and my daughter, Dorena, gave untiringly of their efforts in performing much of the field work and note-taking involved in this research.

And, finally, many site informants throughout the country provided help without which the compilation of the thousands of panels necessary to this study could not have been made.

To all of these people I am deeply grateful.

Index

Symbol Reference List

This symbol reference list has been devised to enable the reader to locate symbol concepts and extensions within the text. Indented words are extensions of the basic concept under which they appear. Extensions are cross-referenced, so they may be located alphabetically. Every page on which a concept occurs is not included; only that page on which the symbol is most clearly explained is noted. This compilation thus serves as both a symbol list and an index to symbol meanings and extensions. Terms are worded as each would normally be translated by itself, not in context, and therefore occasionally differ from wordings used in the text.

Happiness, 65
Hat, 97
  white man, 97
Healing. *See* Fan
Heard, 80
  listened, 80
Heart, 155
Heaped up, 4
  piled up, 101
  pyramid, 5
  rocky mountain, 6, 82
  stepped buildings, 5
Heaven. *See* Flower
Held by many, 66
  owned by many, 66
Held in one place, 37
  a good place, 37
  corraled, 37
  out of reach, 37
  pinned down, 37
  unable to get out, 37
  waterhole, 37
  within, 37
Here, 37
  a fixed position, 37
Hidden (covered), 21
Hidden (head), 99
  behind, 99
High. *See* Mound
High up, 120
Higher, 131
Hit on the head, 103
Hit on the head (not), 95
  not harmed, 95
Hobbled, 97
  difficult traveling, 97
Holding, 37
  pen, 105
Holding (closely), 82
Holding (loosely), 79
Holding firm, 66
  having a firm grip, 74
Hole, 127
Hollow, 38
Horse, 74
Hunchback, 53
Hungry, 74
Hunting magic, 9
Hurt. *See* Arrowhead

I. *See* Flexing arms
I was told, 80
  he told me, 80
Imprisoned. *See* Compressed

In front (symbol), 27
In front (superimposition), 40
Inactive, 51
  idle, 79
Indian, 63
Inferior, 39
  future tense, 39
  last, 39
  later, 40
Inside, 37
Iron, 55
Island, 132

Joining, 133
Joking, 103
  laughing, 103

Keeping someone at a distance, 88
  distrust, 88
Killed. *See* Cut
Kiowa, 72
Knife. *See* Cutting meat
Knocked off, 65
  force, 65
  ramming, 65

Ladle, 93
  deep, 93
  reaching down deep, 93
Lance, 137
  braced for battle, 137
  prepared to fight, 63
Lance head, 66
Land, 99
Last. *See* Inferior
Later. *See* Inferior
Leader, 127
Leading, 89
Learning, 133
Let go of it, 100
Level, 33
  good, 33
Lieing. *See* Forks in a trail
Lined up, 103
Limp, 77
  ready to die, 77
Liquid, 28
Listened. *See* Heard
Listening (not), 99
Little, 35
Locomotive, 125
Long journey by horseback, 61
Long time. *See* Distant
Looking. *See* Eyes and ears (erect)
Looking down, 89

Looking into heaven, 115
Love songs. *See* Flutes
Lying down, 47

Magic. *See* Strong
Many, 56
Many holding, 101
Medicine. *See* Strong
Meeting. *See* Converging
Member (becoming), 113
Mexican, 72
Migrating, 57
   traveling together, 57
Missed. *See* Bent stick
Missing a destination, 105
Mistaken, 79
Moccasin, 88
Moccasin track, 99
   protected, 99
Mound, 27
   high, 27
   mountain, 123
Mountain sheep, 3-14
Mouth, 89
   opening, 89
Movement (broad), 80
Movement (completed), 49
Movement down between, 121
Movement (downhill), 48
Movement (lateral), 48
Movement (straight ahead), 47
Movement (uncompleted), 50
Movement (uphill), 48
Moving, 50
Muddy. *See* Small scattered particles
Mutilated, 100

Naked, 33
   poor, 33
Narrow, 93
Navajo, 99
Near the end, 79
Neck, 125
Necklace, 89
Negation, 51
   not liking it, 51
   not wanting it, 79
New, 113
   children, 113
   young, 113
Night. *See* Black
Not allowed to come close, 131
   keeping others away, 131
Not wanting to leave, 100

North, 43
Nothing there, 49
   clean, 49
   empty space, 49
   good, 49
   light, 49
   off, 49
   taken off, 49
   white, 49
   wiped out, 49

Obeying. *See* Believing
Objectionable area, 79
Off. *See* Nothing there
Often, 75
   repeat, 75
Old man, 33
Old way of life, 65
Omaha, 40
On top, 35
Open, 111
   crack, 90
   opening up, 111
Out of shape, 82
Outnumbered, 131
Outside, 95

Packs, 53
   trade goods, 53
Pants, 133
Part of, 81
Passing in front, 79
Passed through, 120
Passing through (lines), 101
Passing through (dots and line), 24
Past tense. *See* Superior
Pawnee, 41
Peace, 4
Peace pipe, 61
   visiting a friendly tribe, 61
Peeking out, 63
Peeking over, 77
   cautious, 77
People, 116
Pierced through, 74
Pinned down. *See* Held in one place
Plucked crops, 115
Poking it through, 88
   laced, 89
   poked, 89
   sewing, 88
Poor. *See* Naked
Praying, 80, 127
   beseeching, 127